D0849861

Rights, Restitution, and Risk

Rights, Restitution, and Risk

ESSAYS IN MORAL THEORY

Judith Jarvis Thomson

EDITED BY WILLIAM PARENT

HARVARD UNIVERSITY PRESS

Cambridge, Massachusetts,
and London, England   1986

Library of Congress Cataloging-in-Publication Data

Thomson, Judith Jarvis.
  Rights, restitution, and risk.

  Bibliography: p.
  Includes index.
  1. Ethics—Addresses, essays, lectures.
I. Parent, William.   II. Title.
BJ1031.T49   1986   170   85-30204
ISBN 0-674-76980-5 (alk. paper)
ISBN 0-674-76981-3 (pbk. : alk. paper)

170
T483

Contents

Editor's Preface

The publication in 1971 of Judith Jarvis Thomson's "A Defense of Abortion," in the first issue of *Philosophy and Public Affairs*, marked a watershed in contemporary moral philosophy. The putative rights and wrongs of abortion have always been a concern of moral theologians; secular moral philosophers had on the whole ignored the topic. Perhaps they shunned it because it seemed to concern only women, and discussion of it might require attention to such potential embarrassments as The Female Body, but certainly also because of the generalizing tendency in philosophy—the sense many philosophers have had that no problems can be solved until the deepest problems are solved, and thus that it is the task of moral philosophy precisely to look beneath the concerns of ordinary men and women for the foundations, the very sources of good and evil and right and wrong. Mrs. Thomson's essay had a double impact. On the one hand, it brought home to philosophers that the question whether abortion is morally permissible does itself raise deep questions (in particular, it raises the question of what it is to have a right to life), and on the other hand, it asserted that progress can be made, that matters of moral concern to ordinary people can be profitably dealt with by philosophers, even in advance of that long-awaited day when all of the deepest problems are solved. *Philosophy and Public Affairs* has over the years provided a forum for philosophers and their philosophically inclined friends in political science and law who have wished to carry on this enterprise.

"A Defense of Abortion" is an extraordinarily ingenious and inventive essay, and it captured the attention of moral philosophers overnight. It spawned a large literature, and it has by now become the most widely reprinted essay in all of contemporary philosophy.

Since abortion has continued to be (perhaps nowadays increasingly) a matter of public concern, it is time for that essay to be made more widely available to readers outside departments of philosophy, who do not normally come in contact with journals of philosophy or anthologies of philosophical writing.

Mrs. Thomson responded directly to a critic of her essay on abortion only once, in "Rights and Deaths," which is here reprinted as essay number 2. But certain central themes and ideas which she dealt with in "A Defense of Abortion" recur in many of her later essays, in which she takes up a wide variety of other problems in moral philosophy. I hint at those themes and ideas in the title I have given to this collection: *Rights, Restitution, and Risk.* She finds herself confronted again and again, in connection with one issue after another, with the question: what is it to have a right—whether the right to life, or any other right? What shows we have such rights as we take ourselves to have? What is the moral significance of a person's having a right? What do we owe to those whose rights we infringe, or may risk infringing, if we act in this or that way?

Many of Mrs. Thomson's later essays are well known to philosophers, but some are not, in that they initially appeared in publications which do not circulate readily among philosophers—such as conference proceedings and law journals. I have therefore thought that philosophers as well as nonphilosophers would find it useful to have them made available together here.

I have organized the essays I reprint here by way of topic, rather than chronologically. Essays 1 and 2 ("A Defense of Abortion" and "Rights and Deaths") argue that there are circumstances in which it is morally permissible to kill an innocent person, in particular where the innocent person himself constitutes a threat to others—despite the fact that, being innocent, he constitutes a threat to others through no fault of his own. If that is correct, then a certain familiar argument against abortion does not succeed.

Essay 3 ("Self-Defense and Rights") begins with the fact that it is morally permissible to kill in self-defense, even if the aggressor constitutes a threat through no fault of his own; it then asks how we are to understand this fact if we believe that innocent human beings have a right to life, and thus that the innocent aggressor himself has a right to life. It argues, as do essays 4 and 5 ("Some Ruminations on Rights" and "Rights and Compensation"), that a sign or mark that an act of A's infringed a right of B's can be found in A's having a duty to compensate B for harms or losses which his act caused B.

Essay 6 ("Killing, Letting Die, and the Trolley Problem") reminds us of the fact that there are cases in which we may kill a person who constitutes no threat to anybody—that is, cases in which more lives will be saved if we do so. But there are cases in which we may not kill one person to save more lives. Mrs. Thomson asks: Which are which? In which cases may we kill one to save more, and in which cases may we not do this? Having been dissatisfied with her earlier account of the matter, Mrs. Thomson returns to this problem in essay 7 ("The Trolley Problem").

We take ourselves to have rights other than the rights to life and bodily integrity; essay 8 ("The Right to Privacy") asks what it is to have a right to privacy, and what marks that right off from others which we take ourselves to have.

Essay 9 ("Preferential Hiring") asks whether giving preference to blacks and women constitutes an infringement of the rights of others, and more generally, whether it is morally permissible.

Essays 10 and 11 ("Some Questions about Government Regulation of Behavior" and "Imposing Risks") were provoked by attention to government regulation of the imposition of risk—in particular, by regulations intended to decrease risks in the work-place.

Essay 12 ("Remarks on Causation and Liability") attends to situations in which many people imposed risks on a person, and it is not discoverable which risk-imposer in fact caused the harm which the person then suffered; Mrs. Thomson's attention was drawn to this issue by the recent lawsuits against the drug companies which manufactured DES (diethylstilbestrol, a drug used to prevent miscarriage). Along the way, she discussed a problem raised by what is sometimes called "naked statistical evidence"—very roughly, evidence which merely shows it to be probable that this or that particular risk-imposer caused the harm. Essay 13 ("Liability and Individualized Evidence") returns to the question why we, and the law courts, are inclined to feel suspicious of such evidence.

In the Afterword, written especially for this volume, Mrs. Thomson discusses three points which seem to her to be particularly worth emphasizing about these thirteen essays.

I suggested to Mrs. Thomson some years ago that she bring out a collection of her essays in moral philosophy. She said it would be impossible: she could not even reread them without feeling they ought to be completely rewritten. I hope that she will continue to work at, and to rethink afresh, those central themes and ideas which lie at the heart of these essays. But it would be a pity to rewrite them. Some of them have become classics by now; all of them are stimulating, lively, and rich in argument and example. Hence, except for very minor changes, none of which is substantive, the essays appear in their original form. I am most grateful to Mrs. Thomson for permitting me to collect and bring them out here.

Rights, Restitution, and Risk

1 · *A Defense of Abortion*

Most opposition to abortion relies on the premise that the fetus is a human being, a person, from the moment of conception. The premise is argued for, but, as I think, not well. Take, for example, the most common argument. We are asked to notice that the development of a human being from conception through birth into childhood is continuous; then it is said that to draw a line, to choose a point in this development and say "before this point the thing is not a person, after this point it is a person" is to make an arbitrary choice, a choice for which in the nature of things no good reason can be given. It is concluded that the fetus is, or anyway that we had better say it is, a person from the moment of conception. But this conclusion does not follow. Similar things might be said about the development of an acorn into an oak tree, and it does not follow that acorns are oak trees, or that we had better say they are. Arguments of this form are sometimes called "slippery slope arguments"—the phrase is perhaps self-explanatory—and it is dismaying that opponents of abortion rely on them so heavily and uncritically.

I am inclined to agree, however, that the prospects for "drawing a line" in the development of the fetus look dim. I am inclined to think also that we shall probably have to agree that the fetus has already become a human person well before birth. Indeed, it comes as a surprise when one first learns how early in its life it begins to acquire human characteristics. By the tenth week, for example, it already has a face, arms and legs, fingers and toes; it has internal organs, and brain activity is detectable.[1] On the other hand, I think that the prem-

---

1. Daniel Callahan, *Abortion: Law, Choice, and Morality* (New York: Macmillan, 1970), p. 373. This book gives a fascinating survey of the available information on abortion. The Jewish tradition is surveyed in David M. Feldman, *Birth Control in Jewish Law*

ise is false, that the fetus is not a person from the moment of conception. A newly fertilized ovum, a newly implanted clump of cells, is no more a person than an acorn is an oak tree. But I shall not discuss any of this. For it seems to me to be of great interest to ask what happens if, for the sake of argument, we allow the premise. How, precisely, are we supposed to get from there to the conclusion that abortion is morally impermissible? Opponents of abortion commonly spend most of their time establishing that the fetus is a person, and hardly any time explaining the step from there to the impermissibility of abortion. Perhaps they think the step too simple and obvious to require much comment. Or perhaps instead they are simply being economical in argument. Many of those who defend abortion rely on the premise that the fetus is not a person, but only a bit of tissue that will become a person at birth; and why pay out more arguments than you have to? Whatever the explanation, I suggest that the step they take is neither easy nor obvious, that it calls for closer examination than it is commonly given, and that when we do give it this closer examination we shall feel inclined to reject it.

I propose, then, that we grant that the fetus is a person from the moment of conception. How does the argument go from here? Something like this, I take it. Every person has a right to life. So the fetus has a right to life. No doubt the mother has a right to decide what shall happen in and to her body; everyone would grant that. But surely a person's right to life is stronger and more stringent than the mother's right to decide what happens in and to her body, and so outweighs it. So the fetus may not be killed; an abortion may not be performed.

It sounds plausible. But now let me ask you to imagine this. You wake up in the morning and find yourself back to back in bed with an unconscious violinist. A famous unconscious violinist. He has been found to have a fatal kidney ailment, and the Society of Music Lovers has canvassed all the available medical records and found that you alone have the right blood type to help. They have therefore kidnapped you, and last night the violinist's circulatory system was plugged into yours, so that your kidneys can be used to extract poisons from his blood as well as your own. The director of the hospital now tells you, "Look, we're sorry the Society of Music Lovers did this to you—

(New York: Greenwood, 1968), Part 5; the Catholic tradition in John T. Noonan, Jr., "An Almost Absolute Value in History," in *The Morality of Abortion*, ed. John T. Noonan, Jr. (Cambridge, Mass: Harvard University Press, 1970).

we would never have permitted it if we had known. But still, they did it, and the violinist now is plugged into you. To unplug you would be to kill him. But never mind, it's only for nine months. By then he will have recovered from his ailment, and can safely be unplugged from you." Is it morally incumbent on you to accede to this situation? No doubt it would be very nice of you if you did, a great kindness. But do you *have* to accede to it? What if it were not nine months, but nine years? Or longer still? What if the director of the hospital says, "Tough luck, I agree, but you've now got to stay in bed, with the violinist plugged into you, for the rest of your life. Because remember this. All persons have a right to life, and violinists are persons. Granted you have a right to decide what happens in and to your body, but a person's right to life outweighs your right to decide what happens in and to your body. So you cannot ever be unplugged from him." I imagine you would regard this as outrageous, which suggests that something really is wrong with that plausible-sounding argument I mentioned a moment ago.

In this case, of course, you were kidnapped; you didn't volunteer for the operation that plugged the violinist into your kidneys. Can those who oppose abortion on the ground I mentioned make an exception for a pregnancy due to rape? Certainly. They can say that persons have a right to life only if they didn't come into existence because of rape; or they can say that all persons have a right to life, but that some have less of a right to life than others, in particular, that those who come into existence because of rape have less. But these statements have a rather unpleasant sound. Surely the question of whether you have a right to life at all, or how much of it you have, shouldn't turn on the question of whether or not you are the product of a rape. And in fact the people who oppose abortion on the ground I mentioned do not make this distinction, and hence do not make an exception in case of rape.

Nor do they make an exception for a case in which the mother has to spend the nine months of her pregnancy in bed. They would agree that would be a great pity, and hard on the mother; but all the same, all persons have a right to life, the fetus is a person, and so on. I suspect, in fact, that they would not make an exception for a case in which, miraculously enough, the pregnancy went on for nine years, or even the rest of the mother's life.

Some won't even make an exception for a case in which continuation of the pregnancy is likely to shorten the mother's life; they regard abortion as impermissible even to save the mother's life. Such cases are nowadays very rare, and many opponents of abortion do not accept this extreme view. All the same, it is a good place to begin: a number of points of interest come out in respect to it.

1. Let us call the view that abortion is impermissible even to save the mother's life "the extreme view." I want to suggest first that it does not issue from the argument I mentioned earlier without the addition of some fairly powerful premises. Suppose a woman has become pregnant, and now learns that she has a cardiac condition such that she will die if she carries the baby to term. What may be done for her? The fetus, being a person, has a right to life, but as the mother is a person too, so has she a right to life. Presumably they have an equal right to life. How is it supposed to come out that an abortion may not be performed? If mother and child have an equal right to life, shouldn't we perhaps flip a coin? Or should we add to the mother's right to life her right to decide what happens in and to her body, which everybody seems to be ready to grant—the sum of her rights now outweighing the fetus's right to life?

The most familiar argument here is the following. We are told that performing the abortion would be directly killing[2] the child, whereas doing nothing would not be killing the mother, but only letting her die. Moreover, in killing the child, one would be killing an innocent person, for the child has committed no crime, and is not aiming at his mother's death. And then there are a variety of ways in which this might be continued. (1) But as directly killing an innocent person is always and absolutely impermissible, an abortion may not be performed. Or, (2) as directly killing an innocent person is murder, and murder is always and absolutely impermissible, an abortion may not be performed.[3] Or, (3) as one's duty to refrain from directly killing

2. The term "direct" in the arguments I refer to is a technical one. Roughly, what is meant by "direct killing" is either killing as an end in itself, or killing as a means to some end, for example, the end of saving someone else's life. See note 5, below, for an example of its use.

3. See *Encyclical Letter of Pope Pius XI on Christian Marriage*, (Boston: St. Paul Editions, n.d.), p. 32: "however much we may pity the mother whose health and even life is gravely imperiled in the performance of the duty allotted to her by nature, nevertheless what could ever be a sufficient reason for excusing in any way the direct murder of the innocent? This is precisely what we are dealing with here." Noonan (*The Morality of Abortion*, p. 43) reads this as follows: "What cause can ever avail to excuse in any way the direct killing of the innocent? For it is a question of that."

an innocent person is more stringent than one's duty to keep a person from dying, an abortion may not be performed. Or, (4) if one's only options are directly killing an innocent person or letting a person die, one must prefer letting the person die, and thus an abortion may not be performed.[4]

Some people seem to have thought that these are not further premises which must be added if the conclusion is to be reached, but that they follow from the very fact that an innocent person has a right to life.[5] But this seems to me to be a mistake, and perhaps the simplest way to show this is to bring out that while we must certainly grant that innocent persons have a right to life, the theses in (1) through (4) are all false. Take (2), for example. If directly killing an innocent person is murder, and thus is impermissible, then the mother's directly killing the innocent person inside her is murder, and thus is impermissible. But it cannot seriously be thought to be murder if the mother performs an abortion on herself to save her life. It cannot seriously be said that she *must* refrain, that she *must* sit passively by and wait for her death. Let us look again at the case of you and the violinist. There you are, in bed with the violinist, and the director of the hospital says to you, "It's all most distressing, and I deeply sympathize, but you see this is putting an additional strain on your kidneys, and you'll be dead within the month. But you *have* to stay where you are all the same. Because unplugging you would be directly killing an innocent violinist, and that's murder, and that's impermissible." If anything in the world is true, it is that you do not commit murder, you do not do what is impermissible, if you reach around to your back and unplug yourself from that violinist to save your life.

The main focus of attention in writings on abortion has been on what a third party may or may not do in answer to a request from a

4. The thesis in (4) is in an interesting way weaker than those in (1), (2), and (3): they rule out abortion even in cases in which both mother *and* child will die if the abortion is not performed. By contrast, one who held the view expressed in 4 could consistently say that one needn't prefer letting two persons die to killing one.

5. See the following passage from Pius XII, *Address to the Italian Catholic Society of Midwives:* "The baby in the maternal breast has the right to life immediately from God.—Hence there is no man, no human authority, no science, no medical, eugenic, social, economic or moral 'indication' which can establish or grant a valid juridical ground for a direct deliberate disposition of an innocent human life, that is a disposition which looks to its destruction either as an end or as a means to another end perhaps in itself not illicit.—The baby, still not born, is a man in the same degree and for the same reason as the mother" (quoted in Noonan, *The Morality of Abortion*, p. 45).

woman for an abortion. This is in a way understandable. Things being as they are, there isn't much a woman can safely do to abort herself. So the question asked is what a third party may do, and what the mother may do, if it is mentioned at all, is deduced, almost as an afterthought, from what it is concluded that third parties may do. But it seems to me that to treat the matter in this way is to refuse to grant to the mother that very status of person which is so firmly insisted on for the fetus. For we cannot simply read off what a person may do from what a third party may do. Suppose you find yourself trapped in a tiny house with a growing child. I mean a very tiny house, and a rapidly growing child—you are already up against the wall of the house and in a few minutes you'll be crushed to death. The child on the other hand won't be crushed to death; if nothing is done to stop him from growing he'll be hurt, but in the end he'll simply burst open the house and walk out a free man. Now I could well understand it if a bystander were to say, "There's nothing we can do for you. We cannot choose between your life and his, we cannot be the ones to decide who is to live, we cannot intervene." But it cannot be concluded that you too can do nothing, that you cannot attack it to save your life. However innocent the child may be, you do not have to wait passively while it crushes you to death. Perhaps a pregnant woman is vaguely felt to have the status of house, to which we don't allow the right of self-defense. But if the woman houses the child, it should be remembered that she is a person who houses it.

I should perhaps stop to say explicitly that I am not claiming that people have a right to do anything whatever to save their lives. I think, rather, that there are drastic limits to the right of self-defense. If someone threatens you with death unless you torture someone else to death, I think you have not the right, even to save your life, to do so. But the case under consideration here is very different. In our case there are only two people involved, one whose life is threatened, and one who threatens it. Both are innocent: the one who is threatened is not threatened because of any fault, the one who threatens does not threaten because of any fault. For this reason we may feel that we bystanders cannot intervene. But the person threatened can.

In sum, a woman surely can defend her life against the threat to it posed by the unborn child, even if doing so involves its death. And this shows not merely that the theses in (1) through (4) are false; it shows also that the extreme view of abortion is false, and so we need not canvass any other possible ways of arriving at it from the argument I mentioned at the outset.

2. The extreme view could of course be weakened to say that while abortion is permissible to save the mother's life, it may not be performed by a third party, but only by the mother herself. But this cannot be right either. For what we have to keep in mind is that the mother and the unborn child are not like two tenants in a small house which has, by an unfortunate mistake, been rented to both: the mother *owns* the house. The fact that she does adds to the offensiveness of deducing that the mother can do nothing from the supposition that third parties can do nothing. But it does more than this: it casts a bright light on the supposition that third parties can do nothing. Certainly it lets us see that a third party who says "I cannot choose between you" is fooling himself if he thinks this is impartiality. If Jones has found and fastened on a certain coat, which he needs to keep him from freezing, but which Smith also needs to keep him from freezing, then it is not impartiality that says "I cannot choose between you" when Smith owns the coat. Women have said again and again "This body is *my* body!" and they have reason to feel angry, reason to feel that it has been like shouting into the wind. Smith, after all, is hardly likely to bless us if we say to him, "Of course it's your coat, anybody would grant that it is. But no one may choose between you and Jones who is to have it."

We should really ask what it is that says "no one may choose" in the face of the fact that the body that houses the child is the mother's body. It may be simply a failure to appreciate this fact. But it may be something more interesting, namely the sense that one has a right to refuse to lay hands on people, even where it would be just and fair to do so, even where justice seems to require that somebody do so. Thus justice might call for somebody to get Smith's coat back from Jones, and yet you have a right to refuse to be the one to lay hands on Jones, a right to refuse to do physical violence to him. This, I think, must be granted. But then what should be said is not "no one may choose," but only "I cannot choose," and indeed not even this, but "*I* will not *act*," leaving it open that somebody else can or should, and in particular that anyone in a position of authority, with the job of securing people's rights, both can and should. So this is no difficulty. I have not been arguing that any given third party must accede to the mother's request that he perform an abortion to save her life, but only that he may.

I suppose that in some views of human life the mother's body is only on loan to her, the loan not being one which gives her any prior claim to it. One who held this view might well think it impartiality to say "I cannot choose." But I shall simply ignore this possibility. My own view is that if a human being has any just, prior claim to anything at all, he has a just, prior claim to his own body. And perhaps this needn't be argued for here anyway, since, as I mentioned, the arguments against abortion we are looking at do grant that the woman has a right to decide what happens in and to her body.

But although they do grant it, I have tried to show that they do not take seriously what is done in granting it. I suggest the same thing will reappear even more clearly when we turn away from cases in which the mother's life is at stake, and attend, as I propose we now do, to the vastly more common cases in which a woman wants an abortion for some less weighty reason than preserving her own life.

3. Where the mother's life is not at stake, the argument I mentioned at the outset seems to have a much stronger pull. "Everyone has a right to life, so the unborn person has a right to life." And isn't the child's right to life weightier than anything other than the mother's own right to life, which she might put forward as ground for an abortion?

This argument treats the right to life as if it were unproblematic. It is not, and this seems to me to be precisely the source of the mistake.

For we should now, at long last, ask what it comes to, to have a right to life. In some views having a right to life includes having a right to be given at least the bare minimum one needs for continued life. But suppose that what in fact *is* the bare minimum a man needs for continued life is something he has no right at all to be given? If I am sick unto death, and the only thing that will save my life is the touch of Henry Fonda's cool hand on my fevered brow, then all the same, I have no right to be given the touch of Henry Fonda's cool hand on my fevered brow. It would be frightfully nice of him to fly in from the West Coast to provide it. It would be less nice, though no doubt well meant, if my friends flew out to the West Coast and carried Henry Fonda back with them. But I have no right at all against anybody that he should do this for me. Or again, to return to the story I told earlier, the fact that for continued life that violinist needs the continued use of your kidneys does not establish that he has a right to be given the continued use of your kidneys. He certainly has no right against you that *you* should give him continued use of your kidneys. For nobody has any right to use your kidneys unless you give him such a right; and nobody has the right against you that you shall give him this right—if you do allow him to go on using your kidneys, this is a kindness on your part, and not something he can claim from you as his due. Nor has he any right against anybody else that *they* should give him continued use of your kidneys. Certainly he had no right against the Society of Music Lovers that they should plug him into you in the first place. And if you now start to unplug yourself, having learned that you will otherwise have to spend nine years in bed with him, there is nobody in the world who must try to prevent you, in order to see to it that he is given something he has a right to be given.

Some people are rather stricter about the right to life. In their view, it does not include the right to be given anything, but amounts to, and only to, the right not to be killed by anybody. But here a related difficulty arises. If everybody is to refrain from killing that violinist, then everybody must refrain from doing a great many different sorts of things. Everybody must refrain from slitting his throat, everybody must refrain from shooting him—and everybody must refrain from unplugging you from him. But does he have a right against everybody that they shall refrain from unplugging you from him? To refrain from doing this is to allow him to continue to use your kidneys. It could be argued that he has a right against us that *we* should allow him to continue to use your kidneys. That is, while he had no right against us that we should give him the use of your kidneys, it might be argued that he anyway has a right against us that we shall not now intervene and deprive him of the use of your kidneys. I shall come back to third-party interventions later. But certainly the violinist has no right against you that *you* shall allow him to continue to use your kidneys. As I said, if you do allow him to use them, it is a kindness on your part, and not something you owe him.

The difficulty I point to here is not peculiar to the right of life. It reappears in connection with all the other natural rights; and it is something which an adequate account of rights must deal with. For present purposes it is enough just to draw attention to it. But I would stress that I am not arguing that people do not have a right to life—

quite to the contrary, it seems to me that the primary control we must place on the acceptability of an account of rights is that it should turn out in that account to be a truth that all persons have a right to life. I am arguing only that having a right to life does not guarantee having either a right to be given the use of or a right to be allowed continued use of another person's body—even if one needs it for life itself. So the right to life will not serve the opponents of abortion in the very simple and clear way in which they seem to have thought it would.

4. There is another way to bring out the difficulty. In the most ordinary sort of case, to deprive someone of what he has a right to is to treat him unjustly. Suppose a boy and his small brother are jointly given a box of chocolates for Christmas. If the older boy takes the box and refuses to give his brother any of the chocolates, he is unjust to him, for the brother has been given a right to half of them. But suppose that, having learned that otherwise it means nine years in bed with that violinist, you unplug yourself from him. You surely are not being unjust to him, for you gave him no right to use your kidneys, and no one else can have given him any such right. But we have to notice that in unplugging yourself, you are killing him; and violinists, like everybody else, have a right to life, and thus in the view we were considering just now, the right not to be killed. So here you do what he supposedly has a right you shall not do, but you do not act unjustly to him in doing it.

The emendation which may be made at this point is this: the right to life consists not in the right not to be killed, but rather in the right not to be killed unjustly. This runs a risk of circularity, but never mind: it would enable us to square the fact that the violinist has a right to life with the fact that you do not act unjustly toward him in unplugging yourself, thereby killing him. For if you do not kill him unjustly, you do not violate his right to life, and so it is no wonder you do him no injustice.

But if this emendation is accepted, the gap in the argument against abortion stares us plainly in the face: it is by no means enough to show that the fetus is a person, and to remind us that all persons have a right to life—we need to be shown also that killing the fetus violates its right to life, that is, that abortion is unjust killing. And is it?

I suppose we may take it as a datum that in a case of pregnancy due to rape the mother has not given the unborn person a right to the use of her body for food and shelter. Indeed, in what pregnancy could it be supposed that the mother has given the unborn person such a right? It is not as if there were unborn persons drifting about the world, to whom a woman who wants a child says "I invite you in."

But it might be argued that there are other ways one can have acquired a right to the use of another person's body than by having been invited to use it by that person. Suppose a woman voluntarily indulges in intercourse, knowing of the chance it will issue in pregnancy, and then she does become pregnant; is she not in part responsible for the presence, in fact the very existence, of the unborn person inside her? No doubt she did not invite it in. But doesn't her partial responsibility for its being there itself give it a right to the use of her body?[6] If so, then her aborting it would be more like the boy's taking away the chocolates, and less like your unplugging yourself from the violinist—doing so would be depriving it of what it does have a right to, and thus would be doing it an injustice.

And then, too, it might be asked whether or not she can kill it even to save her own life: If she voluntarily called it into existence, how can she now kill it, even in self-defense?

The first thing to be said about this is that it is something new. Opponents of abortion have been so concerned to make out the independence of the fetus, in order to establish that it has a right to life, just as its mother does, that they have tended to overlook the possible support they might gain from making out that the fetus is *dependent* on the mother, in order to establish that she has a special kind of responsibility for it, a responsibility that gives it rights against her which are not possessed by any independent person—such as an ailing violinist who is a stranger to her.

On the other hand, this argument would give the unborn person a right to its mother's body only if her pregnancy resulted from a voluntary act, undertaken in full knowledge of the chance a pregnancy might result from it. It would leave out entirely the unborn person whose existence is due to rape. Pending the availability of some further argument, then, we would be left with the conclusion that unborn persons whose existence is due to rape have no right to the use of their mothers' bodies, and thus that aborting them is not depriving

6. The need for a discussion of this argument was brought home to me by members of the Society for Ethical and Legal Philosophy, to whom this paper was originally presented.

them of anything they have a right to and hence is not unjust killing.

And we should also notice that it is not at all plain that this argument really does go even as far as it purports to. For there are cases and cases, and the details make a difference. If the room is stuffy, and I therefore open a window to air it, and a burglar climbs in, it would be absurd to say, "Ah, now he can stay, she's given him a right to the use of her house—for she is partially responsible for his presence there, having voluntarily done what enabled him to get in, in full knowledge that there are such things as burglars, and that burglars burgle." It would be still more absurd to say this if I had had bars installed outside my windows, precisely to prevent burglars from getting in, and a burglar got in only because of a defect in the bars. It remains equally absurd if we imagine it is not a burglar who climbs in, but an innocent person who blunders or falls in. Again, suppose it were like this: people-seeds drift about in the air like pollen, and if you open your windows, one may drift in and take root in your carpets or upholstery. You don't want children, so you fix up your windows with fine mesh screens, the very best you can buy. As can happen, however, and on very, very rare occasions does happen, one of the screens is defective; and a seed drifts in and takes root. Does the person-plant who now develops have a right to the use of your house? Surely not—despite the fact that you voluntarily opened your windows, you knowingly kept carpets and upholstered furniture, and you knew that screens were sometimes defective. Someone may argue that you are responsible for its rooting, that it does have a right to your house, because after all you *could* have lived out your life with bare floors and furniture, or with sealed windows and doors. But this won't do—for by the same token anyone can avoid a pregnancy due to rape by having a hysterectomy, or anyway by never leaving home without a (reliable!) army.

It seems to me that the argument we are looking at can establish at most that there are *some* cases in which the unborn person has a right to the use of its mother's body, and therefore *some* cases in which abortion is unjust killing. There is room for much discussion and argument as to precisely which, if any. But I think we should side-step this issue and leave it open, for at any rate the argument certainly does not establish that all abortion is unjust killing.

5. There is room for yet another argument here, however. We surely must all grant that there may be cases in which it would be morally indecent to detach a person from your body at the cost of his

life. Suppose you learn that what the violinist needs is not nine years of your life, but only one hour: all you need do to save his life is to spend one hour in that bed with him. Suppose also that letting him use your kidneys for that one hour would not affect your health in the slightest. Admittedly you were kidnapped. Admittedly you did not give anyone permission to plug him into you. Nevertheless it seems to me plain you *ought* to allow him to use your kidneys for that hour—it would be indecent to refuse.

Again, suppose pregnancy lasted only an hour, and constituted no threat to life or health. And suppose that a woman becomes pregnant as a result of rape. Admittedly she did not voluntarily do anything to bring about the existence of a child. Admittedly she did nothing at all which would give the unborn person a right to the use of her body. All the same it might well be said, as in the newly emended violinist story, that she *ought* to allow it to remain for that hour—that it would be indecent in her to refuse.

Now some people are inclined to use the term "right" in such a way that it follows from the fact that you ought to allow a person to use your body for the hour he needs, that he has a right to use your body for the hour he needs, even though he has not been given that right by any person or act. They may say that it follows also that if you refuse, you act unjustly toward him. This use of the term is perhaps so common that it cannot be called wrong; nevertheless it seems to me to be an unfortunate loosening of what we would do better to keep a tight rein on. Suppose that box of chocolates I mentioned earlier had not been given to both boys jointly, but was given only to the older boy. There he sits, stolidly eating his way through the box, his small brother watching enviously. Here we are likely to say "You ought not to be so mean. You ought to give your brother some of those chocolates." My own view is that it just does not follow from the truth of this that the brother has any right to any of the chocolates. If the boy refuses to give his brother any, he is greedy, stingy, callous—but not unjust. I suppose that the people I have in mind will say it does follow that the brother has a right to some of the chocolates, and thus that the boy does act unjustly if he refuses to give his brother any. But the effect of saying this is to obscure what we should keep distinct, namely the difference between the boy's refusal in this case and the boy's refusal in the earlier case, in which the box was given to both boys jointly, and in which the small brother thus had what was from any point of view clear title to half.

A further objection to so using the term "right" that from the fact that A ought to do a thing for B, it follows that B has a right against A that A do it for him, is that it is going to make the question of whether or not a man has a right to a thing turn on how easy it is to provide him with it; and this seems not merely unfortunate, but morally unacceptable. Take the case of Henry Fonda again. I said earlier that I had no right to the touch of his cool hand on my fevered brow, even though I needed it to save my life. I said it would be frightfully nice of him to fly in from the West Coast to provide me with it, but that I had no right against him that he should do so. But suppose he isn't on the West Coast. Suppose he has only to walk across the room, place a hand briefly on my brow—and lo, my life is saved. Then surely he ought to do it, it would be indecent to refuse. Is it to be said "Ah, well, it follows that in this case she has a right to the touch of his hand on her brow, and so it would be an injustice in him to refuse"? So that I have a right to it when it is easy for him to provide it, though no right when it's hard? It's rather a shocking idea that anyone's rights should fade away and disappear as it gets harder and harder to accord them to him.

So my own view is that even though you ought to let the violinist use your kidneys for the one hour he needs, we should not conclude that he has a right to do so—we should say that if you refuse, you are, like the boy who owns all the chocolates and will give none away, self-centered and callous, indecent in fact, but not unjust. And similarly, that even supposing a case in which a woman pregnant due to rape ought to allow the unborn person to use her body for the hour he needs, we should not conclude that he has a right to do so; we should conclude that she is self-centered, callous, indecent, but not unjust, if she refuses. The complaints are no less grave; they are just different. However, there is no need to insist on this point. If anyone does wish to deduce "he has a right" from "you ought," then all the same he must surely grant that there are cases in which it is not morally required of you that you allow that violinist to use your kidneys, and in which he does not have a right to use them, and in which you do not do him an injustice if you refuse. And so also for mother and unborn child. Except in such cases as the unborn person has a right to demand it—and we were leaving open the possibility that there may be such cases—nobody is morally *required* to make large sacrifices, of health, of all other interests and concerns, of all other duties and commitments, for nine years, or even for nine months, in order to keep another person alive.

6. We have in fact to distinguish between two kinds of Samaritan: the Good Samaritan and what we might call the Minimally Decent Samaritan. The story of the Good Samaritan, you will remember, goes like this:

> A certain man went down from Jerusalem to Jericho, and fell among thieves, which stripped him of his raiment, and wounded him, and departed, leaving him half dead.
>
> And by chance there came down a certain priest that way; and when he saw him, he passed by on the other side.
>
> And likewise a Levite, when he was at the place, came and looked on him, and passed by on the other side.
>
> But a certain Samaritan, as he journeyed, came where he was; and when he saw him he had compassion on him.
>
> And went to him, and bound up his wounds, pouring in oil and wine, and set him on his own beast, and brought him to an inn, and took care of him.
>
> And on the morrow, when he departed, he took out two pence, and gave them to the host, and said unto him, "Take care of him; and whatsoever thou spendest more, when I come again, I will repay thee."   (Luke 10:30–35)

The Good Samaritan went out of his way, at some cost to himself, to help one in need of it. We are not told what the options were, that is, whether or not the priest and the Levite could have helped by doing less than the Good Samaritan did, but assuming they could have, then the fact they did nothing at all shows they were not even Minimally Decent Samaritans, not because they were not Samaritans, but because they were not even minimally decent.

These things are a matter of degree, of course, but there is a difference, and it comes out perhaps most clearly in the story of Kitty Genovese, who, as you will remember, was murdered while thirty-eight people watched or listened, and did nothing at all to help her. A Good Samaritan would have rushed out to give direct assistance against the murderer. Or perhaps we had better allow that it would have been a Splendid Samaritan who did this, on the ground that it would have involved a risk of death for himself. But the thirty-eight not only did not do this, they did not even trouble to pick up a phone to call the police. Minimally Decent Samaritanism would call for doing at least that, and their not having done it was monstrous.

After telling the story of the Good Samaritan, Jesus said "Go, and do thou likewise." Perhaps he meant that we are morally required to act as the Good Samaritan did. Perhaps he was urging people to do more than is morally required of them. At all events it seems plain that it was not morally required of any of the thirty-eight that he rush out to give direct assistance at the risk of his own life, and that it is not morally required of anyone that he give long stretches of his life— nine years or nine months—to sustaining the life of a person who has no special right (we were leaving open the possibility of this) to demand it.

Indeed, with one rather striking class of exceptions, no one in any country in the world is *legally* required to do anywhere near as much as this for anyone else. The class of exceptions is obvious. My main concern here is not the state of the law in respect to abortion, but it is worth drawing attention to the fact that in no state in this country is any man compelled by law to be even a Minimally Decent Samaritan to any person; there is no law under which charges could be brought against the thirty-eight who stood by while Kitty Genovese died. By contrast, in most states in this country women are compelled by law to be not merely Minimally Decent Samaritans, but Good Samaritans to unborn persons inside them. [This essay first appeared in 1971, and thus prior to the decision in *Roe v. Wade*—ed.] This doesn't by itself settle anything one way or the other, because it may well be argued that there should be laws in this country—as there are in many European countries—compelling at least Minimally Decent Samaritanism.[7] But it does show that there is a gross injustice in the existing state of the law. And it shows also that the groups currently working against liberalization of abortion laws, in fact working toward having it declared unconstitutional for a state to permit abortion, had better start working for the adoption of Good Samaritan laws generally, or earn the charge that they are acting in bad faith.

I should think, myself, that Minimally Decent Samaritan laws would be one thing, Good Samaritan laws quite another, and in fact highly improper. But we are not here concerned with the law. What we should ask is not whether anybody should be compelled by law to be a Good Samaritan, but whether we must accede to a situation in which somebody is being compelled—by nature, perhaps—to be a Good Samaritan. We have, in other words, to look now at third-party interventions. I have been arguing that no person is morally required to make large sacrifices to sustain the life of another who has no right

7. For a discussion of the difficulties involved, and a survey of the European experience with such laws, see *The Good Samaritan and the Law*, ed. James M. Ratcliffe (New York: Peter Smith, 1966).

to demand them, and this even where the sacrifices do not include life itself; we are not morally required to be Good Samaritans or anyway Very Good Samaritans to one another. But what if a man cannot extricate himself from such a situation? What if he appeals to us to extricate him? It seems to me plain that there are cases in which we can, cases in which a Good Samaritan would extricate him. There you are, you were kidnapped, and nine years in bed with that violinist lie ahead of you. You have your own life to lead. You are sorry, but you simply cannot see giving up so much of your life to the sustaining of his. You cannot extricate yourself, and ask us to do so. I should have thought that—in light of his having no right to the use of your body—it was obvious that we do not have to accede to your being forced to give up so much. We can do what you ask. There is no injustice to the violinist in our doing so.

7. Following the lead of the opponents of abortion, I have throughout been speaking of the fetus merely as a person, and what I have been asking is whether or not the argument we began with, which proceeds only from the fetus's being a person, really does establish its conclusion. I have argued that it does not.

But of course there are arguments and arguments, and it may be said that I have simply fastened on the wrong one. It may be said that what is important is not merely the fact that the fetus is a person, but that it is a person for whom the woman has a special kind of responsibility issuing from the fact that she is its mother. And it might be argued that all my analogies are therefore irrelevant—for you do not have that special kind of responsibility for that violinist, Henry Fonda does not have that special kind of responsibility for me. And our attention might be drawn to the fact that men and women both *are* compelled by law to provide support for their children.

I have in effect dealt (briefly) with this argument in section 4 above; but a (still briefer) recapitulation now may be in order. Surely we do not have any such "special responsibility" for a person unless we have assumed it, explicitly or implicitly. If a set of parents do not try to prevent pregnancy, do not obtain an abortion, and then at the time of birth of the child do not put it out for adoption, but rather take it home with them, then they have assumed responsibility for it, they have given it rights, and they cannot *now* withdraw support from it at the cost of its life because they now find it difficult to go on providing for it. But if they have taken all reasonable precautions against having a child, they do not simply by virtue of their biological relationship to the child who comes into existence have a special responsibility for it. They may wish to assume responsibility for it, or they may not wish to. And I am suggesting that if assuming responsibility for it would require large sacrifices, then they may refuse. A Good Samaritan would not refuse—or anyway, a Splendid Samaritan, if the sacrifices that had to be made were enormous. But then so would a Good Samaritan assume responsibility for that violinist; so would Henry Fonda, if he is a Good Samaritan, fly in from the West Coast and assume responsibility for me.

8. My argument will be found unsatisfactory on two counts by many of those who want to regard abortion as morally permissible. First, while I do argue that abortion is not impermissible, I do not argue that it is always permissible. There may well be cases in which carrying the child to term requires only Minimally Decent Samaritanism of the mother, and this is a standard we must not fall below. I am inclined to think it a merit of my account precisely that it does *not* give a general yes or a general no. It allows for and supports our sense that, for example, a sick and desperately frightened fourteen-year-old schoolgirl, pregnant due to rape, may *of course* choose abortion, and that any law which rules this out is an insane law. And it also allows for and supports our sense that in other cases resort to abortion is even positively indecent. It would be indecent in the woman to request an abortion, and indecent in a doctor to perform it, if she is in her seventh month, and wants the abortion just to avoid the nuisance of postponing a trip abroad. The very fact that the arguments I have been drawing attention to treat all cases of abortion, or even all cases of abortion in which the mother's life is not at stake, as morally on a par ought to have made them suspect at the outset.

Secondly, while I am arguing for the permissibility of abortion in some cases, I am not arguing for the right to secure the death of the unborn child. It is easy to confuse these two things in that up to a certain point in the life of the fetus it is not able to survive outside the mother's body; hence removing it from her body guarantees its death. But they are importantly different. I have argued that you are not morally required to spend nine months in bed, sustaining the life of that violinist; but to say this is by no means to say that if, when you unplug yourself, there is a miracle and he survives, you then have a right to turn round and slit his throat. You may detach yourself even if this costs him his life; you have no right to be guaranteed his death, by some other means, if unplugging yourself does not kill him. There are some people who will feel dissatisfied by this feature of my argument. A woman may be utterly devastated by the thought of a child, a bit of herself, put out for adoption and never seen or heard of again. She may therefore want not merely that the child be detached from her, but more, that it die. Some opponents of abortion are inclined to regard this as beneath contempt—thereby showing insensitivity to what is surely a powerful source of despair. All the same, I agree that the desire for the child's death is not one which anybody may gratify, should it turn out to be possible to detach the child alive.

At this place, however, it should be remembered that we have only been pretending throughout that the fetus is a human being from the moment of conception. A very early abortion is surely not the killing of a person, and so is not dealt with by anything I have said here.[8]

8. I am very much indebted to James Thomson for discussion, criticism, and many helpful suggestions.

2 · Rights and Deaths

In an article in *Philosophy and Public Affairs* (2, Winter 1973), John Finnis makes a great many adverse remarks about my views about abortion (see Essay 1). I cannot take them all up: there are too many. I shall instead concentrate on certain of his positive proposals. One of them (I take it up in section 2) would, if true, make abortion impermissible in cases in which I think it permissible; and another (I take it up in section 3) would, if true, undercut an argument I had used to support the permissibility of abortion in those cases, and in others as well. Both proposals have consequences well beyond the abortion issue, and so on any view call for close attention.

1. But first, some things Finnis says about rights. I *think* his main complaint against me in the part of his paper which deals with rights is that I was wrong to discuss them at all—my doing so "needlessly complicates and confuses the issue." I find this puzzling. My aim was to raise doubts about the argument that abortion is impermissible because the fetus is a person, and all persons have a right to life; and how is one to do that without attending to rights? But this is merely by the way. More interesting, I think, is this: I had said that the right to life was not unproblematic—that a man's having a right to life does not guarantee either that he has a right to be given the use of whatever he needs for life, or that he has a right to continued use of whatever he is currently using, and needs for life. So, I said, the right to life will not serve the opponents of abortion in the very simple and clear way in which they seem to have thought it would. Finnis thinks my point about the right to life is correct and familiar enough: he has an explanation of it. He says that he will call, for example, one man's

right to slit another's throat a "Hohfeldian right"; presumably one man's right to hit another on the nose is also a Hohfeldian right. Hohfeldian rights have the same "logical structure," he says: "to assert a Hohfeldian right is to assert a three-term relation between two persons and the action of one of those persons insofar as that action concerns the other person." So (I suppose) to assert:

(1) Alfred has a right to hit Bill on the nose,

is to assert that a three-term relation holds between Alfred, Bill, and a certain action. By contrast, to assert:

(2) Charles has a right to life,

is to assert that a two-term relation holds between Charles and a certain thing ("or state of affairs"). Rights such as are attributed by assertions of (2) "cannot be completely analyzed in terms of some unique combination of Hohfeldian rights"—that is, sentences such as (2) are not analyzable into any function of sentences such as (1). And (he says) this fact is, though I did not recognize it, the explanation of what I drew attention to in the right to life.

Now I am inclined to think that this account of what one asserts when one asserts (1) and (2) has no future. Finnis has simply not noticed the difficulties which lie in wait for it.[1] What precisely is supposed to be the third term in the case of (1)? An actual, particular action of Alfred's, namely, his hitting Bill on the nose? But what if there never is any such action, since Alfred never exercises his right? Or perhaps, instead, the third term is an act-kind? But if so, which? And what precisely is supposed to be the second term in the case of (2)? Life? Charles's continuing to live? And what if his continuing to live does not exist, since he does not continue to live, since he gets killed? The mind reels.

I suspect that what lurks behind Finnis's account is a grammatical difference: in (1), the phrase "right to" is followed by a verb phrase, and indeed a verb phrase whose main verb ("hit") is what some philosophers call an "action verb." By contrast, in (2), the phrase "right to" is followed by a noun phrase ("life"). And perhaps his point, then, is this: that sentences like (2) in this respect are not

1. Actually, a rather dark footnote (10) suggests that Finnis may not really mean what he said. For in the footnote it appears that "inadequate specifications" of the action someone had a right to have done for him may make for trouble. Whereas if a relation holds amongst three things, it holds amongst them however they are specified.

analyzable into sentences like (1) in this respect. ("He has a right to life" is presumably equivalent to "He has a right to live"; but I suppose it would be said that the verb "live" is not an "action verb.") If this is his point, he may for all I know be right—we should need to be told how to recognize an "action verb" when we meet one, but perhaps Finnis could tell us this.

But for present purposes, it doesn't matter whether he can or not, or even whether this is his point or not: for his aim was to explain what I drew attention to in the right to life, and *that* is not explainable by *any* difference between the logic or grammar of (2) on the one hand, and sentences such as (1) on the other.

For the fact is, I was simply over-fascinated by the example currently on the table. I said that a man's having a right to life does not guarantee either that he has a right to be given the use of whatever he needs for life, or that he has a right to continued use of whatever he is currently using, and needs for life. The right to life is a natural right; and being fascinated by the right to life, I noticed only that analogous points hold of all the natural rights. I should have noticed that analogous points hold of *all* rights. If Alfred very much wants to hit Bill on the nose, Bill might well sell him the right to do so— Bill sells, Alfred buys, and then has the right. Does he have a right to be given the use of whatever it is he needs if he is to hit Bill on the nose? If Bill has been carried off by an eagle, and can only be reached by helicopter, does Alfred have a right to be given a helicopter? Hardly. If Alfred steals your helicopter, and is on his way to Bill, does he have a right to continued use of your helicopter? Scarcely.

The situation about rights, it seems to me, is really this: *all* of them are problematic in the way I mentioned—none of them will serve anybody in the very simple and clear way in which opponents of abortion have seemed to think the right to life would serve them. Unlike Mr. Finnis, I think there does not exist any even remotely plausible theory of the logic of rights. And yet, again unlike Mr. Finnis, I think there does not exist any issue of importance in ethics in which we can avoid or side-step them.

2. I had suggested in my article that it is morally permissible for you to unplug the ailing violinist from yourself to save your life, even though to unplug him is to kill him. "Quite so," says Finnis. I had then asked: so why not abortion in analogous circumstances? What if a woman is pregnant due to rape, and allowing the child to remain

inside her endangers her life? May she not arrange for an abortion to save her life? Finnis replies: (1) That would be *direct* killing of the innocent, and direct killing of the innocent is always impermissible. (2) Your unplugging the violinist from yourself to save your life is only *indirect* killing. Indirect killing is not always permissible, but it sometimes is—in particular, indirectly killing that violinist is.

A very important difference, then, this difference between direct and indirect killing: it bears a heavy moral weight. And I am not convinced that Finnis has made clear how it is able to carry that weight.

He puts it like this. Your killing of someone is direct if your choice in acting is "a choice against life"; and he says—anyway, I *think* he means to say[2]—that a choice is a choice against life where it is a choice to bring about a death, either as an end in itself, or as a means to some further end. You directly kill a person if your choice in acting is a choice to bring about a death, either as end or means. By contrast, you only indirectly kill a person if, though you foresee his death will be a consequence of what you do, your choice in acting is not a choice to bring about his death, either as end or means. (I had said in footnote 2 that what matters is whether or not the *killing* is the agent's end or means; Finnis says that what matters is whether or not the *death* is the agent's end or means. There are reasons to prefer my account, but I am content to adopt his in what follows.)

Two questions present themselves: (1) Why should it be thought that this difference makes a moral difference? (2) If it makes a moral difference, does it make the moral difference Finnis wants it to?

The difficulties to which question (2) points are familiar enough, and I shall not spend much time over them.[3] I suppose Finnis is right to say that if you unplug the violinist, you only indirectly kill him:

2. Because on p. 135 he asks himself: "When *should* one say that the expected bad effect or aspect of an action is not intended either as end or as means and hence does not determine the moral character of the act as a choice not to respect one of the basic human values?" I take it that if an expected bad effect, say a death, is *not* intended as end or as means, then the act which causes the death does not issue from a choice against life, and hence the agent does not directly kill.

3. See, for example, Philippa Foot, "The Problems of Abortion and the Doctrine of the Double Effect," *The Oxford Review 5 (1967)*, and Thomas Nagel, "War and Massacre," in his *Mortal Questions* (Cambridge: Cambridge University Press, 1979), pp. 53–74. I should at this place mention how much I have learned about the matters dealt with in this section, not merely from these two articles, but from the discussions of them at the Society for Ethical and Legal Philosophy.

since you unplug him to save your life, his death is not your end (your end is the saving of your life), and it is not your means either (your means to the saving of your life is the unplugging you do). But what if a woman is pregnant due to rape, and allowing the child to remain inside her endangers her life? Suppose she takes a medicine known to cause miscarriage,[4] and takes it in order to cause miscarriage in order to save her life? The child's death is not her end (her end is the saving of her life), and it is not her means either (her means to the saving of her life is the medicine she takes and the miscarriage it causes). So here too the killing should be indirect. But if it is indirect, it should be permissible, for just as you unplug the violinist to save your life, she takes the medicine to save her life. Yet on Finnis's view *she* acts wrongly, she does the impermissible.

Finnis needs to have the woman's killing of the child turn out to be direct killing, and your killing of the violinist to be indirect killing. And I am afraid he has not succeeded in getting what he needs. He mentions four questions we should ask about a putative indirect killing. (a) "Would the chosen action have been chosen if the victim had not been present?" If so, there is reason to say the killing is indirect: the death is not the agent's end, but is a mere (foreseen) side effect of the action he takes to reach his end. But as Finnis himself grants, *this* will not distinguish between the cases we are looking at: "in both situations, the oppressive presence of the victim is what makes one minded to do the act in question." (b) "Is the person making the choice the one whose life is threatened by the presence of the victim?" Yes, in both cases. (c) "Does the chosen action involve not merely a denial of aid and succor to someone but an actual intervention that amounts to an assault on the body of that person?" No more in the one case than in the other. What Finnis has in mind in raising this question is that we should contrast with your unplugging the violinist, not a woman's neatly and cleanly taking a teaspoon of medicine, but rather a craniotomy: an operation in which the child's skull is crushed to make it possible to get it out of its mother. (And a craniotomy, of course, the mother is not likely to be limber enough to perform herself.) You can unplug the violinist, thereby killing him, while wearing white gloves; in a craniotomy you have actually to take hold, and it is far

4. I had not known there were such medicines. But Finnis tells us that if a pregnant woman's life is threatened by fever, it is permissible for her to take or be given a medicine to reduce the fever, even though it is known that the medicine causes miscarriage. (In *this* case, then, the killing must be indirect.) So perhaps there are.

too messy for that. But I cannot think that Finnis means us to take this point very seriously. Abortifacients one could take by teaspoon would then be morally safe, and the existing procedure for a late abortion (the use of a saline solution) only slightly less so. Jonathan Bennett poured scorn on this kind of consideration in the article which Finnis cites, and I think he was quite right to do so. (d) "But is the action against someone who had a duty not to be doing what he is doing, or not to be present where he is present?" I think Finnis supposes there is more fault in the case of you and the violinist than in the case of the woman and child: in the former case, "the whole affair is a gross injustice." I should have thought there was no need to remind anyone of the injustice of rape. But more important, it is hard to see how anyone could think that this question has any bearing at all on the question whether a given death is, on the one hand, an agent's end or means, or on the other hand, a mere foreseen consequence of what he does to save his life.

Still, it might be said that perhaps the killing in the case of woman and child (but not in the case of you and the violinist) really is a direct killing, even though Finnis has just not argued very well for it. Or again, it might be said (Germaine Grisez, for example, would say) that the killings in both cases are indirect, and Finnis has simply been wrong in thinking that while one is permissible, the other is not. So it seems to me that we should turn back to question (1), and ask— Mr. Finnis, his arguments, his moral views apart—why it should be thought that the difference between a direct and an indirect killing makes a moral difference.

Some people may think that Finnis has already sufficiently answered this question when he asked us to notice that a direct killing involves a choice "against life." Isn't that bad? And isn't it plain that a man's choices, intentions, reasons have a bearing on the moral evaluation proper to what he does?

Of course they do. But a man who kills only indirectly foresees perfectly clearly that he will bring about a death, and chooses the act he knows will bring it about. What we need to know is why it should matter so crucially whether the death a man foresees is, on the one hand, his end or means, or on the other hand, a merely foreseen consequence.

Sometimes what is done for us is just this: we are given sample acts in which a death is a man's end or means. Here a man kills for nothing further, he kills merely out of hate; there a man kills for money. And the acts are indeed horrendous. Alongside these are set acts in which though a man kills, and the death he brings about is foreseen, it is neither his end nor his means. Here is a bombardier, assigned the task of destroying a missile site which has been launching a rain of deadly missiles onto his country. Unfortunately there is a child on the site, the two-year-old daughter of the missile site's commanding officer. If the bombardier drops his bombs, that child will be killed. Most regrettable that the thing has to be done, yet plainly not a horrendous act if he goes ahead.

But this enterprise, fascinating though it may be, proves nothing at all. A man may perform a dreadful deed while wearing boots, and a permitted, even a quite good deed, while barefoot. This hardly establishes the (hitherto unnoticed) moral significance of boots.

What is needed is to show that the difference *makes* the moral difference, or at least contributes to it. And the best way to test such a claim is to isolate the difference so far as possible. We should try to get as clear a direct killing and as clear an indirect killing as we can, which so far as possible differ only in that respect, and then see if a moral difference emerges.

Imagine the following:

(3) A violent aggressor nation has threatened us with death unless we allow ourselves to be enslaved by it. It has, ready and waiting, a monster missile launcher, which it will use on us unless we surrender. The missile launcher has interior tunnels, each leading to a missile. For technical reasons, the tunnels had to be very small; for technical reasons also, each missile has to be triggered by a human hand. Midgets are too large. So it was necessary to train a team of very young children, two-year-olds in fact, to crawl through and trigger the missiles.

There are two possible continuations of this story. We might imagine two worlds, in both of which (3) is true, but in one of which (4) is, and in the other of which (5) is:

(4) Their technology being what it is, they were able to build only one missile launcher; it will take at least two years to produce another. (By contrast, training the team of children was easy, indeed, was done in a day.) We are capable of bombing the site. Unfortunately, if we bomb to destroy the launcher to save our lives, we kill the children.

(5) Their psychology being what it is, they were able to train only one team of children; it will take at least two years to train another. (By contrast, building the launcher was easy, indeed, was done in a day.) We are capable of bombing the site. Unfortunately, bombing the site will save our lives only if by bombing we kill the children.

Now I take it that if (4) is true, and we act, we only indirectly kill the children: their deaths are not our end, nor do we need their deaths if we are to achieve our end—our end would be just as well achieved if by some miracle the children survive the bombing. Cases such as this have standardly been regarded as cases of indirect killing in the literature on this topic. By contrast, if (5) is true, and we act, we directly kill the children: their deaths are necessary to the achieving of our end, and if, by a miracle, they survive the bombing, we must bomb again.

Of course some very high-minded people may say we must not bomb in either case: after all, the children are innocent! Lower-minded people, like me, will say we can bomb in either case: after all, it is the violent aggressor nation which itself imposed that risk on the children. But what I think no one can say is that we may bomb if (4) is true, but not if (5) is. If that were true, a violent aggressor nation would do well to aspire to such a missile launcher. Careful engineering of tasks and supplies so as to insure the truth of (5) would guarantee it could swallow the virtuous at leisure.

I suspect that the most likely response to what I have said is: those children are not really innocent in the sense intended in the principle "Direct killing of the innocent is always impermissible." "Innocent" here does not mean "free of guilt," but has a technical sense:[5] perhaps "not currently doing harm, or about to do harm in the immediate future," perhaps "not part of the threat directed at others." The children on the launching team are no doubt free of guilt (they mean no one any harm), but they are part of the threat to us, for they are precisely the ones who will launch the missiles against us.

But how is this supposed to bear on the issue at hand? Finnis seemed to think that the innocence or lack of innocence of the victim has a bearing on the question whether he is killed directly or indirectly—see his question (d) above. But then were we misled as to the difference between direct and indirect killing? We were told it was a

5. Thomas Nagel, in "War and Massacre," draws attention to this.

matter of whether the victim's death is end or means, or merely a foreseen consequence; and how could the victim's innocence, in the technical, or perhaps in any other, sense bear on *that?* After all, the children are not innocent in the technical sense in either (4) or (5); yet the one killing is indirect, the other direct.

I did indeed take a liberty when I said, above, that cases such as our act in (4) have standardly been regarded as cases of indirect killing in the literature on this topic. What we have standardly been offered are cases in which the victims are innocent in this technical sense. (Compare the little girl on the missile site in the case of the bombardier, cited above.) Whereas the children in (4) are not innocent in the technical sense. Nevertheless it was appropriate to take that liberty, for our act in (4) is exactly like the cases we have standardly been offered in those respects which define "indirect killing." It is unlike them in other respects—which only makes clear that the cases we have been offered did not isolate the difference whose moral significance they were intended to convince us of.

In the absence of a new account of the difference between direct and indirect killing, I suspect that innocence is best seen as having a bearing, not on whether a killing is direct or indirect, but rather on whether or not a given direct killing is permissible. Anyone who accepts this is then in a position to explain why the act in (5) is permitted, just as the act in (4) is: though the act in (5) is, unlike the act in (4), a direct killing, still its victims are not innocent in the technical sense and it is only direct killing *of the innocent* in the technical sense which is categorically ruled out.

But on the other hand, to accept this is also to grant that the difference between direct and indirect killing does not have the moral significance which has been claimed for it. The acts in (4) and (5) are both permitted, though one is a direct, the other an indirect killing.

And to accept it is also to open the door for abortions in cases in which the child itself is part of the threat to the mother, and hence is not in the technical sense innocent. Such abortions no longer fall under the categorical ban, it having been only a play on the word "innocent" which made it seem that they did fall under it.

3. Finnis rightly says that it was my intention to assimilate certain cases in which a woman allows a pregnancy to continue to cases in which a man is a Good Samaritan to another; and similarly, to assimilate her refusing to allow the pregnancy to continue, to cases in which

a man refuses to be a Good Samaritan to another. My further intention was to draw attention to the fact that there are circumstances in which it is morally acceptable for a man—and similarly for the pregnant woman—to refuse, to say "No, the cost is too great, and I will not pay it."

Finnis believes he has a crushing proof I was wrong to do this. "And here," he says, "we have perhaps the decisive reason why abortion cannot be assimilated to the range of Samaritan problems and why Thomson's location of it within that range is a mere (ingenious) novelty." So we should look where he points.

What we find is this: "The child, like his mother, has a 'just prior claim to his own body,'[6] and abortion involves laying hand on, manipulating, that body." I *think* his point is this. A man who refuses to be a Good Samaritan lays hands on no one, he manipulates no one, he does harm to no one; he merely refrains from giving aid. By contrast, the woman who aborts herself (if she can) does lay hands on and manipulate the child. Well, perhaps she does not actually *touch* it. But she certainly does it harm: she kills it, in fact. So the decisive reason why I am wrong in making the assimilation is this: a reluctant Samaritan merely does not save a life, whereas the mother actually kills the child.

Now it had not actually escaped my notice that the mother who aborts herself kills the child, whereas a man who refuses to be a Good Samaritan—on the traditional understanding of Good Samaritanism—merely does not save. My suggestion was that from a moral point of view these cases should be assimilated: the woman who allows the pregnancy to continue, at great cost to herself, is entitled to praise in the same amount, and, more important, of the same kind, as is the man who sets forth, at great cost to himself, to give aid. That is why I proposed we attend to the case of you and the violinist: surely if you allow the violinist to remain plugged into you, at great cost to yourself, you deserve praise in the same amount, and of the same kind, as any traditional Good Samaritan—and how does this

---

6. Here I feel the waters rising. Finnis had said in a footnote that a right to decide what happens in and to one's body is "to be equated, apparently" with a just prior claim to one's own body; so here he is saying that both child and mother have a right to decide what happens in and to their bodies. Earlier, however, he had said, with éclat, that "traditional Western ethics simply does not accept that a person has 'a right to decide what shall happen in and to his body.' " Has traditional Western ethics changed its mind? and so quickly?

differ from the case of woman and child? To say "Ah, but if she refuses, she kills, whereas a man who refuses to set forth to give aid merely refrains from saving" is not only not decisive against my assimilation, it is *no* reason at all to think it improper—in the absence of a showing that (a) the difference between killing and not saving makes a moral difference, and indeed that (b) the difference between killing and not saving makes a sufficiently profound moral difference as to make the assimilation improper, and of course also that (c) the truth of (b) does not conflict with its being permissible for you to refuse to sustain the violinist, that is, with its being permissible for you to unplug him, thereby killing him.[7]

Finnis has not only not produced these showings, he seems not to have seen they are needed. This *may* be because he thinks that not saving is the same as indirect killing, and therefore already shown to differ morally from real (read: direct) killing. Why else, after all, would he have advised us that if we want to know whether an agent kills directly or indirectly, we should ask whether he makes an assault, or merely denies aid? (Compare question [c] of the preceding section.) But it is, simply, a *mistake* to think that not saving is indirect killing. An indirect killing is perforce a killing, whereas it is quite possible that a man has never killed, and yet that there are many lives he did not save.

Or, alternatively, it *may* be because he thinks (a), (b), and (c) so obvious as to need no argument. My own view is that none of them is obvious. It seems to me to be an interesting, and open, question whether or not (a) is true, and I want to make a few brief suggestions about it below. However, (b) strikes me as false, and in fact as shown to be false by the story of you and the violinist; so as is plain, I think (c) false too. As I cannot see that any reasons have been advanced to think (b) true, I shall from here on ignore it, and therefore (c) as well.

Is (a) true? Once again it is noteworthy that the sample acts offered to convince us of the moral significance of the difference do not isolate

---

7. Finnis must show (c) as well as (a) and (b), since he agrees with me that you may unplug the violinist. It *may* be that Baruch Brody ("Thomson on Abortion," *Philosophy and Public Affairs* 1 [Spring 1972]) does not have to show (c) as well as (a) and (b). Brody puts forward the same ground for rejecting the assimilation as Finnis does, but unlike Finnis, does not say you may unplug the violinist. On the other hand, he does not explicitly say you may not. All he explicitly says on the matter is that my "account of the violinist" is "very problematic."

it.[8] Here is a man who commits a gross and bloody murder; horrendous, isn't it? There is a man who is asleep, and therefore is not saving lives; scarcely horrendous, surely permissible for a man to sleep! But of course there are other things at work here besides the fact that one kills and the other does not save. For one thing, the sleeper does not know he is not saving, whereas the murderer knows he kills. So let us instead compare:

(6) David is walking across a field. Unbeknownst to him, a sick baby has burrowed its way under a clump of hay ahead of him. He steps on the clump, thereby killing the baby.

(7) Edward is walking across a field. Unbeknownst to him, a sick baby has burrowed its way under a clump of hay alongside his path. He walks on; the baby dies; he did not save it.

Is there a moral difference here? This brings me to the first point I wished to make about (a): its defenders will have to make a decision. Do they wish to say that although neither David nor Edward is at fault or to blame for what he does, or for what happens, still their acts differ morally? Or do they wish to say that the acts do not differ morally, that the important difference is not between killing and not saving, but between knowingly killing and knowingly not saving?

I propose we side-step this, and restrict ourselves to cases in which both men act knowingly. A second difference between committing murder, and not saving while asleep, is that the murderer aims at a death whereas the sleeper does not, and this too contributes to the moral difference between them. So let us instead compare:

(8) Frank hates his wife and wants her dead. He puts cleaning fluid in her coffee, thereby killing her.

(9) George hates his wife and wants her dead. She puts cleaning fluid in her coffee (being muddled, thinking it's cream). George happens to have the antidote to cleaning fluid, but he does not give it to her; he does not save her life, and she dies.

Horrendous, both!—but if (a) is true, what Frank did should be worse than what George did, and is it? I suspect that if anyone feels that it

8. Michael Tooley ("Abortion and Infanticide," *Philosophy and Public Affairs* 2 [Fall 1972]) also draws attention to this, and tries to isolate the difference in order to show it is not morally significant.

is, this is because he thinks of Frank as having done *two* morally significant things: first he imposed a risk on his wife by poisoning her coffee, and then, like George, he did not save her. (Maybe he did not have an antidote, but surely he could have called for an ambulance.) So he and George both did not save; but Frank had imposed the risk because of which his wife needed saving, and it is plainly bad to impose risks on people even if no harm actually comes to them. I suspect that it may, ultimately, be this[9] which inclines people to opt for (a). But should we? What if there were no room at all for saving once the agent had made his move?

Whatever we think about Frank and George, it does seem to be very difficult to construct a clear and convincing pair of cases in which the difference is isolated (knowledge, intentions, and reasons are so far as possible the same), but in which the one who kills acts badly, and the one who refrains from saving does not. I suppose that (a) could be true, even if this could not be done; but it does cast doubt on it.

What does seem plain is just this: the question of (a)'s truth is so far an open one. It needs attention of a kind of which Mr. Finnis has certainly not paid it, and in the absence of which his objection to the assimilation I made is merely so much hand waving.

9. And the connected point that a man who wants not to save, and did not impose the risk, can always ask that fascinating question "Why me?"

3 · *Self-Defense and Rights*

1. Suppose Agressor has got hold of a tank. He had told Victim that if he gets a tank, he's going to get in it and run Victim down. Victim sees Aggressor get in his tank and start towards Victim. It is open country, and Victim can see that there is no place to hide, and nothing he can put between himself and Aggressor which Aggressor cannot circle round. Fortunately, Victim happens to have an anti-tank gun with him, and it is in good working order, so he can use it to blow up the tank, thereby saving his life, but of course thereby also killing Aggressor. I think that most people would say that it is morally permissible for Victim to use that anti-tank gun: surely it is permissible to kill a man if that is the only way in which you can prevent him from killing you!

On the other hand, one of the things we are firmly wedded to is the belief that human beings have a right to life, and this presumably includes the right to not be killed. Aggressor is a human being; so he, like the rest of us, has a right to life, and presumably, therefore, the right to not be killed. So how *can* Victim kill him? Precisely *why* is it permissible for Victim to use that anti-tank gun on Aggressor? I propose we look at three replies which I think come fairly readily to mind.

2. The first reply I am going to call "forfeit," and it goes like this. "We good folk all do have a right to life, and that does include the right to not be killed. But there is such a thing as forfeiting a right. We say such things as that the right to life, liberty, and the pursuit of happiness are 'natural rights,' and therefore unconditionally possessed by all people; but that is just so much high-minded rhetoric.

What has happened in the case described is that Aggressor, by virtue of his attack on Victim, has forfeited his right to not be killed, and therefore his right to life. And *that* is why Victim may use his anti-tank gun on Aggressor, thereby killing him: he violates no right of Aggressor's in doing so."

But this very natural first reply is not at all satisfactory. Suppose that as Victim raises his anti-tank gun to fire it, Aggressor's tank stalls. Aggressor gets out to examine the engine, but falls and breaks both ankles in the process. Victim (let us suppose) now has time to get away from Aggressor, and is in no danger. I take it you will not think that Victim may all the same go ahead and kill Aggressor. But why not?—if Aggressor really has forfeited his right to not be killed by virtue of his attack on Victim.[1]

It could, of course, be said that at this point utilitarian considerations come into play. That is, it could be said that yes, Aggressor has forfeited his right to life, but no, Victim cannot now kill him, and that this latter is true because Victim now has no need to kill Aggressor—indeed, because killing Aggressor would mean the loss of a life, whereas not killing Aggressor would mean no loss at all.

But I think this cannot be right. Suppose Victim is a great transplant surgeon. There is Aggressor, lying helpless next to his tank, with two broken ankles—but the rest of him physically fine and healthy. Can Victim now cart Aggressor off to surgery, cut him up, and give his one heart, two kidneys, and two lungs to five who need the parts? If Aggressor now has no right to not be killed (having forfeited it by his attack on Victim), so that utilitarian considerations are all we have to weigh here, it is hard to see why not. After all, five lives would be saved at a cost of only one. Yet surely Victim cannot do this.

I am inclined to think that it would no more be permissible for Victim to cut Aggressor up and parcel out his parts to save five than it would be for Victim to cut *you* up and parcel out *your* parts to save five. He cannot do this to you; and it is often said that the reason why he cannot (despite the fact that utilities might be maximized by doing so) is the fact that you have a right to life, and thus, presumably, the right to not be killed.[2] I should imagine that the very same thing makes it impermissible for Victim to do this to Aggressor, namely,

1. This question is asked by Sanford H. Kadish, in "Respect for Life and Regard for Rights in the Criminal Law," *California Law Review* 64 (July 1976).
2. But it is not at all obvious that this is what explains the fact that Victim cannot cut you up and parcel out your parts to save five. See footnote 6 below.

the fact that Aggressor, now helpless and no danger to anyone, has a right to life, and thus, presumably, the right not to be killed.

There are, of course, those who think it permissible for a state to impose death, as a penalty, on one who commits one or another very serious crime. If any one of them is a friend of the reply I am calling "forfeit," he will no doubt say that what makes it permissible is the fact that one who commits such a crime has forfeited his right to not be killed. But in the first place, I doubt that those who think of death as an acceptable penalty would think it an acceptable penalty for an (unsuccessful) attempt on the life of another, and it will be remembered that an (unsuccessful) attempt is all that Aggressor is guilty of. More important, even if it could be made out that it *will* be permissible, after trial and conviction, for an agent of the state to kill Aggressor, no agent of the state can kill him *now* (prior to trial and conviction). And Victim not only cannot kill him now, Victim—unless he is himself an agent of the state—is not going to be able to kill him at any time. So while it is (I suppose) open to those who regard death as an acceptable penalty for Aggressor's crime to say that he *will* (after trial and conviction) have no right to not be killed by an agent of the state, he at any rate *now* has a right to not be killed by Victim, indeed a right to not be killed by anybody at all, and thus a right to not be killed.

There are two moves open to a friend of "forfeit." He can say (1) that the fact that the tank stalled and Aggressor broke both ankles shows that it never was necessary for Victim to kill Aggressor, so that Aggressor never did forfeit his right to not be killed. Or he can say (2) that Aggressor did forfeit his right to not be killed when he launched his attack on Victim, but that he regained this right at the moment at which he ceased to pose a threat to Victim's life.

Alternative (1) would be an unfortunate choice for the purpose of "forfeit." For surely Victim could, permissibly, have killed Aggressor at any time between the launching of Aggressor's attack and the stall of the tank. (Who in such circumstances could be expected to know that the tank would stall? Who in such circumstances could be expected to wait in hopes of so freakish an accident?) That indeed was where we began: i.e., with the fact that it was then permissible for Victim to shoot. "Forfeit" proposed to explain this fact by saying that Aggressor forfeited a right; yet (1) denies that he did.

For the purpose of this reply (2) seems preferable. If Aggressor did forfeit his right to not be killed when he launched the attack, that would explain why, between the launching of it and the stall of the tank, Victim could shoot; and if Aggressor re-acquired that right when he ceased to pose a threat to Victim, that would explain why, after the stall of the tank, Victim could no longer shoot.

But it is a far from happy choice. If it were by virtue just of the launching of that attack that Aggressor forfeited his right, then it would seem possible to say that when the attack ceases, Aggressor re-acquires his right—the right being, as it were, in abeyance throughout the time of the attack. But it surely cannot be said to have been by virtue *just* of the launching of that attack that Aggressor forfeited his right. Compare a second aggressor and a second victim. Suppose that Second Aggressor launches a similar attack on Second Victim, but that Second Aggressor (by contrast with Aggressor) is innocent. Second Aggressor, let us suppose, is a schizophrenic, and he is under a hallucination that Second Victim is in a tank of his own, driving towards Second Aggressor's home and family, so that, as Second Aggressor sees it, he is merely trying to ward off an attack. Morality may not protect us from getting run down by lunatics in tanks, but it does permit our protecting ourselves from such a fate; and it seems plain that poor Second Victim, who is himself innocent, may permissibly use his anti-tank gun on Second Aggressor. Why is this permissible? It is an excellent question. But presumably "forfeit" would be a most implausible reply in this case.[3] Perhaps Aggressor, being a villain, can be thought to have forfeited a right; Second Aggressor, however, being himself innocent, cannot. But then it is not by virtue *just* of launching an attack on Victim that Aggressor forfeits his right; Aggressor's bad intention figures too. Yet Aggressor's bad intention may be supposed to remain even after he becomes helpless—we may imagine him continuing to plot as he is carried off to jail—and if that remains, how can he be thought to have re-acquired the right he forfeited at least in part because of that bad intention?

There is room for maneuver here. It could be said that the point is this: both Aggressor and Second Aggressor simply cease to have a right to not be killed when they launch their attacks on their victims, and both of them re-acquire that right when their tanks stall. (On this view, while Aggressor is guilty and Second Aggressor is not, this does not matter: launching an attack by itself—whether guilty or not—is what makes one lose the right to not be killed.) I shall

3. See Kadish, "Respect for Life . . ."

come back to this idea later. For the moment, it should be noted that saying that Aggressor simply ceased to have the right is not the same as saying that Aggressor has forfeited the right. That is, *this* reply is entailed by the reply I am calling "forfeit," but is not identical with it.

3. The second reply I am going to call "specification." Actually I mean to use the term "specification" so as to cover two connected replies. Both begin in the same way. "You only think there's a problem here because you think that 'Aggressor has a right to life' entails 'Aggressor has a right to not be killed.' But it doesn't. We all do have a right to life, but that right to life is a more complicated business than it at first may appear to be. In particular, having a right to life *doesn't* include having a right to not be killed. Indeed, *nobody* has a right to not be killed: all you have is—" and here there are two ways in which the speaker may go on. I will call the first "moral specification": ". . . all you have is the right to not be wrongly, unjustly killed." I will call the second "factual specification": ". . . all you have is the right to not be killed if you are not in process of trying to kill a person, where that person has every reason to believe he can preserve his life only by killing you." There is what seems to me a serious objection, which bears against both of these equally. But first let us look at difficulties specific to each.

I used to think that the reply I have called "moral specification" was the right reply to make in the case I described, as in other, similar, cases. That is, I used to think it just a mistake to suppose that anyone has a right to not be killed. It is so obvious that there are cases in which it is permissible, and therefore no violation of anyone's rights, to kill a person that it seems right to say that the most we can plausibly be thought to have is a right to not be wrongly or unjustly killed. But if so, then it is hard to see how appeal to rights which we do or do not have can *explain* why it is or is not permissible for a person to kill. Consider Victim. We were asked to explain why it is permissible for Victim to use his anti-tank gun on Aggressor, thereby killing him; and consider the following answer: "The reason why it is permissible for Victim to kill Aggressor is that Aggressor has no right to not be killed—he only has a right to not be killed wrongly or unjustly—and in killing Aggressor, Victim would not be killing Aggressor wrongly or unjustly." One does not mind all circles, but this circle is too small. For it to be permissible for Victim to kill Aggressor *is* for it to be the case that in killing Aggressor, Victim does not act wrongly or unjustly;

and we cannot say that the reason *why* Victim is not acting wrongly or unjustly in killing Aggressor is the fact that in killing Aggressor, Victim is not acting wrongly or unjustly.

The reply I have called "factual specification" is, I think, even less satisfactory. Let us look at it again. "Nobody has a right to not be killed: all you have is a right to not be killed if you are not in process of trying to kill a person, where that person has every reason to believe he can preserve his life only by killing you." Hence Victim can kill Aggressor. For Victim violates no right of Aggressor's in killing him, for Aggressor *is* in process of trying to kill Victim, where Victim has every reason to believe he can preserve his life only by killing Aggressor.

But the fact is that there are a great many other cases in which it is permissible to kill a man—defense of your life against a villain is by no means the only one. Consider Second Aggressor again. Second Aggressor is no villain; yet Second Victim can shoot to kill.

Again, consider a case which involves what Robert Nozick calls an "innocent shield of a threat."[4] Third Aggressor is driving his tank at you. But he has taken care to arrange that a baby is strapped to the front of the tank, so that if you use your anti-tank gun, you will not only kill Third Aggressor, you will kill the baby. Now Third Aggressor, admittedly, is in process of trying to kill you; but that baby isn't. Yet you can presumably go ahead and use the gun, even though this involves killing the baby as well as Third Aggressor.

It would, of course, be consistent to opt for "factual specification" in the original case of Aggressor and Victim, and yet not opt for a similar reply in these other cases. Yet it is hard to see what reason there could be for distinguishing. And if a similar reply is opted for in these other cases, we shall find ourselves having to say, not only that nobody has a right to not be killed, but also that you do not even have a right to not be killed if you are not in process of trying to kill a person, where that person has every reason to believe he can preserve his life only by killing you. We shall find ourselves having to say that the most you have is a right to not be killed if (a) you are not a villain who is trying to kill a person, and (b) you are not a schizophrenic who is trying to (as he sees it) ward off an attack on his home and family, and (c) you are not tied to a tank which will kill a person—where the threatened person in (a), (b), and (c) has

4. See his *Anarchy, State, and Utopia* (New York: Basic Books, 1974), p. 35.

every reason to believe he can preserve his life only by killing you.

And this is obviously not the end of it. Consider a case of a quite different kind, which I borrow from Philippa Foot.[5] You are the driver of a trolley. On the track ahead of you are five track workmen. The banks are very steep at that point, and the men are not able to get off the track. Well, it is plain enough: you had better put on your brakes. Alas, the brakes do not work. You notice just then that there is a spur of track leading off to the right, and you can turn off onto it. But again alas, you can see that there is one track workman on that spur, and he too cannot get off the track. If you do nothing, you kill five; if you turn off to the right, you kill one. Presumably it is morally permissible—some would even say it was morally required— that you turn the trolley off to the right, thereby killing one. But *why* is it permissible to kill that one? Does he not have a right to life?[6] Notice that *he* is not threatening anybody at all; nor is he an innocent shield of a threat. A friend of "factual specification" will then presumably have to expand still further his list of conditions under which killing is permissible, and thus make still more complicated the right which—as he says—is the most we have in respect of life.

Where is this to end? Is there anybody who knows what right it is which (it is here suggested) is the most we have in respect of life?

Moreover, it is worth noticing that a kind of circle is going to turn up here too. What the friend of factual specification has to do is to figure out when it is permissible to kill, and then tailor, accordingly, his account of what right it is which is the most we have in respect of life. But if that is the only way anyone can have of finding out what right it is we have in respect of life, how can anyone then *explain* its being permissible to kill in such and such circumstances by appeal to the fact that killing in those circumstances does not violate the right which is the most the victim has in respect of life?

But I think there is a still more serious objection, which bears equally against both moral specification and factual specification. What I have in mind is that both replies issue from what I think is an incorrect

---

5. See her "Abortion and the Doctrine of the Double Effect," *Oxford Review* 5 (1967).

6. If the workman on the right-hand track has a right to life (and it seems plain that if we do, he does), then we cannot explain the fact that a surgeon cannot cut you up and parcel out your parts to save five by appeal to the fact that you have a right to life. For so does the workman, yet the driver *can* turn the trolley onto him to save five. Mrs. Foot (ibid.) has an explanation; others may be found in Essays 6 and 7 of this volume.

view of rights: neither would be opted for by anyone who did not take the view that rights are, in a certain sense, *absolute*. What this sense is may best be brought out if we make a terminological distinction. Suppose a man has a right that something or other shall be the case; let us say he has a right that p, where p is some statement or other, and now suppose that we make p false. So, for example, if his right is the right that he is not punched in the nose, we make that false, that is, we bring about that he *is* punched in the nose. Then, as I shall say, we *infringe* his right. But I shall say that we *violate* his right if and only if we do not merely infringe his right, but more, are acting wrongly, unjustly in doing so. Now the view that rights are absolute in the sense I have in mind is the view that every infringing of a right is a violating of a right.

This view of rights seems to me, as I said, to be incorrect. That it is comes out in the following case. You are rich, and therefore own lots of steak, which you keep in a locked freezer on your back porch. Here is a child with a terrible protein deficiency: he will die if I do not get some protein into him fast. I have none myself at the moment. I call you to see if you will lend or sell me a steak, but your answering service says you are out of town for the weekend, and they do not know where. The only way in which I can get some protein for that child is to break into your freezer and take a steak. Now most people would say it is okay, I can go ahead. But why? Don't you have a right that people will not break into your freezer and take a steak? If anyone thinks that rights are absolute, then he is committed to saying that you do not after all have a right that people will not break into your freezer and take a steak, and this on the ground that I do not act wrongly or unjustly if I do so—and I surely do not act wrongly or unjustly if I do so, since it is permissible for me to do so. This is not to say he has to deny you have *any* rights over your freezer and your steak. We are all familiar by now with the kind of right he can say you have. He can engage in moral specification: he can say that although you do not have a right that people will not break into your freezer and take a steak, you do have a right that people will not do this wrongly or unjustly. Or, alternatively, he can engage in factual specification: he can say that the right you do have is that people will not do this except where they have in hand a child with a protein deficiency, who will die if it is not done. But the point, I think, is that the wrong move was made from the start. Surely you *do* have a right that people will not break into your freezer and take a steak. If you had no such right, why would I have to compensate you later for having done so? And surely I do have to compensate you: I have to pay for the damage I caused to the freezer, and I have to replace, or pay you for, the steak I took.

If all you had was a right that I not wrongly or unjustly break into the freezer and take a steak, then I would have done nothing at all you have a right I not do; in which case, why would I owe you anything for what I did? Similarly, if all you had was a right that I not break into the freezer and take a steak when I do not have a starving child to feed, then since I did have a starving child to feed, I would have done nothing at all you had a right I not do; so once again, no compensation would be owing. The fact that compensation *is* owing shows (and it seems to me, shows conclusively) that I did do something you had a right that I not do. How are we to square this fact with the fact that I did not act wrongly or unjustly in doing so? I think we had better allow that there are cases in which a right may be infringed without being violated—i.e., cases in which one does a thing another has a right he not do, and yet in which one does not violate a right.

Now I do not suppose that if Victim kills Aggressor in the circumstances I described at the outset, then Victim must pay compensation to Aggressor's heirs. I do not suppose that if the trolley driver turns off to the right, killing the one, then he must pay compensation to the one's heirs. But there surely are cases in which it is permissible to kill, and in which compensation *is* owed. If you are an "innocent threat"[7] to my life (you threaten it through no fault of your own), and I can save my life only by killing you, and therefore do kill you, I think I do owe compensation, for I take your life to save mine. If so, I infringe a right of yours but do not violate it. And this means that at least some rights in respect of life—as well as at least some rights in respect of property—are not absolute.

It could, of course, be insisted that Victim (supposing he killed Aggressor) not only violated no right of Aggressor's, but also infringed no right of Aggressor's. And as I said, there is no need for Victim to compensate Aggressor's heirs, so there is not available *that* ground for saying that Victim infringed a right of Aggressor's. On the other hand, if we do say that Victim infringed a right of Aggressor's (and that the trolley driver infringed a right of the one on the

---

7. The term is Robert Nozick's: see *Anarchy, State, and Utopia,* p. 34.

right-hand track, and . . .), then it is open to us to say—what had certainly seemed plausible at the outset—that we all of us do have a right to not be killed. Quite simply: a right to not be killed. Not an absolute right to not be killed, of course, only a nonabsolute right to not be killed. And saying this would be entirely consistent with saying that we also have the (absolute) right to not be killed wrongly or unjustly, which the moral specifier attributes to us, and the (absolute) right to not be killed if (a) we are not a villain who is trying to kill a person, and (b) we are not a schizophrenic who . . . , which the factual specifier will attribute to us if and when he ever finishes specifying it.

It is not surprising that people are inclined to opt for the view that rights are absolute: if a person has a *right* to such and such how can it be that anyone may, permissibly, deprive him of it? Isn't a right something one can positively *demand* accordance with? But the fact is that there are occasions on which a right is infringed but not violated; and a moral philosopher has to find some way of explaining what makes this be the case when it is. A move which is familiar enough is to say that what makes this be the case when it is is the fact that the right in question is "overridden." It is a natural idea, then, that we should make the same move in respect of Victim and Aggressor. Ths brings us to the third of the three replies to the question I asked: for obvious reasons, I will call it "overriding."

4. An overrider begins as follows. "Yes, Aggressor does, like the rest of us, have a right to not be killed. A nonabsolute right is all it is, however. And the reason why it is permissible for Victim to kill Aggressor is the fact that, the circumstances being what they are, Aggressor's right to not be killed is overridden." But what does "His right is overridden" mean? If it means only "It is permissible to infringe his right," then—so far as explanatory force is concerned—the overrider might as well have instead said "And the reason why it is permissible for Victim to kill Aggressor is the fact that, the circumstances being what they are, it is permissible for Victim to kill Aggressor."

Moreover, by what is Aggressor's right supposed to be overridden? That is (as I take it), what in the circumstances makes it permissible for Victim to kill Aggressor? An overrider may be expected to answer in one or another of two ways. He may say "Aggressor's right to not be killed is overridden by the fact that a great lot of utility will get produced if Victim kills Aggressor—much more utility than if Victim does not kill Aggressor." Or he may instead say "Aggressor's right to not be killed is overridden by a more stringent right of Victim's." I find the first of these two answers uninteresting: it is easy enough to add details to the story which, *prima facie*, at any rate, suggest that the utilities are not as the answer claims they are, and I think that a dispute as to whether or not they really do is not theoretically fruitful. So I shall attend only to the second of the two answers.

The answer obviously invites a question: "What makes one right be more stringent than another?" If what makes Victim's right (whatever it is) be more stringent than Aggressor's right to not be killed is merely the very fact that it is permissible for Victim to kill Aggressor, then it is hard to see how we can explain the fact that it is permissible for Victim to kill Aggressor by appeal to a right in Victim which is more stringent than Aggressor's right to not be killed. I do not say that no independent account of relative stringency among rights can be given; I say only that an overrider plainly needs one.

Moreover, there is a second question which the answer invites, and which we should take note of, namely the question "*What* right is it which Victim has, and which is more stringent than Aggressor's right to not be killed, and which is such that, the circumstances containing the fact that that right of Victim's is more stringent than Aggressor's right to not be killed, it is permissible for Victim to kill Aggressor?" It is a good question, I think.

We might begin with this: the right which Victim has, and which meets those further conditions, is the right to preserve his life. But *is* Victim's right to preserve his life more stringent than Aggressor's right to not be killed? Certainly it just is not the case, quite generally, that one person's right to preserve his life is more stringent than another person's right to not be killed. Suppose I am starving, and need food or else I die. Suppose further that the only available food is *you*. I should imagine I do have a right to preserve my life; but surely your right to not be killed is more stringent than my right to preserve my life—surely it is not permissible for me to kill you to preserve my life!

Well, perhaps we simply fastened on the wrong right; perhaps we should instead have said that the right which Victim has, and which meets those further conditions, is the right to self-defense—more precisely, perhaps, the right to preserve his life against an attack on it. (Your being the only available food does not make it be the case that you are *attacking* me.) But *is* Victim's right to preserve his life against an attack on it more stringent than Aggressor's right to not be killed? Certainly it just is not the case, quite generally, that one person's right to preserve his life against an attack on it is more stringent than another person's right to not be killed. Suppose I am being threatened with a gun, and the only way in which I can preserve my life against that attack on it is by grabbing some innocent bystander and shoving him in front of me. I should imagine I do have a right to preserve my life against an attack on it; but surely the innocent bystander's right to not be killed is more stringent than my right to preserve my life against an attack on it—surely it is not permissible for me to shove the innocent bystander in front of me!

I suppose it could be said that Aggressor's right to not be killed is less stringent than yours is, and than the innocent bystander's is, and that that is why Victim may act though I may not. Aggressor is a villain, after all, and neither you nor the innocent bystander is.

But then are we to suppose that after the stall of the tank, and Aggressor's breaking of his ankles, Aggressor's right to not be killed sweeps back to being just as stringent as yours is, and as the innocent bystander's is? For after that time, Victim may not kill Aggressor on any weaker grounds than would permit of his killing you or an innocent bystander.

The right to not be killed (as well as the right to preserve one's life, the right to preserve one's life against an attack on it, and the right to life itself) is traditionally thought to be a natural right, that is, a right a human being has simply by virtue of being a human being.[8] Now if a right is a right which we have simply by virtue of being human beings, it is not possible that some human beings possess it and others do not. Moreover, it is not possible that a human being possesses it at one time and not at another, so long as he remains a human being throughout.

Suppose the time now is after the start of Aggressor's attack on Victim, but before the time at which Aggressor ceases to pose a threat to Victim. If the right to not be killed is a natural right, so defined (henceforth I shall take this qualification to be understood), then we plainly cannot say

8. See H. L. A. Hart's definition of "natural right" in "Are There Any Natural Rights?" *The Philosophical Review* 64 (April 1955). See also Joel Feinberg's definition of what he calls "human rights" in *Social Philosophy* (Englewood Cliffs, N.J.: Prentice-Hall, 1973).

(1) Aggressor had (before launching his attack) and will again have (after breaking his ankles) a right to not be killed, but he does not have this right now. *That* is why Victim may now kill him.

But *is* the right to not be killed a natural right? It is by no means obvious that it is. Perhaps the right to not be killed is forfeitable. Hobbes thought that the right to not be killed is inalienable, but perhaps even this is wrong. Could one not voluntarily relinquish one's right to not be killed? Suppose I am terminally ill, and want to be able to provide for my children. Here is a rich man, who likes to kill. I say "For so and so much, to be given to my children, you may kill me now." Suppose, then, that he accepts my offer, and kills me. No doubt he does not act *well*. Perhaps he does what it is impermissible for him to do. But I think it arguable that he violates—even that he infringes—no right of mine, and that if he does act impermissibly, it is nothing to do with my rights that makes this so.

Moreover, even if the right to not be killed is a natural right, this does not settle what we are to say about the case in hand. Of course we may not say (1). I should imagine also that we cannot say

(2) Aggressor has (at all times) a right to not be killed, but Aggressor's right to not be killed is (at all times) less stringent than any innocent person's is—so much less stringent as to be less stringent than Victim's right to preserve his life against an attack on it. *That* is why Victim may now kill him.

It is not inconsistent to suppose that a certain right is a right which we all have by virtue of being human beings, and nevertheless that it varies in stringency between human beings—in particular, between the innocent and the villains. We do of course say about natural rights that they are "equal" in both of the following two senses: every human being has them, and no one human being's are any more stringent than any other human being's. But only the first follows from the definition of "natural right" which I gave above. So taking the right to not be killed to be a natural right does not rule out opting for (2). But I take it that what I drew attention to a moment ago *does* rule out opting for (2). What I have in mind is the fact that after the stall of the tank, and Aggressor's breaking of his ankles, Aggressor's right to not be killed is surely just as stringent as yours is, and as the innocent bystander's is—for after that time, Victim may not kill Aggressor on any weaker grounds than would permit of his killing you or an innocent bystander.

This points, however, to a further possibility. It is not inconsistent to suppose that a certain right is a right which we all have by virtue of being human beings, and nevertheless that it sweeps back and forth from one degree of stringency to another in one human being— according as he is or is not threatening another. I do not think it is as commonly said that natural rights are also equal in the following (third) sense: no one human being's are any more stringent at one time than they are at any other time. That they are equal in this sense certainly does not follow from the definition of "natural right" I gave, or even from their being equal in either of the two senses I pointed to. So it would be consistent to say that the right to not be killed is a natural right, and yet also opt for

(3) Aggressor has (at all times) a right to not be killed, and Aggressor's right to not be killed was (before launching his attack) and will again be (after breaking his ankles) as stringent as any innocent person's is, but it is less stringent now—so much less stringent now as to be less stringent than Victim's right to preserve his life against an attack on it. *That* is why Victim may now kill him.

So far as I can see, nothing in the case rules this out.

But there is plainly yet another alternative. Don't we all of us have a right to kill a person who is currently giving us every reason to believe that he will kill us unless we kill him? And isn't this right as good a candidate for the status of natural right as the right to not be killed is? And isn't it, moreover, *always* more stringent than the right to not be killed? If so, there is a fourth alternative:

(4) Aggressor has (at all times) an equally stringent right to not be killed, but that right is (always) less stringent than the right— possessed by Victim—to kill a person who is currently giving every reason to believe that he will kill Victim unless Victim kills him. *That* is why Victim may now kill him.

Is there any principled ground for choosing between (3) and (4)? Indeed, between (1), (3), and (4)?—since, as I said, it is by no means obvious that the right to not be killed is a natural right.

The other side of the same coin is that (1), (3), and (4) are marvelously *ad hoc*. Consider the appeal in (1) to loss of, and then re-acquisition of, the right to not be killed; is there any reason to opt for (1) other than the fact that if we do, we seem to have in hand an explanation of why Victim may kill Aggressor? Similarly for the appeal in (3) to difference in stringency in one person across time. And what of that right to kill a person who is currently giving every reason to believe that he will kill you unless you kill him? Can there be any reason to suppose we have such a right other than the fact that it is permissible for a victim to kill an aggressor who is currently giving every reason to believe that he will kill the victim unless the victim kills him? Notice how carefully tailored to its explanatory purpose this right is.

Notice, moreover, how difficult it would be to find a lesson in any of this in respect of permitted killings generally. Take the case of the trolley driver I mentioned earlier. Surely the trolley driver may turn his trolley, to save five at a cost of one. Does it seem at all plausible to say that the reason why he may is that the one has ceased to have a right to not be killed, or that his right to not be killed is now less stringent than it was before he started work on that particular stretch of track? Of course we could say that the reason why the trolley driver may turn the trolley is that he has a right to turn his trolley onto one to save five, and that that right is always more stringent than the right to not be killed—compare (4) above. But you might as well say: Leave me alone, I'm too busy to do moral philosophy this afternoon.

5. Many people who do moral philosophy these days appeal to rights to *explain* why this or that piece of behavior is or is not permissible. For example, it is common to say that the reason why you cannot maximize utility in such and such a case is the fact that the utility-maximizing course of action would involve infringing a right—indeed, violating a right, since the right in question is a stringent one, and the utility to be got not sufficiently great to override the right. But when we say that, in that case, the utility-maximizing course of action would involve violating a right, *are* we saying anything more than that, in that case, it is not permissible to take the utility-maximizing course of action? If not, then we can hardly take ourselves to have explained why it is not permissible, in that case, to take the utility-maximizing course of action. It is arguable that if there is to be any point at all in appealing to rights in such discussions, there had better be something independent of permissibilities and impermissibilities which fixes their existence and degree of stringency. It is not obvious that this is true. It might be that to attribute a right is only

to talk about permissibilities and impermissibilities, but in a way that groups or collects them, and brings whole clusters of cases to bear on each other. I do not for a moment think it a novel idea that we stand in need of an account of just how an appeal to a right may be thought to function in ethical discussion. What strikes me as of interest, however, is that the need for such an account shows itself even in a case which might have been thought to be transparent.[9]

9. I am indebted to the students and faculty of the Department of Philosophy at the University of Kansas, and to the members of the Society for Ethical and Legal Philosophy, for criticisms of earlier versions of this essay.

4 · Some Ruminations on Rights

In *Anarchy, State, and Utopia*, Robert Nozick says that a government which imposes taxes for the purpose of redistribution violates the rights of its citizens.[1] The word "imposes" perhaps needs no stress: Nozick could hardly object to a government's withholding a percentage of income for this purpose if its citizens had unanimously requested it to do so. What he objects to—on the ground of its constituting a violation of rights—is forcing payment for this purpose on those who do not wish to pay. What we might expect Nozick to give us, then, is a theory of rights, or at least a clear picture of why this should be so. In fact, we get neither.

Nozick makes two quite general points about rights, both of them important. He says, first, that the fact that if we bring about that such and such is the case there will be more good in the world than there otherwise would be does not by itself justify our bringing about that it is the case, and this on the ground that to bring it about may be to violate a right. This seems to me to be wholly right. Suppose, for example, that if we bring about that Alfred takes a certain aspirin tablet there will be more good in the world than there otherwise would be. This does not by itself justify our bringing about that Alfred takes it, for it might be that to do so would be to violate a right. For example, it might be that Bert owns that aspirin tablet and does not wish Alfred to take it; in that case, to bring about that Alfred takes it would be to violate a right of Bert's. Indeed, it might be that Alfred himself owns it but does not wish to take it; in that case, to bring about that he does would be to violate, paternalistically, a right of Alfred's.

---

1. Robert Nozick, *Anarchy, State, and Utopia* (New York: Basic Books, 1974), pp. 171–174.

This point, though important, is familiar enough. What is perhaps less familiar is Nozick's second point: That the fact that if we bring about that such and such is the case there will be more good in the world than there otherwise would be does not by itself justify our bringing about that it is the case—even if we require that, in assessing how much good there will be in the world, account be taken of which rights, if any, will be infringed and of how stringent those rights are. This point too seems to me to be wholly right. If we do opt for this requirement on an assessment of how much good there will be in the world, then it seems to me we may suppose that if we bring about that Alfred takes a certain aspirin tablet there will *not* be more good in the world than there otherwise would be, however bad Alfred's headache may be: for there would have to be considered in arriving at the assessment, not merely the fact that if we bring about that Alfred takes the aspirin his headache will go away, but also (as it might be) the fact that a right of Bert's will be infringed, or (as it might be) the fact that a right of Alfred's will be infringed. If so, this is not really a case in which, even though there will be more good in the world if we act than there otherwise would be, it is not morally permissible for us to act. But there are other cases. Suppose that a villain threatens to kill five people if you will not kill Charles. Even prima facie it seems that if you act, there will be more good in the world than there otherwise would be since five lives are four more than one life. And now let us include in our assessment infringements of rights. If you act, fewer rights will be infringed than if you do not, for five violations of the right to not be killed are four more than one violation of the right to not be killed. Therefore, if we require that in assessing how much good there will be in the world account be taken of which rights, if any, will be infringed and of how stringent those rights are, *this* is a case in which there will be more good in the world if you act than if you do not. Yet you surely cannot act, since you surely cannot kill in response to such a threat.

This kind of case has been appearing fairly often in recent literature.[2] The kind of case I mean is this: For the agent to act would require him to infringe a right, but he is under threat that if he does not act, others will infringe more, equally stringent rights. Most people agree that the agent in such a case cannot act. What is particularly good in

2. A typical example is the following: You are a sheriff in a small southern town. A murder has been committed, and you do not have the least idea who committed it, but a lynch mob will hang five others if you do not fasten the crime on one individual.

Nozick's treatment of these matters is the connection he makes between cases of this kind on the one hand, and the case of Alfred on the other hand. Nozick's discussion brings out that if a utilitarian saves his theory in face of putative countercases such as that of Alfred by claiming that right infringements themselves have disvalue, which disvalue must be counted in assessing how much good there will be in the world if the agent acts, he thereby ensures that cases where the agent must infringe a right to avoid greater right infringement on the part of others *will* be countercases.

As I say, I think these points are wholly correct. Nozick does not argue for them; nor shall I. But to have arrived here is to be miles away from Nozick's thesis about government and taxation for the purpose of redistribution. What we have so far is that the fact that if we bring about that such and such is the case there will be more good in the world than there otherwise would be does not by itself justify our bringing about that it is the case. Thus suppose redistribution is, in one way or another, a good, and that if we make a certain redistributive move there will in fact be more good in the world than there otherwise would be. What we have is that that fact does not by itself justify our making that redistributive move. However, this leaves it wide open that something which includes—or even something entirely other than—that fact *does* justify our making it.

Let us begin with a point of terminology. Suppose that someone has a right that such and such shall not be the case. I shall say that we infringe a right of his if and only if we bring about that it is the case.[3] I shall say that we violate a right of his if and only if *both* we bring about that it is the case *and* we act wrongly in so doing. The difference I have in mind comes out in the following case, which I shall call A:

(A)   There is a child who will die if he is not given some drug in the near future. The only bit of that drug which can be obtained for him in the near future is yours. You are out of town, and

3. This is a simplified account of what I mean by "infringe a right." For example, someone might have a right that such and such shall be the case, and we might bring about that it is not the case, but our act might at one and the same time bring about both that it is not the case and that he no longer has a right that it is the case. It is possible that in some cases (that is, those in which we infringe no other right of his in bringing about that he no longer has that right), no right of his is "infringed," in the sense I mean this word to have. But the difficulties I point to here are of no interest for present purposes, so I ignore them.

hence cannot be asked for consent within the available time. You keep your supply of the drug in a locked box on your back porch.

In this case the box is yours, you have a right that it not be broken into without your consent; since the drug is yours, you have a right that it shall not be removed and given to someone without your consent. So if we break into the box, remove the drug, and feed it to the child, we thereby infringe a number of rights of yours. But I take it that a child's life being at stake, we do not act wrongly if we go ahead; that is, though we infringe a number of your rights, we violate none of them.

It might be said that we do violate one or more of your rights if we go ahead, but that our act, though wrongful, is excusable. In other words, although we act wrongly if we go ahead, we are not to be blamed for doing so. It is true that for clarity about rights we need, and do not have, a general account of when one should say "a non-wrongful infringement of a right" and when one should instead say "a wrongful, but excusable, infringement of a right." I think (but without great confidence) that the difference lies in this: The former may not be said where, and the latter may only be said where the agent ought not act or ought not have acted. If so, then the proposal we are considering is false: For it surely is plain that a third party would not speak truly if he said to us, given we are in (A): "You ought not go ahead."

In any case, the proposal in a certain sense hangs in midair. What I have in mind is this. It is presumably agreed universally that if we go ahead in (A), we are not to be blamed, punished, scolded, or the like, for doing so. Now the question is: Why? One possible answer is: If we go ahead in (A) we do not act wrongly, and that is why we are not to be blamed for doing so. That this is my answer shows itself in the paragraph in which I first set out (A). But how is a proponent of the proposal we are now considering to answer? On his view, we act wrongly if we go ahead; what, on his view, is the reason why we are not to be blamed for doing so? There are cases in which there is an answer to an analogous question. Thus if I break your box in a rage which you provoked, then I acted wrongly, but perhaps excusably, and the reason why I am not to be blamed (if I am not) is at hand: you yourself provoked the rage out of which I acted. Again, a reason why I am not to be blamed in another case might be: I was not fully aware of what I was doing; or I was so frantic with worry I could not think clearly; or I was so frantic with worry, nothing else seemed to matter. If (A) had read: "*Our* child will die if he is not given . . . ," then there might have been a toehold for an answer of the kind just pointed to. But (A) says: "There is a child who will die if he is not given . . . ," and it is possible to suppose that we go ahead in (A)—break the box, and give the drug to the child—calmly, coolly, carefully weighing all the relevant considerations. If so, just what is a proponent of the proposal we are now considering to give as an answer to the question of why we are not to be blamed for doing so?

So I shall simply assume that this proposal is false, and I shall take it, then, that while we infringe some of your rights if we go ahead, we do not violate them.[4]

A second way of responding to what I said of our act if we go ahead in (A) is this: True, we violate no rights if we go ahead, but we also infringe no rights if we go ahead. What I have in mind is the possibility of saying that you do not have either of the rights it might have been thought you had—that you do not have a right that your box not be broken into without your consent, and that you do not have a right that your drug not be removed and given to someone without your consent—on the ground that it is morally permissible for us to go ahead in (A). What rights do you have over your box and drug on this view? Well, I suppose it would be said that what you have is at most a right that your-box-not-be-broken-into-and-your-drug-not-taken-without-your-consent-when-there-is-no-child-who-needs-that-drug-for-life. The inclination to take, everywhere, either the view discussed just above, or the view indicated here, is the inclination to regard all rights as "absolute." That is, it is the inclination to take it that if a man has a right that such and such shall not be the case, then if we bring about that it is the case, we act wrongly in so doing. As the point might be put, every infringing of a right is a violation of a right. So if a man really does have a right that such and such shall not be the case (as it might be, that his drug not be

---

4. It is worth noticing, in passing, that for present purposes it would not matter if I were wrong to make this assumption. There are acts which Nozick says are violation of rights. I shall say that some of them, anyway, are nonwrongful infringements of rights. Suppose I am mistaken in this way: That what I should have said is that they are wrongful, though excusable, infringements of rights. Since Nozick plainly thinks those acts are not merely wrongful, but inexcusable, what I shall say would still conflict with what he thinks.

removed from his box), then we act at best excusably if we bring about that it is the case—as in the view discussed just above. If we do not act wrongly in bringing it about, then he did not really have a right that it not come about, but at most a right that it-not-come-about-when-the-circumstances-are-so-and-so, as in the view indicated here.

It seems to me, however, that you do have a right that your box not be broken into without your consent and a right that your drug not be removed and given to someone without your consent, and that what shows this is the fact that if we go ahead in (A)—break into your box and give some of the drug to the child—we shall have later to pay you some, if not all, of the cost we imposed on you by doing so. We shall have to pay some, if not all, of the cost of repairing or replacing the box and of replacing the drug we removed.[5] You may reject payment: you may say, on your return, that, the circumstances having been what they were, all is well, and that you do not mind bearing the costs yourself. But we must at least offer. If you had no right that we not do these things without your consent, why would we have to pay you some of the costs we imposed on you by doing them?

It is sometimes said (see Essay 3) that if we go ahead in (A) we shall have to *compensate* you for the costs we imposed on you by doing so, and that *that* is what shows that we infringed some of your rights by going ahead—for compensation is repayment for a wrong. But I think that this is not a good way to put the point, and will bring out my reason for thinking so later.

In any case, it seems to me we do well to agree that rights are not all absolute: There are rights which can be infringed without being violated. In particular, it seems to me that if we go ahead in (A), we infringe some of your property rights, but do not violate any of them.

What people who would agree with me on this matter would say is this: If we go ahead in (A), we will infringe your property rights, but we would not violate them, since those rights are "overridden" by the fact that the child will die if we do not go ahead.

A more stringent right than your property rights over your box and drug might not have been overridden by this fact. For example, if it had been necessary for the saving of the child's life that we kill you, then it would not have been morally permissible that we go ahead. Your right to not be killed is considerably more stringent than any of

5. It is of the greatest interest whether or not we have to pay *all* this back, a question to which I shall return later.

your property rights, and would not have been overridden by the child's need.

The question just how stringent our several rights are is obviously a difficult one. It does not even seem to be obvious that there is any such thing as *the* degree of stringency of any given right. Perhaps a right may be more or less stringent, as the rightholder's circumstances vary, and also, in the case of special rights, as the means by which he acquired the right vary. One thing only is plain: Only an absolute right is infinitely stringent. For only an absolute right is such that every possible infringement of it is a violation of it. Indeed, we may re-express the thesis that all rights are absolute as follows: all rights are infinitely stringent.

There are passages in *Anarchy, State, and Utopia* which suggest that Nozick thinks all rights are infinitely stringent. He say: "[O]ne might place [rights] as side constraints upon the actions to be done: don't violate constraints C. The rights of others determine the constraints upon your actions. . . . The side-constraint view forbids you to violate these moral constraints in the pursuit of your goals."[6] If you use "violate" in the way I suggested we should use it, this "side-constraint view" does not amount to much—under that reading of the term, all Nozick says is that we may not wrongly infringe a right. Of course we may not. But I think he does not mean so to use the term "violate," in this passage at any rate. I think that in this passage all he means by it is "infringe." Thus I think that we are to take this "side-constraint view" to say that we may not ever infringe a right. Accordingly, every infringing of a right is wrong. Compare what Nozick says a few pages on:

> A specific side constraint upon action toward others expresses the fact that others may not be used in the specific ways the side constraint excludes. Side constraints express the inviolability of others, in the ways they specify. These modes of inviolability are expressed by the following injunction: "Don't use people in specified ways."[7]

Now Nozick does not in fact say that his view is the "side-constraint view," so interpreted, but he implies that it is. Certainly his thesis about redistribution suggests it: for according to that thesis it is not morally permissible to tax people for the purpose of redistribution, however dire the human need which makes redistribution seem called

6. Nozick, *Anarchy, State, and Utopia*, p. 29.
7. Ibid., p. 32.

for, and if dire human need does not override a right, what on earth would?

There are also passages which suggest that Nozick thinks that rights *may* be overrideable, and thus not infinitely stringent, though *very* stringent all the same. He says that it is an open question "whether these side constraints are absolute, or whether they may be violated in order to avoid catastrophic moral horror."[8] Catastrophic moral horror is pretty horrible moral horror; so even if rights are overrideable, as the passage suggests is possible, it is likely to be a rare occasion on which they are overridden. Unfortunately, Nozick leaves the question unanswered; he says it "is one I hope largely to avoid."[9]

There are also passages which suggest that Nozick thinks that some rights at least are overrideable even where catastrophic moral horror is not in the offing. In the course of a discussion of what may be done to animals, he asks: "Can't one save 10,000 animals from excruciating suffering by inflicting some slight discomfort on a person who did not cause the animals' suffering?"[10] And he adds: "One may feel the side constraint is not absolute when it is *people* who can be saved from excruciating suffering. So perhaps the side constraint also relaxes, though not as much, when animals' suffering is at stake."[11] Of course Nozick does not *say* the side constraint relaxes when animals' suffering is at stake, but he seems to think so, and it would surely be mad to think it did not. Well, perhaps 10,000 animals suffering excruciating pain counts as catastrophic moral horror. But does it require 10,000 of them, in excruciating pain, to override your right to not be caused some slight discomfort? I take it you have a right to not be pinched without your consent. But surely we can pinch you without your consent, if doing so is required to save even one cow from excruciating suffering. Indeed I should have thought we could do so if doing so is required to save just one cow from suffering which is considerably less than excruciating.

This wobbling about the degree of stringency of rights makes a reader feel nervous. It also makes it very unclear just how Nozick is to get from his starting point, which is that we have rights, to his thesis that a government which imposes taxes for the purpose of redistribution violates the rights of its citizens. I am inclined to think

8. Ibid., p. 30n.
9. Ibid.
10. Ibid., p. 41.
11. Ibid. (emphasis in original).

that what happens is this: At the outset, he is unclear what degree of stringency should be assigned to rights (and hopes to avoid having to take a stand on the matter), but by the time he gets to government, all is forgotten, and rights—at any rate, property rights—are infinitely stringent. It is my impression that his argument for his thesis rests entirely on the supposition that they are.

But surely it is plain as day that property rights are not infinitely stringent. It hardly needs argument to show they are not. In any case, the fact that it is morally permissible for us to go ahead in (A) would show—if it needed showing—that they are not.

Consider now case (B), which is in an interesting way different from (A):

(B) There is a child who will die if he is not given some drugs in the future. The only bit of that drug which can be obtained for him in the near future is yours. You are out of town, so we telephone you to ask. You refuse consent. You keep your supply of the drug in a locked box on your back porch.

"They did it without Jones' consent" covers two interestingly different kinds of cases: In the one kind, they were unable to get Jones' consent because he was not available to be asked for his consent; in the other kind, they were unable to get Jones' consent because he refused to give it. In the latter kind of case they acted, not merely without Jones' consent, but against his wishes. (A) is a case of the first kind; we cannot reach you to ask for consent. (B) is a case of the second kind; if we go ahead in (B) we act, not merely without your consent, but against your wishes. I said it is morally permissible for us to go ahead in (A); is it morally permissible for us to go ahead in (B)?

The fact is that our going ahead in (B)—our breaking into the box and removing the drug to give it to the child—seems morally suspect in a way in which our going ahead in (A) does not. Why? And should it?

Anyone who thinks that it is morally permissible for us to go ahead in (A) but not in (B) must think that there is at least a good chance that in (A), you would give consent if we were able to reach you to ask for consent. Surely if it were known that if we were to ask for consent in (A) you would refuse to give it, then it would be no better to go ahead in (A) than it is to go ahead in (B). For then (A) too would be a case in which going ahead would be acting against your wishes— though not against any wish that was in fact given expression.

Anyone who thinks that it is not morally permissible for us to go ahead in (B) must think that the box and the drug in it are in some way very important to you—that you place a very high value on the box not being broken into, and on the drug not being taken away from you. Suppose, however, that there is a toothpick on your desk, and it is in no way special to you. By virtue of some peculiarity in nature, we can save a life if we snap it in two. We ask if we can, but you are feeling refractory and say "No." Can we nót go ahead and snap it in two, despite your expressed wish that we not do so? By contrast, suppose what is on your desk is the last remaining photograph of your dead mother, and what we need to do to save the life is to burn it. Well, some people would say we can go ahead all the same. Suppose that what we need to do is to destroy *all* the now existing beautiful works of art, and that their owners (individuals, museums, governments) say, "Alas no, we are very sorry, but no." Could we go ahead all the same?

If (X), "The box and drug are, at most, of little value to you," is true, then we may surely go ahead in both (A) and (B). If (X) is true and we are in (A), then in the absence of information to the contrary, we shall rightly assume you would consent if we were able to ask. But even if we have information to the effect that you would not consent—even if we were in (B) instead of (A)—it is morally permissible for us to go ahead all the same. Why? Because if (X) is true, then it would be indecent for you to refuse consent in (A), and it is indecent for you to refuse consent in (B). I said you might be feeling refractory; alternatively, you might think: "What is that child to me?" There are other possible sources of refusal, but none of them bears looking at.

What if, instead, (Y), "The box and drug are of immense value to you," is true? Some would say we can go ahead all the same. I feel considerable sympathy for this view, but I do not hold it myself. It seems to me that if (Y) is true, we may not go ahead in (B), and in the absence of reason to think you would consent despite the truth of (Y), we may not go ahead in (A) either. I hope that when I first produced (A) above, your intuition agreed with mine; if so, I think that was because you were assuming that nothing so strong as (Y) was true. Why may we not go ahead if (Y) is true? It is not morally splendid to value bits of property more than human lives; but if there are some which you do—and this for no morally suspect reason—then it seems to me that there are cases, and that this is one of them, in which we must withdraw.

There are all manner of possibilities between (X) and (Y), but it is not necessary for our purposes that we attend to them.

It is also not necessary for our purposes that we attend to a very interesting question which is raised by consideration of the difference (which I take there to be) between what we may do if (X) is true and what we may do if (Y) is true, but I suggest we have a brief look at it all the same. What I have in mind is the question in precisely what way the difference between (X) and (Y) makes such a difference. One way of explaining it is this: If (Y) is true, then your rights that your box not be broken and drug not be taken are more stringent than they would be if (X) were true. More generally, that

(T) The stringency of A's right that x not be broken and y not taken away from him varies with the degree to which he values x's not being broken and y's not being taken away from him.

If so, then more is required to override your rights over your box and drug if (Y) is true than is required to override them if (X) is true. In particular, the fact that a human life may be saved by going ahead overrides your rights if (X) is true, but not if (Y) is true.

I think, myself, that this is how we should explain the difference (which I take there to be) between what we may do if (X) is true and what we may do if (Y) is true. Indeed, I think we should adopt (T).[12] But the question whether or not (T) is true is very important for the logic of rights; and so it should be noticed that there is yet another way of explaining the difference even if (T) is rejected. What might be said is this: The stringency of your rights that your box not be broken and your drug not be taken is no greater whether (Y) is true or (X) is true; and these rights are overridden by the fact that a human life may be saved by going ahead. But if (Y) is true, then it is less likely, perhaps even impossible, that we are going to be able to reimburse you for all of the costs we impose on you by going ahead; and if we take "immense" *very* seriously, it is less likely, perhaps even impossible, that we are even going to be able to pay you a meaningful part of those costs. Now it will be remembered that I said earlier that if we go ahead in (A) we are going to have to pay you some, if not all, of the costs we impose on you by going ahead. This means that you have a right, not merely that your-box-not-be-broken-and-drug-

12. Or something like (T), for of course we shall want to allow for irrationality, preferences immorally inculcated, and so forth. I do not for a moment want to suggest that I think the proper spelling out of the thesis would be easy; it is merely that the difficulties are irrelevant for present purposes.

taken-without-consent, but also that your-box-not-be-broken-and-drug-taken-without-consent-without-reimbursement-for-some-if-not-all-of-the-costs-imposed-by-the-breaking-and-taking. The former, simpler right is overridden by the fact that a human life may be saved by going ahead; the latter, more complex, right is more stringent, and is not overridden by this fact—indeed, it would be violated if we went ahead without reimbursing you. If (X) is true we can easily make the required payment; but if (Y) is true we cannot. So if (X) is true we may go ahead without violating any right of yours, for we can pay later; but if (Y) is true, then if we go ahead we shall violate, not the simpler right, but the move complex one, for we cannot pay later. And *that* is why we may go ahead if (X) is true, but not if (Y) is.

I have no objection to the supposition that you do have this more complex right as well as the simpler one. And I imagine that it is more stringent than the simpler one.[13] But, as I said, I think we should adopt (T), and if we do, we can explain the difference in the simpler manner I pointed to earlier. If (T) is *not* true, then the stringency of a right is independent of the value the rightholder places on its being accorded to him, and that makes the source of rights very dark indeed. If (T) is true, then we can understand *why* one's right to life is more stringent than one's right to not have, for example, an arm broken, and why one's right to not have an arm broken is more stringent than most of one's property rights; if (T) is not true, it is obscure why this should be so. The truth of (T) is just what you would expect if rights issue from interests in some way or another. And if they do not issue from interests, what on earth do they issue from?

However, this is no argument for (T). Fortunately it is not necessary for our purposes that we decide on the truth or falsity of (T). It is enough for our purposes that if (X) is true, then we may go ahead in (B) as well as in (A). For with that in hand we are in a position to return to Nozick's thesis that a government which imposes taxes for the purpose of redistribution violates the rights of its citizens.

I said that it is my impression that Nozick's argument for this thesis rests entirely on the supposition that property rights are infinitely stringent, and I said also that it is plain as day that they are not. Well, setting aside Nozick's argument for the thesis, what about the thesis itself?

---

13. Surely, however, it is not infinitely stringent: I should imagine it is overrideable, even if not overridden in the cases at which we are looking.

The rights which Nozick thinks would be violated by a redistributive move are property rights. I shall make no criticism here of his account of the source and content of those rights. However, it is perhaps worth just drawing attention to the fact that Nozick allows that title to property is clouded in existing states: He grants that injustices lie behind their current property distributions.[14] This means, then, that a redistributive move in an existing state may very well not really conflict with property rights, and in fact there is no practical moral lesson about redistributive moves in existing states to be learned from Nozick's book.

In light of that fact we had better take Nozick to be speaking only of governments in "ideal" states—states in which property rights are not clouded; more precisely, states in which the distribution of property satisfies Nozick's principles of distributive justice.

One thing we know is that there are circumstances in which it is morally permissible, and hence no violation of any right, to take from Smith—even against his wishes—to give to Jones. Any case in which Jones needs something, and he needs it for *life*, and the only way of providing him with it is by taking it from Smith, and Smith places at most little value on it, is such a case. Suppose we live in an ideal state. Then there are circumstances in which agents of government can arrange this redistributon. Would that count as imposing a tax for the purpose of redistribution? It is hard to see why not.

Something of great interest comes out if we consider, now, a second kind of case. Suppose there is an "ideal" state of only eleven people. One person will die if he is not provided with a certain amount of a particular drug. Eight of the remaining ten people would very much like for him to get that amount of that drug. (I make it a large majority, though I have no very clear idea how its being a majority matters. I also made the sick one be a citizen of the state, though I have no very clear idea how his being so matters.) The eight can scrape together the needed amount of the drug from among their own supplies, but to do so would require each of them to deplete his supply drastically—not to the point at which any of their lives is at risk, but to the point at which they would have a bare sufficiency. By contrast, the remaining two people have ample supplies; each of them could, himself, easily supply the needed amount. But these two individuals refuse to contribute.

14. See Nozick, *Anarchy, State, and Utopia*, pp. 152–153.

This case is different from (A) and (B): In this case, by contrast with those we have been looking at, the agents do not have to take anything from anyone else in order to meet the need of the eleventh. They can meet his need themselves. Does this mean that they must meet it themselves? On Nozick's view they must. On Nozick's view, the meeting of human needs is a consumer good like any other. Or rather, it is like any other expensive consumer good.[15] If you want a color television set, and buying one will deplete your assets to the point at which you have a bare sufficiency to live on, well, so be it, it is up to you whether or not a color television is worth that much to you. You certainly cannot take from anyone else in order to be able to buy one without having to deplete your assets! Similarly for the meeting of human needs.

It is plain enough, however, that the meeting of human needs is not a consumer good like any other. I hasten to say I have no account of what marks needs off from mere wants. But certainly if a man will die unless he gets something, then that thing is something he needs. And we know that if we cannot provide him with that thing which he needs for life without taking it from Smith, then—at least in such cases as Smith places at most little value on it—it is permissible for us to take it from Smith. This marks a difference. For even if you cannot get a color television at all unless you take from someone else, then all the same you cannot take from him in order to buy one, even if he has plenty of money.

But is this difference relevant to the case at hand? Suppose Nozick were to grant it, and say: "Very well, the meeting of human needs is not a consumer good like any other—it differs from color televisions in the way you indicate. [He would thus acknowledge that property rights are not infinitely stringent.] Still, if the eight *can* meet the need of the eleventh by themselves, how can they presume to take from the two who do not care if the need is met?"

Nozick might go on: "In those cases you have been describing in which Jones needs something for life, and it is permissible to take it from Smith and give it to Jones, what overrides Smith's right that the thing not be taken from him is not the mere fact that Jones needs it for life, but the complex fact that Jones needs it for life *and* we can provide it in no other way than by taking it from Smith. Suppose what Jones needs for life is a drug which you have ample supplies

15. Ibid., pp. 160–164, 168–172.

of and Smith has only a little of; surely you cannot say: 'How nice! The fact that Jones needs that drug for life overrides Smith's right that his drug not be taken away from him, so I do not have to provide for Jones myself—I can take from Smith to provide for Jones.' Surely you cannot take from Smith if you have plenty yourself! But if it is the complex fact I pointed to which is doing the real work in the cases you describe—if it is that fact which really does the overriding—then those cases have no bearing at all on the case now at hand. So I repeat: Given the eight can meet the need of the eleventh by themselves, how can they presume to take from the two who do not care if the need is met?''

Nozick might go on: "And wouldn't it be like that in ideal states generally? In other words, that those who refuse to contribute would be few enough so that those willing to contribute could, by themselves, meet such needs as they wanted met?[16] If so, nothing so far said counts against my thesis that a government of an ideal state which imposes taxes for the purpose of redistribution violates the rights of its citizens."

It is hard to know what to say about people who would live in "ideal" states if there were any. What would they be like? But I join the many other readers of *Anarchy, State, and Utopia* who have doubts about their generosity.[17]

Moreover, the instability of the situation I invited you to imagine is obvious. Suppose that if only one of the eight ceased to be willing to contribute, then the remaining seven could no longer meet the need of the eleventh by themselves, so that the case would then collapse into a case of the kind we were looking at earlier. Would it not pay them to draw straws to choose one among them to volunteer to say he has changed his mind? Then, instead of the eight having to deplete their own supplies of the drug, the remaining seven could take from the two who are rich in it. Would they even need to draw straws to choose a liar? If the eight were given the information that if there were only seven, the seven could take from the two, would there not be at least one who would *really* change his mind? It would

16. Ibid., pp. 182, 265–268.
17. Thomas Nagel, in his review of Nozick's book, makes the interesting suggestion that insisting that contributions be voluntary is "an excessively demanding moral position" and that "excessive demands on the will . . . can be more irksome than automatic demands on the purse." Nagel, Book Review, *Yale Law Journal* 85 (November 1975), pp. 136, 145–146.

be an odd moral theory that yielded either the conclusion that the eight must not be given that information, or the conclusion that the eight must meet the need of the eleventh by themselves unless they are lucky enough to get that information, in which case they do not have to.

All the same, the question my hypothetical Nozick raises is a hard one. If the eight can meet the need of the eleventh by themselves, how can they presume to take from the two who do not care if the need is met? I am sure that the instability I pointed to should figure in the answer, but I do not see clearly how.

One's intuition, I think, is that it just is not *fair* that the eight should have to deplete their supplies so drastically in order to meet the need of the eleventh. The source of that intuition is, I think, this: One thinks of the needs as *having* to be met by the citizens of that state, and therefore thinks that the burden of meeting it should be shared, as in the case of any other project which the citizens have to carry out.

Why does the need *have* to be met by the citizens of the state? By hypothesis, the need is one which can be met by them at little cost to any of them, for each of the two with ample supplies could easily meet the need by himself. But if a need can be met at little cost— remembering that it is a need for something to sustain life itself— then it is indecent that the need not be met. (I here say something of a community which would be true of an individual.) So it has to be met. So, as in the case of any other project which the citizens of a state have to carry out, it is only fair that the burden of doing so be shared. But if the two with ample supplies give nothing at all, the entire burden falls on the remaining eight, who can least afford to share it. Hence it is not fair that it should fall on them alone.

If the two with ample supplies can each meet the need at very little cost, then it makes little difference whether or not one takes the whole amount needed from one, or takes half the needed amount from each, or imposes a proportional tax on all ten of them, under which the two pay the lion's share, and the remaining eight pay a grain or two each. Another possibility is that each of the two might be ordered to provide half, and the remaining eight suffer a comparable loss by having to pay the two, or the community at large, in some commodity other than the drug.

There are cases, however, in which it will make a difference. Let us look back again at case (A). I said that if we go ahead, and break into the box and give the drug to the child, we shall have later to pay you some, if not all, of the cost we imposed on you by doing so. Kindhearted students sometimes look askance at this proposal—for if we go ahead, we do so to save the life of a child, after all. But the idea that the burdens must be fairly shared cuts both ways. If we go ahead, we must share, with you, the burden of meeting that child's need: We must not impose the entire burden of meeting its need on you. If I am right, it follows that we need not reimburse you for the entire cost of repairing or replacing the box and replacing the drug, but only such part of that cost as leaves you to pay the same amount as each of the rest of us. It is for this reason that I preferred not to speak of that payment as *compensation:* its point is not so much to compensate for a loss as to reduce that loss to the point at which it is no greater than ours.

I should stress, however, that the cases I have drawn attention to are all cases in which the redistribution aimed at is aimed at in order to meet the human needs. None of them is a case in which the redistribution aimed at is aimed at simply in order that there be less inequality. Taxation for redistribution for that purpose is a wholly different matter.

5 · Rights and Compensation

1. Suppose, following Joel Feinberg,

that you are on a back-packing trip in the high mountain country when an unanticipated blizzard strikes the area with such ferocity that your life is imperiled. Fortunately, you stumble onto an unoccupied cabin, locked and boarded up for the winter, clearly somebody else's private property. You smash in a window, enter, and huddle in a corner for three days until the storm abates. During this period you help yourself to your unknown benefactor's food supply and burn his wooden furniture in the fireplace to keep warm.[1]

Feinberg thinks it is morally permissible for you to do all these things, and he is surely right.

"Yet," as he also says, having done them, "you have infringed the clear rights of another person." Why does he think that if you act as he imagines you to act, you infringe another's "clear rights?" Well, as he said, that cabin is "clearly somebody else's private property."

It seems to me that Feinberg is right in thinking that in so acting you infringe the rights of the cabin owner. It seems to me that if I own a piece of property, then, unless and until I give you permission, I have a right against you that you not burn it. In Feinberg's story, the cabin owner did not give you permission to burn his furniture: the cabin owner was not there to be asked for permission. So it seems to me that in acting as Feinberg imagines you to do, you infringe at least this right of the owner's: the right that you not burn his furniture.

Let us go in for a closer look. Suppose that I am the cabin owner,

---

1. Joel Feinberg, "Voluntary Euthanasia and the Inalienable Right to Life," *Philosophy and Public Affairs* 7 (Winter 1978), p. 102.

and that you have just broken into my cabin, and that you have not yet burned any of the furniture. Among the bits of furniture is an old wooden chair. Feinberg's view is that I have a right against you that you not burn that chair—a claim, of course, rather than a privilege, in Hohfeld's sense of these terms. Let us abbreviate "x has claim against y that p" as "$C_{x,y}$ p." Then we may say that it is Feinberg's, and my, view that

(1) $C_{I,you}$ You do not burn the chair

is true.

But some people would say that if you burn my furniture in circumstances of the kind which Feinberg describes, then you do not infringe any right of mine. They would remind us of the fact that

(2) It is morally permissible for you to burn the chair

is true in circumstances of the kind which Feinberg describes; and if (2) is true, how can (1) also be true?

In fact, some—perhaps all—of them would say that (2) *entails* that (1) is false. They would say, quite generally, that the question what claims one person has against another is settled by the answer to the question what it is morally permissible for that other person to do; so that, in particular, if he *may* burn my chair, then it is not the case that I have a claim against him that he not burn it.

Our theory of rights would, after all, be considerably simpler if we could adopt the general view that the question of what claims one person has against another is settled by the answer to the question about what is morally permissible for that other person to do. No puzzling clashes: no cases in which A has a right against B which B may permissibly infringe.

One would have to pay something for that simplification. In particular, one would have to allow that ownership is a little more complicated than might have been thought. But ownership is already, and on any view, a complicated business—more complicated, certainly, than a hasty first thought suggests. To own something is to have a cluster of rights in respect of it. Which rights? I own a certain chair. One's hasty first thought is that it follows that I have a right to sit in it whenever I choose. A second thought makes clear that this does not follow. For I might own a chair, and yet have rented it to Jones—and if I have rented it to Jones, then, though I still own it, I do not (for the duration of Jones's lease on it) have a right to sit in it whenever I choose. Again, does it follow from the fact that I own a chair that I have a right to sell it? I should think not: it seems to me eminently possible that I should own a chair and have committed myself to not selling it—that is, waived my right to sell it.

It is clear that the range of rights included in ownership of a piece of property is constrained by rental or loan or other kinds of commitment. And we *can* say that the range of rights included in ownership is narrower even than these considerations suggest it is. I said that if I own a piece of property, then, unless and until I give you permission, I have a right against you that you not burn it. But we can say that this is just a mistake. If you are in circumstances of the kind which Feinberg describes, you are in dire need; that is what makes (2) true. We *can* say that that also makes (1) false. Perhaps we should say that (1) *was* true, but became false when you stumbled onto my cabin, needing to burn the chair; perhaps we should say that (1) is not now true, and never was true—that I at no time have a claim against you that you not burn it, but only a claim that you not-burn-it-when-you-are-in-no-need-of-burning-it. In any case, we *can* say that, though I do still own the chair, (1) is now false. And isn't a simpler general theory of rights worth buying at the cost of a more complicated theory of that small branch of it which has to do with ownership?

2. A number of people have suggested that there is yet another reason to suppose (1) is false. What they would draw our attention to is the fact that it is not morally permissible for me to *prevent* you from burning the chair. Suppose, that is, that I have been watching you stumble toward my cabin via television. Suppose that I have a device in place, by the activation of which I can prevent you from burning my chair—for example, pressing the switch will cause all the furniture to be coated with fire-proof foam. Would it be morally permissible for me to activate that device? Surely not; surely it would be wrong to prevent you from burning the chair.

If Jones is drowning, Smith cannot pull his rope out of reach and say "Mine!"

Now friends of the simplification can easily accommodate the truth of

(3) It is not morally permissible for me to prevent you from burning the chair,

for on their view, (1) is false since (2) is true. But how are Feinberg and his friends to accommodate it? If (1) is true—if I really do have a claim against you that you not burn the chair—how can it be morally impermissible for me to prevent you from burning it? We Feinberg-friends thus seem to be committed to further puzzling clashes, for we are committed, not merely to there being cases in which A has a right against B which B may permissibly infringe, but also to there being cases in which A has a right against B that B not do a thing, though it is not permissible for A to prevent him fom doing it.

But we ought not let this sail by too quickly. *Does* the truth of (3) cast doubt on (1)? Suppose I own a concrete garden gnome. Is

(1') $C_{I, you}$ You do not smash my gnome

true? Well, why would you want to smash it? Let us suppose that you simply dislike me, or my gnome, or both. But let us suppose also that I can prevent you from smashing my gnome only by killing you. (You are bigger than me, but I have an anti-tank gun.) Surely I cannot, surely it would be bad, wrong, morally impermissible for me to prevent you from smashing it in those circumstances. Thus

(3') It is not morally permissible for me to prevent you from smashing my gnome

is true in this case. Should we say that since (3') is true, (1') is false? Really? So that if out of moral compunction I do not kill you, and thus do not prevent you from smashing my gnome, you infringe no right of mine in smashing it?

I think we really must grant that (3') is entirely compatible with (1'). No call for puzzlement *here*: it is perfectly possible that A have a right against B that B not do a thing, and that it not be permissible— the circumstances being what they are—for A to prevent him from doing it.

It is a good question why people have thought otherwise. *Why* has it seemed to people that the truth of (3) casts doubt on (1)? One possible, and I think interesting, source of the idea that it does comes out as follows.

It is a very plausible idea that if I have a *claim* against you that you not burn my chair, then I have the *privilege* as regards you of preventing you from burning it—so that (1) entails

(4) I have the privilege, as regards you, of preventing you from burning the chair.

I'll call the thesis that (1) entails (4) "the claim/privilege thesis."

Now as I said, our theory of rights would be considerably simpler if we could adopt the general view that the question what claims one person has against another is settled by the answer to the question what it is morally permissible for that other person to do. And shouldn't what is true of claims have an analogue true of privileges? And don't we obtain a comparable further simplification if we suppose also that the question what privileges a person has is settled by the answer to the question what it is permissible for *him* to do? So shouldn't we say, not merely that (2) entails that (1) is false, but also that (3) entails that (4) is false?

The argument now emerges. Suppose you like this simplification. Then you accept that (3) entails that (4) is false. To accept that is to accept that (4) entails that (3) is false. Suppose you also like the claim/privilege thesis that (1) entails (4). It would be no surprise if you drew the conclusion that (1) entails that (3) is false, and therefore that (3) entails that (1) is false.

I am inclined to think that this is not merely a *possible* source of the idea that the truth of (3) casts doubt on (1): I am inclined to think that its adherents have reached that idea in just this way.

The simplification to be got in this way is very attractive indeed. It is worth noticing that if we say both that the question what claims a person has is settled by what is permissible for others to do, and also that the question what privileges a person has is settled by what it is permissible for him to do, we do not merely have a simpler theory of rights, we have a simpler moral theory, for to take this line is to commit oneself to the view that rights do not have an independent bearing in moral assessment of action.

And isn't the claim/privilege thesis plausible?

Unfortunately we cannot have both the simplification and the claim/privilege thesis. An argument exactly analogous to the one we just went through yields that (3') entails that (1') is false, which simply is not so—for in the case I imagined, (3') and (1') are both true.

Which should be given up? Feinberg and his friends say: Alas, the simplification must be given up. They say: (1) is entirely compatible with (2) and (3) with (4). They say: the question what claims a person has is not settled by what others may do, and the question what privileges a person has is not settled by what he may do—rights do have an independent bearing in moral assessment of action, so we must learn to live with whatever moral clutter that fact produces.

Indeed, they have an argument to the effect that the simplification must be given up—for they have an argument to the effect that we must suppose that (1) is true. We should now turn to it.

3. Let me remind you of what is being supposed. You were caught by a blizzard; you stumbled onto my cabin; you broke in, and have it in mind to burn my furniture for warmth—among other bits of furniture, an old wooden chair. Feinberg says: if you go ahead and burn that chair, you will later owe me *compensation* for doing so.[2] He says:

> [You will later owe] compensation here for the same reason one must repay a debt or return what one has borrowed. If the other had no right that was infringed in the first place, one could hardly have a duty to compensate him. Perhaps he would be an appropriate object of your sympathy or patronage or charity, but those are quite different from compensation.[3]

Thus Feinberg thinks that if you go ahead and burn that chair, I will have a claim against you for compensation—thus that if you go ahead and burn that chair,

(5) $C_{I,you}$ You compensate me for the loss of the chair

will be true. Moreover, Feinberg thinks (5) will be true *because* (1) is now true, and that (5) would not become true if (1) were not true now.

The proposal is of considerable importance, since accepting it blocks accepting that attractive simplification I drew attention to.

It seems plain that Feinberg is right in thinking that if you go ahead and burn the chair, (5) will be true. What we must ask first, however, is whether he is right in thinking that if (1) were not now true, then (5) would not become true when you burned the chair. In other words, is there no other way of explaining the fact that (5) will be true than by supposing (1) to be true now, and appealing to *that* fact to explain it?

2. A similar point, about an example similar to Feinberg's, was made in Essay 3. I have preferred, for a number of reasons, to use Feinberg's example here rather than my own.

3. Feinberg, "Voluntary Euthanasia."

4. Robert E. Keeton's discussion of similar cases in tort law suggests an alternative explanation.[4] On this view, we do not need to suppose that (1) is now true. We need not suppose that I have a claim against you that you not burn the chair; it is enough if we suppose that I have a claim against you that you not do something complex, namely, burn-the-chair-without-compensating-me-for-the-loss-of-it. More precisely, it is enough if we suppose that

(6) $C_{I,you}$ (If you burn the chair, then you compensate me for the loss of the chair)

is now true.

And why should we think that enough? It is a very natural idea that the conjunction of (6) with

(7) You burn the chair

entails (5). So the alternative explanation goes like this: why will (5) be true if you make (7) true? Well, (6) is true, and the conjunction of (6) with (7) entails (5).

This *is* a very natural idea—and it is therefore most unfortunate that we cannot make a permanent home for it.

What I have in mind is this. There is a principle governing the relations among ascriptions of claims, namely,

(P_1) "$C_{A,B}$ p" entails "$C_{A,B}$ q" if "p" entails "q,"

which I think we really ought to accept. I do not have space to defend it here; I shall simply assume it true. Suppose that

(CP_1) "$[C_{A,B} (p \rightarrow q)]$ & p" entails "$C_{A,B}$ q"

were also true. ("CP_1" is an abbreviation for "first candidate principle.") Then

(α) $[C_{A,B} (-p)]$ & p

would entail

(β) $C_{A,B}$ q

for "$C_{A,B} (-p)$" entails "$C_{A,B} (p \rightarrow q)$" by (P_1), and the conjunction of that with "p" entails "$C_{A,B}$ q" by (CP_1). But we really cannot have

4. Robert E. Keeton, "Conditional Fault in the Law of Torts," *Harvard Law Review* 72 (January 1959).

it that (α) entails (β). For if (α) entails (β), then if A has a claim against B that B does not kick A, and if also B *does* kick A, then for any sentence S you choose, A has a claim against B that S be true—the sentences "B murders A's father," "B starts World War III," and so on. This is, to say the least, an unacceptable consequence. You do not give me a claim against you to anything and everything simply by bringing about some one thing which I have a claim against you that you not bring about.

So we may not accept (CP_1); and I should imagine we must, therefore, reject that very natural idea that the conjunction of (6) with (7) entails (5). So this putative alternative explanation of what will make (5) true if you burn the chair is a nonstarter.

5.   There is a possible source of worry about what I just said which is worth attending to. What I have in mind is that if we reject (CP_1), we may seem to be in trouble elsewhere in ethics. There are cases and cases, and in some there is a duty to compensate where there is no plausibility whatever to the idea that anyone infringed anyone's rights. Suppose, for example, that A owns a restaurant. B enters and sits down at a table. A hands B a menu, and let us for simplicity imagine that there is only one thing written on it: "Stew. . . . $1.50." B says "Yes, please." A brings B some stew, and then, later, when B has eaten the stew, a bill for $1.50. It is now surely true to say:

(5*) $C_{A,B}$ B pays A $1.50.

What makes (5*) be true? It is a plausible idea that

(6*) $C_{A,B}$ (If A gives B stew, then B pays A $1.50)

was true, and by hypothesis,

(7*)   A gives B stew

is true. But if the conjunction of (6) with (7) does not entail (5), then the conjunction of (6*) with (7*) does not entail (5*). How *are* we to account for the truth of (5*), if we cannot suppose that (CP_1) is true?

Such situations are common enough, and it is—quite apart from our concerns here—an interesting question how the debt gets generated in them. One thing which is plain is that no one infringes anyone's rights in such situations: we cannot say that what makes (5*) true is the fact that B infringed a right of A's.

A and B seem to have made a deal. Neither *said* anything about a deal; they did not have to, the custom in such things being what it is. What they made was an unwritten, unspoken contract.

How precisely did they do that? The most plausible account of what happened is, I think, H. A. Prichard's.[5] On Prichard's view, we must take A and B to have made promises to each other. What promises? It cannot be supposed that in handing B the menu, A was promising (all simply) to give B stew; A wants to give B stew only if he can suppose B to be committed to paying for it if he gets it. On Prichard's view, A was, in handing B the menu, making an (unspoken) promise reportable in the words

(8) A promises B that [if B promises A that (if A gives B stew, then B pays A $1.50), then A gives B stew];

and B was, in saying, "Yes, please," making an (unspoken) promise reportable in the words

(9) B promises A that (if A gives B stew, then B pays A $1.50).

I think this is a plausible account of what went on between them. In any case, it is easy to see *roughly* how B's debt got generated under this account of what went on between them. By making the promise reported in (8), A commits himself to the truth of what is in the square brackets in (8); by making the promise reported in (9), B makes its antecedent true, and commits himself to the truth of what is in the round brackets in (9). Since B made the antecedent of what is in the square brackets true, A must give him some stew. By giving him some stew, A makes the antecedent of what is in the round brackets true, and B must therefore pay A $1.50.

But this *is* rough. We must look at it a little more closely. I shall concentrate on the second half of the drama, that is, on the source of B's debt to A.

Suppose B has made the promise reported in (9). I said B thereby committed himself to the truth of what is in the round brackets in (9). I might have put it: B thereby gave A a claim against him to the truth of what is in the round brackets in (9). It seems a plausible idea, that is, that we should accept

(P_2) "$\text{Prom}_{A,B}$ p" entails "$C_{B,A}$ p,"

5. H. A. Prichard, "Exchanging," in *Moral Obligation* (Oxford: The Clarendon Press, 1949).

and thus take (9) to entail (6*). After B made the promise reported in (9), A gave him some stew; so he made (7*) true. I said: by giving B some stew, A made the antecedent of what is in the round brackets true, and B must therefore pay A $1.50—that is, (5*) is now true. But without (CP₁) in hand, we cannot deduce (5*) from the conjunction of (6*) with (7*). So what warrants my use of that word "must"? How does the debt reported in (5*) get generated?

It seems to me we need, and should adopt, a second principle governing the relations between promises and claims, namely

(P₃)   "[Prom$_{A,B}$ (p $\longrightarrow$ q)] & p" entails "C$_{B,A}$ q."[6]

Let us first see that if we can adopt (P₃), all is well. Suppose B has made the promise reported in (9), and that A has therefore given B some stew. The conjunction of (9) with (7*) is now true; and (P₃) tells us that it entails (5*). So if we have (P₃) in hand, all is well: what generates the debt reported in (5*) is the fact that B made his promise, and that A gave B stew.

Can we adopt (P₃)? Compare it with (CP₁). They look very like—and yet we had to reject (CP₁).

We would have to reject (P₃) for analogous reasons if

(CP₂)   "Prom$_{A,B}$ p" entails "Prom$_{A,B}$ q" if "p" entails "q"

were true. For if (P₃) and (CP₂) were both true,

(α*) [Prom$_{A,B}$ (−P)] & p

would entail

(β*) C$_{B,A}$ q.

And we can no more have it that (α*) entails (β*) than we can have it that (α) entails (β).

6. The following principle is stronger than (P₃):

"[Prom$_{A,B}$ (p $\longrightarrow$ q)] & p" entails "Prom$_{A,B}$ q."

Is it acceptable? I think not. "I promise you that if you go, I'll go," I say; and you do go. No doubt you have a claim against me that I go, but I do not think I at any time promised to go. It is an interesting question what is "the internal logic of promising"—if anything merits so grand a name.

"Prom$_{A,B}$ (p & q)" entails "Prom$_{A,B}$ p,"

for example, is surely plausible enough. But since (CP₂)—see the text, below—is not at all plausible, the logic is at best slim.

Fortunately, however, (CP$_2$) is on its face a false principle. I may promise you that a state of affairs S will obtain without having *promised* you that every state of affairs S* will obtain such that S's obtaining entails S*'s obtaining. Compare some other "speech-activities." Suppose "p" entails "q." I may say that p without thereby having said that q; I may ask you whether p without thereby having asked you whether q; and so on. Claims are different. If you have a claim against me that S will obtain, then you have a claim against me to the obtaining of every state of affairs which must obtain if S is to obtain. Promising, like other "speech-activities," involves intentionality; the generating of claims does not.

So I think we *can* adopt (P$_3$). Moreover, it really does seem a plausible principle. If I promise you that if p then q, and it turns out to be the case that p, then I surely am committed to you to its being the case that q—you have a claim against me that it be the case that q, and can complain to me if it is not.

If so, then we do not make trouble for ourselves by giving up (CP$_1$). We *can* explain B's debt to A without it.

6. Let us go back to the case we began with. If we could suppose that you promised me that if you burn my chair, then you will compensate me for the loss of it, we could explain the fact that (5) will be true if you burn my chair in the same way as we explained B's debt to A. But we cannot suppose this. If memory serves, nobody has ever made me a promise, written or unwritten, spoken or unspoken, to the effect that if he burns any of my furniture, he will compensate me for the loss of it. So what makes it be the case that if you burn that chair, (5) will be true?

I gather that some legal writers would say that if you burn the chair, you will have "unjustly enriched" yourself, and that *that* is why you will have to compensate me for the loss of it. Unjust enrichment? I am taking it to be a datum that it is—in the circumstances—morally permissible, not bad, not wrong for you to burn that chair. It could be said that if you burn the chair then, although you act permissibly, you do nevertheless act unjustly—since I have a right that you not burn the chair, which right you therefore infringe in acting. If they take this line, they are friends of Feinberg's: they explain the fact that (5) will be true by appeal to the fact that (1) is now true.

The idea of unjust enrichment could enter at a different place. It could be said that burning my chair would not be a case of unjust enrichment, but that burning-my-chair-without-compensating-me-for-the-loss-of-it would be. As I said, Robert E. Keeton is one who takes this line. Unfortunately it does not succeed.

7. Feinberg says that (5) will be true if you burn the chair because (1) is now true. I think he must be right. I certainly have not canvassed all the possibilities, but it does seem to me that there is no way of explaining the fact that (5) will be true which does not, somewhere, pass through the truth of (1). It is perhaps just worth saying explicitly that to take this view is not to commit oneself to the view that (5) entails (1). (5) plainly does not entail (1). (5) does not even entail that you infringed any right of mine. Compensation may be owed in cases in which no one infringed anyone's rights: see, for example, B's duty to compensate A for the stew he ate in A's restaurant. The duty to compensate is at best a sign of an infringed right—and probably not even a very good one at that. What has been in question here is only this: what could explain the fact that (5) will be true *in these circumstances* if we cannot suppose that (1) is true.

There remains a second question, namely *how* the fact that (1) is true—supposing now that (1) is true—explains the fact that (5) will be true if you burn that chair. It is not obvious how it does. I am sorry to have to leave this question for discussion elsewhere.

8. My main aim has been to give ground for thinking that we cannot have that simplification in moral theory which I drew attention to earlier. If, as I think, we must suppose that (1) is true if we are to be able to explain the fact that you will have a duty to compensate me if you burn the chair, then we must suppose that (1) is compatible with (2). More generally, we cannot have it that the question what claims a person has is settled by the answer to the question what it is permissible for other people to do. Moral theory is more cluttered than we might have wished for it to be.[7]

7. This essay was written during my tenure of an NEH Fellowship and a sabbatical leave from MIT. Many people made helpful criticisms and suggestions; I am especially grateful to Charles Fried.

6 · Killing, Letting Die, and the Trolley Problem

1. Morally speaking it may matter a great deal how a death comes about, whether from natural causes, or at the hands of another, for example. Does it matter whether a man was killed or only let die? A great many people think it does: they think that killing is worse than letting die. And they draw conclusions from this for abortion, euthanasia, and the distribution of scarce medical resources. Others think it doesn't, and they think this shown by what we see when we construct a pair of cases which are so far as possible in all other respects alike, except that in the one case the agent kills, in the other he only lets die. So, for example, imagine that

(1) Alfred hates his wife and wants her dead. He puts cleaning fluid in her coffee, thereby killing her,

and that

(2) Bert hates his wife and wants her dead. She puts cleaning fluid in her coffee (being muddled, thinking it's cream). Bert happens to have the antidote to cleaning fluid, but he does not give it to her; he lets her die.[1]

Alfred kills his wife out of a desire for her death; Bert lets his wife die out of a desire for her death. But what Bert does is surely every bit as bad as what Alfred does. So killing isn't worse than letting die.

But I am now inclined to think that this argument is a bad one. Compare the following argument for the thesis that cutting off a man's

1. See Essay 2, section 3. See also Michael Tooley, "Abortion and Infanticide," *Philosophy and Public Affairs* 2 (Fall 1972), sec. 5, and James Rachels, "Active and Passive Euthanasia," *New England Journal of Medicine* 292 (January 9, 1975).

head is no worse than punching a man in the nose. "Alfrieda knows that if she cuts off Alfred's head he will die, and, wanting him to die, cuts it off; Bertha knows that if she punches Bert in the nose he will die—Bert is in peculiar physical condition—and, wanting him to die, punches him in the nose. But what Bertha does is surely every bit as bad as what Alfrieda does. So cutting off a man's head isn't worse than punching a man in the nose." It's not easy to say just exactly what goes wrong in this argument, because it's not clear what we mean when we say, as we do, such things as that cutting off a man's head is worse than punching a man in the nose. The argument brings out that we don't mean by it anything which entails that for every pair of acts, actual or possible, one of which is a nose-punching, the other of which is a head-cutting-off, but which are so far as possible in all other respects alike, the second is worse than the first. Or at least the argument brings out that we can't mean anything which entails this by "Cutting off a man's head is worse than punching a man in the nose" if we want to go on taking it for true. Choice is presumably in question, and the language which comes most readily is perhaps this: if you can cut off a man's head or punch him in the nose, then if he is in "normal" condition—and if other things are equal—you had better not choose cutting off his head. But there is no need to go into any of this for present purposes. Whatever precisely we do mean by "Cutting off a man's head is worse than punching a man in the nose," it surely (a) is not disconfirmed by the cases of Alfrieda and Bertha, and (b) is confirmed by the fact that if you can now either cut off my head, or punch me in the nose, you had better not choose cutting off my head. This latter is a fact. I don't say that you had better choose punching me in the nose: best would be to do neither. Nor do I say it couldn't have been the case that it would be permissible to choose cutting off my head. But things being as they are, you had better not choose it.

I'm not going to hazard a guess as to what precisely people mean by saying "Killing is worse than letting die." I think the argument of the first paragraph brings out that they can't mean by it anything which entails that for every pair of acts, actual or possible, one of which is a letting die, the other of which is a killing, but which are so far as possible in all other respects alike, the second is worse than the first—they can't, that is, if they want to go on taking it for true. I think here too that choice is in question, and that what they mean by it is something which is not disconfirmed by the cases of Alfred and Bert. And isn't what they mean by it confirmed by the fact—isn't it a fact?—that in the following case, Charles must not kill, that he must instead let die:

> (3) Charles is a great transplant surgeon. One of his patients needs a new heart, but is of a relatively rare blood-type. By chance, Charles learns of a healthy specimen with that very blood-type. Charles can take the healthy specimen's heart, killing him, and install it in his patient, saving him. Or he can refrain from taking the healthy specimen's heart, letting his patient die.

I should imagine that most people would agree that Charles must not choose to take out the one man's heart to save the other: he must let his patient die.

And isn't what they mean by it further confirmed by the fact—isn't it a fact?—that in the following case, David must not kill, that he must instead let die:

> (4) David is a great transplant surgeon. Five of his patients need new parts—one needs a heart, the others need, respectively, liver, stomach, spleen, and spinal cord—but all are of the same, relatively rare, blood-type. By chance, David learns of a healthy specimen with that very blood-type. David can take the healthy specimen's parts, killing him, and install them in his patients, saving them. Or he can refrain from taking the healthy specimen's parts, letting his patients die.

If David may not even choose to cut up one where *five* will thereby be saved, surely what people who say "Killing is worse than letting die" mean by it must be right!

On the other hand, there is a lovely, nasty difficulty which confronts us at this point. Philippa Foot says[2]—and seems right to say—that it is permissible for Edward, in the following case, to kill:

> (5) Edward is the driver of a trolley, whose brakes have just failed. On the track ahead of him are five people; the banks are so steep that they will not be able to get off the track in time. The track has a spur leading off to the right, and Edward can turn

---

2. In her very rich article, "Abortion and the Doctrine of the Double Effect," *Oxford Review* 5 (1967). Most of my examples are more or less long-winded expansions of hers. See also G. E. M. Anscome's brief reply, "Who is Wronged?" in the same issue of the *Oxford Review*.

the trolley onto it. Unfortunately there is one person on the right-hand track. Edward can turn the trolley, killing the one; or he can refrain from turning the trolley, killing the five.

If what people who say "Killing is worse than letting die" mean by it is true, how is it that Edward may choose to turn that trolley?

Killing and letting die apart, in fact, it's a lovely, nasty difficulty: why is it that Edward may turn that trolley to save his five, but David may not cut up his healthy specimen to save his five? I like to call this the trolley problem, in honor of Mrs. Foot's example.

Mrs. Foot's own solution to the trolley problem is this. We must accept that our "negative duties," such as the duty to refrain from killing, are more stringent than our "positive duties," such as the duty to save lives. If David does nothing, he violates a positive duty to save five lives; if he cuts up the healthy specimen, he violates a negative duty to refrain from killing one. Now the negative duty to refrain from killing one is not merely more stringent than the positive duty to save one, it is more stringent even than the positive duty to save five. So of course Charles may not cut up his one to save one; and David may not cut up his one even to save five. But Edward's case is different. For if Edward "does nothing," he doesn't just do nothing; he kills the five on the track ahead, for he drives right into them with his trolley. Whichever Edward does, turn or not turn, he kills. There is, for Edward, then, not a conflict between a positive duty to save five and a negative duty to refrain from killing one; there is, for Edward, a conflict between a negative duty to refrain from killing five and a negative duty to refrain from killing one. But this is no real conflict: a negative duty to refrain from killing five is surely more stringent than a negative duty to refrain from killing one. So Edward may, indeed must, turn that trolley.

Now I am inclined to think that Mrs. Foot is mistaken about why Edward may turn his trolley, but David may not cut up his healthy specimen. I say only that Edward "may" turn his trolley, and not that he must: my intuition tells me that it is not required that he turn it, but only that it is permissible for him to do so. But this isn't important now: it is, at any rate, permissible for him to do so. Why? Compare (5) with

(6) Frank is a passenger on a trolley whose driver has just shouted that the trolley's brakes have failed, and who then died of the shock. On the track ahead are five people; the banks are so

steep that they will not be able to get off the track in time. The track has a spur leading off to the right, and Frank can turn the trolley onto it. Unfortunately there is one person on the right-hand track. Frank can turn the trolley, killing the one; or he can refrain from turning the trolley, letting the five die.

If Frank turns his trolley, he plainly kills his one, just as if Edward turns his trolley, he kills his one: anyone who turns a trolley onto a man presumably kills him. Mrs. Foot thinks that if Edward does nothing, he kills his five, and I agree with this: if a driver of a trolley drives it full speed into five people, he kills them, even if he only drives it into them because his brakes have failed. But it seems to me that if Frank does nothing, he kills no one. He at worst lets the trolley kill the five; he does not himself kill them, but only lets them die.

But then by Mrs. Foot's principles, the conflict for Frank is between the negative duty to refrain from killing one, and the positive duty to save five, just as it was for David. On her view, the former duty is the more stringent: its being more stringent was supposed to explain why David could not cut up his healthy specimen. So by her principles, Frank may no more turn that trolley than David may cut up his healthy specimen. Yet I take it that anyone who thinks Edward may turn his trolley will also think that Frank may turn his. Certainly the fact that Edward is driver, and Frank only passenger could not explain so large a difference.

So we stand in need, still, of a solution: why can Edward and Frank turn their trolleys, whereas David cannot cut up his healthy specimen? One's intuitions are, I think, fairly sharp on these matters. Suppose, for a further example, that

(7) George is on a footbridge over the trolley tracks. He knows trolleys, and can see that the one approaching the bridge is out of control. On the track back of the bridge there are five people; the banks are so steep that they will not be able to get off the track in time. George knows that the only way to stop an out-of-control trolley is to drop a very heavy weight into its path. But the only available, sufficiently heavy weight is a fat man, also watching the trolley from the footbridge. George can shove the fat man onto the track in the path of the trolley, killing the fat man; or he can refrain from doing this, letting the five die.

Presumably George may not shove the fat man into the path of the trolley; he must let the five die. Why may Edward and Frank turn their trolleys to save their fives, whereas George must let his five die? George's shoving the fat man into the path of the trolley seems to be very like David's cutting up his healthy specimen. But what is the relevant likeness?

Further examples come from all sides. Compare, for example, the following two cases:

(8) Harry is President, and has just been told that the Russians have launched an atom bomb towards New York. The only way in which the bomb can be prevented from reaching New York is by deflecting it; but the only deflection-path available will take the bomb onto Worcester. Harry can do nothing, letting all of New York die; or he can press a button, deflecting the bomb, killing all of Worcester.

(9) Irving is President, and has just been told that the Russians have launched an atom bomb towards New York. The only way in which the bomb can be prevented from reaching New York is by dropping one of our own atom bombs on Worcester: the blast of the American bomb will pulverize the Russian bomb. Irving can do nothing, letting all of New York die; or he can press a button, which launches an American bomb onto Worcester, killing all of Worcester.

Most people, I think, would feel that Harry may act in (8): he may deflect the Russian bomb from its New York path onto Worcester, in order to minimize the damage it does. (Notice that if Harry doesn't deflect that bomb, he kills no one—just as Frank kills no one if he doesn't turn his trolley.) But I think most people would feel that Irving may not drop an American bomb onto Worcester: a President simply may not launch an atomic attack on one of his own cities, even to save a larger one from a similar attack.

Why? I think it is the same problem.

2. Perhaps the most striking difference between the cases I mentioned in which the agent may act, and the cases I mentioned in which he may not, is this: in the former what is in question is deflecting a threat from a larger group onto a smaller group, in the latter what is in question is bringing a different threat to bear on the smaller

group. But it is not easy to see why this should matter so crucially. I think it does, and have a suggestion as to why, but it is no more than a suggestion.

I think we may be helped if we turn from evils to goods. Suppose there are six men who are dying. Five are standing in one clump on the beach, one is standing further along. Floating in on the tide is a marvelous pebble, the Health-Pebble, I'll call it: it cures what ails you. The one needs for cure the whole Health-Pebble; each of the five needs only a fifth of it. Now in fact that Health-Pebble is drifting towards the one, so that if nothing is done to alter its course, the one will get it. We happen to be swimming nearby, and are in a position to deflect it towards the five. Is it permissible for us to do this? It seems to me that it is permissible for us to deflect the Health-Pebble if and only if the one who has no more claim on it than any of the five does.

What could make it be the case that the one has more claim on it than any of the five does? One thing that I think *doesn't* is the fact that the pebble is headed for the one, and that he will get it if we do nothing. There is no Principle of Moral Inertia: there is no prima facie duty to refrain from interfering with existing states of affairs just because they are existing states of affairs. A burglar whose burgling we interfere with cannot say that since, but for our interference, he would have got the goods, he had a claim on them; it is not as if we weigh the burglar's claim on the goods against the owner's claim on them, and find the owner's claim weightier, and therefore interfere— the burglar has no claim on the goods to be weighed.

Well, the Health-Pebble might actually belong to the one. (It fell off his boat.) Or it might belong to us, and we had promised it to the one. If either of these is the case, the one has a claim on it in the sense of a right to it. If the one alone owns it, or if we have promised it only to the one, then he plainly has more claim on it than any of the five do; and we may not deflect it away from him.

But I mean to be using the word "claim" more loosely. So, for example, suppose that the five are villains who had intentionally caused the one's fatal illness, hoping he would die. (Then they became ill themselves.) It doesn't seem to me obvious that a history like this gives the one a *right* to that pebble; yet it does seem obvious that in some sense it gives the one a claim on it—anyway, more of a claim on it than any of the five has. Certainly anyway one feels that if it comes to a choice between them and him, he ought to get it. Again, suppose the six had played pebble-roulette: they had seen the pebble floating in, and agreed to flip a coin for positions on the beach and take their chances. And now the pebble is floating in towards the one. It doesn't seem to me that a history like this gives the one a *right* to that pebble; yet it does seem obvious that in some sense it gives him a claim on it, anyway, more claim on it than any of the five has. (While the fact that a pebble is floating towards one does not give him more claim on it, the compound fact that a pebble is floating towards him and that there was a background of pebble-roulette does, I think, give him more claim. If two groups have agreed to take what comes, and have acted in good faith in accordance with that agreement, I think we cannot intervene.)

I leave it open just precisely what sorts of things might give the one more claim on that Health-Pebble than any of the five has. What seems clear enough, however, is this: if the one has no more claim on it than any of the five has, we may deflect it away from him and towards the five. If the one has no more claim on it than any of the five has, it is permissible for us to deflect it in order to bring about that it saves more lives than it would do if we did not act.

Now that Health-Pebble is good to those dying men on the beach: if they get to eat it, they live. The trolley is an evil to the living men on the tracks: if they get run down by it, they die. And deflecting the Health-Pebble away from one and towards five is like deflecting the trolley away from five and towards one. For if the pebble is deflected, one life is lost and five are saved; and if the trolley is deflected, so also is one life lost and five saved. The analogy suggests a thesis: that Edward (or Frank) may deflect his trolley if and only if the one has no more claim against the trolley than any of the five has—that is, that under these circumstances he may deflect it in order to bring about that it takes fewer lives than it would do if he did not.

But while it was at least relatively clear what sorts of things might give the one more of a claim *on* the Health-Pebble, it is less clear what could give the one more of a claim *against* a trolley. Nevertheless there are examples in which it is clear enough that the one has more of a claim against the trolley than any of the five does. Suppose that

(i) The five on the track ahead are regular track workmen, repairing the track—they have been warned of the dangers of their job, and are paid specially high salaries to compensate. The right-hand track is a dead end, unused in ten years. The Mayor, representing the City, has set out picnic tables on it, and invited the convalescents at the nearby City Hospital to have lunch there, guaranteeing them safety from trolleys. The one on the right-hand track is a convalescent having his lunch there; it would never have occurred to him to have his lunch there but for the Mayor's invitation and guarantee of safety. And Edward (Frank) is the Mayor.

The situation if (i) is true is very like the situation if we own the Health-Pebble which is floating in on the tide, and have promised it to the one. If we have promised the Health-Pebble to the one and not to the five, the one has more claim on it than any of the five does, and we therefore may not deflect it away from him; if Edward (Frank) has promised that no trolley shall run down the one, and has not made this promise to the five, the one has more claim against it—more claim to not be run down by it—than any of the five does, and Edward therefore may not deflect it onto him.

So in fact I cheated: it isn't permissible for Edward and Frank to turn their trolleys in *every* possible instance of (5) and (6). Why did it seem as if it would be? The cases were underdescribed, and what you supplied as filler was that the six on the tracks are on a par: that there was nothing further true of any of them which had a bearing on the question whether or not it was permissible to turn the trolleys. In particular, then, you were assuming that it was not the case that the one had more claim against the trolleys than any of the five did.

Compare, by contrast, the situation if

(ii) All six on the tracks are regular track workmen, repairing the tracks. As they do every day, they drew straws for their assignments for the day. The one who is on the right-hand track just happened to draw the straw tagged "Right-hand track."

Or if

(iii) All six are innocent people whom villains have tied to the trolley tracks, five on one track, one on the other.

If (ii) or (iii) is true, all six are on a par in the relevant respect: the one has no more claim against the trolley than any of the five has and so the trolley may be turned.

Again, consider the situation if

(iv) The five on the track ahead are regular track workmen, repairing the track. The one on the right-hand track is a schoolboy, collecting pebbles on the track. He knows he doesn't
belong there: he climbed the fence to get onto the track, ignoring all warning signs, thinking "Who could find it in his
heart to turn a trolley onto a schoolboy?"

At the risk of seeming hardhearted about schoolboys, I have to say
I think that if (iv) is true, the trolley not only may be, but must be
turned. So it seems to me arguable that if—as I take to be the case if
(iv) is true—the five have more claim against the trolley than the one
does, the trolley not only may be, but must be turned. But for present
purposes what counts is only what makes it permissible to turn it
where it is permissible to turn it.

President Harry's case, (8), is of course like the cases of Edward
and Frank. Harry also deflects something which will harm away from
a larger group onto a smaller group. And my proposal is that he may
do this because (as we may presume) the Worcesters have no more
claim against a Russian bomb than the New Yorkers do.

The situation could have been different. Suppose an avalanche is
descending towards a large city. It is possible to deflect it onto a small
one. May we? Not if the following is the case. Large City is in avalanche country—the risk of an avalanche is very high there. The
founders of Large City were warned of this risk when they built there,
and all settlers in it were warned of it before settling there. But lots
and lots of people did accept the risk and settle there, because of the
beauty of the countryside and the money to be made there. Small
City, however, is not in avalanche country—it's flat for miles around;
and settlers in Small City settled for a less lovely city, and less money,
precisely because they did not wish to run the risk of being overrun
by an avalanche. Here it seems plain we may not deflect that avalanche onto Small City to save Large City: the Small Cityers have
more claim against it than the Large Cityers do. And it could have
been the case that New York was settled in the teeth of Russian-
bomb-risk.

The fact that is is permissible for President Harry in (8) to deflect
that atom bomb onto Worcester brings out something of interest. Mrs.
Foot had asked us to suppose "that some tyrant should threaten to
torture five men if we ourselves would not torture one." She then
asked: "Would it be our duty to do so, supposing we believed him . . .?"

Surely not, she implies: for "if so anyone who wants us to do something we think wrong has only to threaten that otherwise he himself will do something we think worse. A mad murderer, known to keep his promises, could thus make it our duty to kill some innocent citizen to prevent him from killing two."[3] Mrs. Foot is surely right. But it would be unfair to Mrs. Foot to summarize her point in this way: we must not do a villain's dirty work for him. And wrong, in any case, for suppose the Russians don't really care about New York. The city they really want to destroy is Worcester. But for some reason they can only aim their bomb at New York, which they do in the hope that President Harry will himself deflect it onto Worcester. It seems to me it makes no difference what their aim is: whether they want Worcester or not, Harry can still deflect their bomb onto Worcester But in doing so, he does the villains' dirty work for them: for if he deflects their bomb, he kills Worcester for them.

Similarly, it doesn't matter whether or not the villains in (iii) want the one on the right-hand track dead: Edward and Frank can all the same turn their trolleys onto him.That a villain wants a group dead gives them no more claim against a bomb or a trolley than these in the other group have.

Mrs. Foot's examples in the passages I quoted are of villains who have not yet launched their threat against anyone, but only threaten to: they have not yet set in train any sequence of events—e.g., by launching a bomb, or by starting a trolley down a track—such that if we don't act, a group will be harmed. The villains have as yet only *said* they would set such a sequence of events in train. I don't object to our acting on the ground of uncertainties: one may, as Mrs. Foot supposes, be perfectly certain that a villain will do exactly what he says he will do. There are two things that make it impermissible to act in this kind of case. In the first place, there are straightforward utilitarian objections to doing so: the last thing we need is to give further villains reason to think they'll succeed if they too say such things.[4] But this doesn't take us very far, for as I said, we may deflect an already launched threat away from one group and onto another, and we don't want further villains thinking they'll succeed if they only manage to get such a sequence of events set in train. So the second point is more important: in such cases, to act is *not* to deflect

3. Foot, ibid., p. 10.

4. See D. H. Hodgson, *Consequences of Utilitarianism: A Study in Normative Ethics & Legal Theory* (Oxford: Oxford University Press, 1967), pp. 77–87.

a threat away from one group and onto another, but instead to bring a different threat to bear on the other group. It is to these cases we should now turn.

3. Edward and Frank may turn their trolleys if and only if the one has no more claim against the trolleys than any of the five do. Why is it impermissible for David to cut up his healthy specimen?

I think the Health-Pebble helps here. I said earlier that we might suppose that the one actually owns the Health-Pebble which is floating in on the tide. (It fell off his boat.) And I said that in that case, he has more claim on it than any of the five has, so that we may not deflect it away from him and towards the five. Let's suppose that deflecting isn't in question any more: the pebble has already floated in, and the one has it. Let's suppose he's already put it in his mouth. Or that he's already swallowed it. We certainly may not cut him open to get it out—even if it's not yet digested, and can still be used to save five. Analogously, David may not cut up his healthy specimen to give his parts to five. One doesn't come to own one's parts in the way in which one comes to own a pebble, or a car, or one's grandfather's desk, but a man's parts are his all the same. And therefore that healthy specimen has more claim on those parts than any of the five has—just as if the one owns the Health-Pebble, he has more claim on it than any of the five do.

I do not, and did not, mean to say that we may *never* take from one what belongs to him to give to five. Perhaps there are situations in which we may even take from one something that he needs for life itself in order to give to five. Suppose, for example, that the healthy specimen had caused the five to catch the ailments because of which they need new parts—he deliberately did this in hope the five would die. No doubt a legal code which permitted a surgeon to transplant in situations such as this would be open to abuses, and bad for that reason; but it seems to me it would not be unjust.

So perhaps we can bring David's case in line with Edward's and Frank's, and put the matter like this: David may cut up his healthy specimen and give his parts to the five if and only if the healthy specimen has no more claim on his parts than any of the five do. This leaves it open that in some instances of (4), David may act.

But I am inclined to think there is more to be said of David's case than this. I suggested earlier that if George, in (7), shoves the fat man into the path of the trolley, he does something very like what David does if David cuts up his healthy specimen. Yet George wouldn't be taking anything away from the one in order to give it to the five. George would be "taking" the fat man's life, of course; but what this means is only that George would be killing the fat man, and Edward and Frank kill someone too. And similarly for Irving, in (9): if he bombs Worcester, he doesn't take anything away from the Worcesters in order to give it to the New Yorkers.

Moreover, consider the following variant on David's case:

(4') Donald is a great diagnostician. Five of his patients are dying. By chance Donald learns of a healthy specimen such that if Donald cuts him up into bits, a peculiar physiological process will be initiated in the five, curing them. Donald can cut his healthy specimen up into bits, killing him, thereby saving his patients. or he can refrain from doing this, letting his patients die.

In (4'), Donald does not need to give anything which belongs to his healthy specimen to his five; unlike David, he need only cut his healthy specimen up into bits, which can then be thrown out. Yet presumably in whatever circumstances David may not act, Donald may not act either.

So something else is involved in George's, Irving's, and Donald's cases than I drew attention to in David's; and perhaps this other thing is present in David's too.

Suppose that in the original story, where the pebble is floating in on the tide, we are for some reason unable to deflect the pebble away from the one and towards the five. All we can do, if we want the five to get it instead of the one, is to shove the one away, off the beach, out of reach of where the pebble will land; or all we can do is to drop a bomb on the one; or all we can do is to cut this one up into bits.

I suppose that there might be circumstances in which it would be permissible for us to do one or another of these things to the one— even circumstances which include that the one owns the pebble. Perhaps it would be permissible to do them if the one had caused the five to catch the ailments because of which they need the pebble, and did this deliberately, in hope the five would die. The important point, however, is this. The fact that the one has no more claim on the pebble than any of the five do does make it permissible for us to deflect the pebble away from the one and towards the five; it does not make it permissible for us to shove the one away, bomb him, or cut him to bits in order to bring about that the five get it.

Why? Here is a good, up for distribution, a Health-Pebble. If we do nothing, one will get it, and five will not; so one will live and five will die. It strikes us that it would be better for five to live and one die than for one to live and five die, and therefore that a better distribution of the good would be for the five to get it, and the one not to. If the one has no more claim on the good than any of the five has, he cannot complain if we do something to *it* in order to bring about that it is better distributed; but he can complain if we do something to *him* in order to bring about that it is better distributed.

If there is a pretty shell on the beach and it is unowned, I cannot complain if you pocket it to give to another person who would get more pleasure from it than I would. But I can complain if you shove me aside so as to be able to pocket it to give to another person who would get more pleasure from it than I would. It's unowned; so you can do to it whatever would be necessary to bring about a better distribution of it. But a *person* is not something unowned, to be knocked about in order to bring about a better distribution of something else.

Here is something bad, up for distribution, a speeding trolley. If nothing is done, five will get it, and one will not; so five will die and one will live. It strikes us that it would be better for five to live and one to die than for one to live and five to die, and therefore that a better distribution of the bad thing would be for the one to get it, and the five not to. If the one has no more claim against the bad thing than any of the five has, he cannot complain if we do something to *it* in order to bring about that it is better distributed: that is, it is permissible for Edward and Frank to turn their trolleys. But even if the one has no more claim against the bad thing than any of the five has, he can complain if we do something to *him* in order to bring about that the bad thing is better distributed: that is, it is not permissible for George to shove his fat man off the bridge into the path of the trolley.

It is true that if Edward and Frank turn their trolleys, they don't merely turn their trolleys: they turn their trolleys onto the one, they run down and thereby kill him. And if you turn a trolley onto a man, if you run him down and thereby kill him, you certainly do something to *him*. (I don't know whether or not it should be said that if you deflect a Health-Pebble away from one who needs it for life, and would get it if you didn't act, you have killed him; perhaps it would be said that you killed him, perhaps it would be said that you didn't kill him, but only caused his death. It doesn't matter: even if you only caused his death, you certainly did something to him.) So haven't their ones as much ground for complaint as George's fat man? No, for Edward's (Frank's) turning his trolley onto the one, his running the one down and thereby killing him, isn't something he does to the one to bring about that the trolley is better distributed. The trolley's being better distributed *is* its getting onto the one, it *is* running the one down and thereby killing him; and Edward doesn't turn his trolley onto the one, he doesn't run the one down and thereby kill him, in order to bring this about—what he does to bring it about is to turn his trolley. You don't bring about that a thing melts or breaks by melting or breaking it; you bring about that it melts or breaks by (as it might be) putting it on the stove or hitting it with a brick. Similarly, you don't bring about that a thing gets to a man by getting it to him; you bring about that it gets to him by (as it might be) deflecting it, turning it, throwing it—whatever it is you do, by the doing of which you will have got it to the man.

By contrast, George, if he acts, does something to the fat man (shoves him off the bridge into the path of the trolley) to bring about the better distribution of the trolley, namely, that the one (the fat man) gets it instead of the five.

A good bit more would have to be said about the distinction I appeal to here if my suggestion is to go through. In part we are hampered by the lack of a theory of action, which should explain, in particular, what it is to bring something about by doing something. But perhaps the intuition is something to take off from: that what matters in these cases in which a threat is to be distributed is whether the agent distributes it by doing something to it, or whether he distributes it by doing something to a person.

The difference between Harry's case and Irving's is, I think, the same. Harry, if he acts, does something to the Russian bomb (deflect it), in order to bring about that it is better distributed: the few Worcesters get it instead of the many New Yorkers. Irving, however, does something to the Worcesters (drops one of our own bombs on them) in order to bring about that the Russian bomb is better distributed: instead of the many New Yorker's getting it, nobody does. Hence the fact that the Worcesters have no more claim against the Russian bomb than the New Yorkers do makes it permissible for Harry to act; but not for Irving to.

If we can speak of making a better distribution of an ailment, we can say of Donald too that if he acts, he does something to his healthy specimen (cut him up into bits) in order to bring about a better distribution of the ailments threatening his five patients: instead of the five patients getting killed by them, nobody is.

And then the special nastiness in David, if he acts, lies in this: in the first place, he gives to five what belongs to the one (bodily parts), *and* in the second place, in order to bring about a better distribution of the ailments threatening his five—that is, in order to bring about that instead of the five patients getting killed by them, nobody is— he does something to the one (cuts him up).

4. Is killing worse than letting die? I suppose that what those who say it is have in mind may well be true. But this is because I suspect that they do not have in mind anything which is disconfirmed by the fact that there are pairs of acts containing a killing and letting die in which the first is no worse than the second (for example, the pair containing Alfred's and Bert's) *and* also do not have in mind anything which is disconfirmed by the fact that there are cases in which an agent may kill instead of letting die (for example, Frank's and Harry's). What I suspect they have in mind is something which is confirmed by certain cases in which an agent may not kill instead of letting die (for example, David's and Donald's). So as I say, I think they may be right. More generally, I suspect that Mrs. Foot and others may be right to say that negative duties are more stringent than positive duties. But we shan't be able to decide until we get clearer what these things come to. I think it's no special worry for them, however. For example, I take it most people think that cutting a man's head off is worse than punching a man in the nose, and I think we aren't any clearer about what this means than they are about their theses. The larger question is a question for all of us.

Meanwhile, however, the thesis that killing is worse than letting die cannot be used in any simple, mechanical way in order to yield conclusions about abortion, euthanasia, and the distribution of scarce medical resources. The cases have to be looked at individually. If nothing else comes out of the preceding discussion, it may anyway serve as a reminder of this: that there are circumstances in which— even if it is true that killing is worse than letting die—one may choose to kill instead of letting die.

7 · *The Trolley Problem*

1. Some years ago, Philippa Foot drew attention to an extraordinarily interesting problem.[1] Suppose you are the driver of a trolley. The trolley rounds a bend, and there come into view ahead five track workmen, who have been repairing the track. The track goes through a bit of a valley at that point, and the sides are steep, so you must stop the trolley if you are to avoid running the five men down. You step on the brakes, but alas they don't work. Now you suddenly see a spur of track leading off to the right. You can turn the trolley onto it, and thus save the five men on the straight track ahead. Unfortunately, Mrs. Foot has arranged that there is one track workman on that spur of track. He can no more get off the track in time than the five can, so you will kill him if you turn the trolley onto him. Is it morally permissible for you to turn the trolley?

Everybody to whom I have put this hypothetical case says, Yes, it is.[2] Some people say something stronger than that it is morally *permissible* for you to turn the trolley: They say that morally speaking, you *must* turn it—that morality requires you to do so. Others do not agree that morality requires you to turn the trolley, and even feel a certain discomfort at the idea of turning it. But everybody says that

1. See Philippa Foot, "The Problem of Abortion and the Doctrine of the Double Effect," *Oxford Review* 5 (1967).
2. I think it possible (though by no means certain) that John Taurek would say No, it is not permissible to (all simply) turn the trolley; what you ought to do is flip a coin. See John Taurek, "Should the Numbers Count?" *Philosophy and Public Affairs* 6 (Summer 197), p. 293. (But he is there concerned with a different kind of case, where the question is not whether we may do what harms one to avoid harming five, but whether we may or ought to choose to save five in preference to saving one.) For criticism of Taurek's article, see Derek Parfit, "Innumerate Ethics," *Philosophy and Public Affairs* 7 (Summer 1978), p. 285.

it is true, at a minimum, that you *may* turn it—that it would not be morally wrong in you to do so.

Now consider a second hypothetical case. This time you are to imagine yourself to be a surgeon, a truly great surgeon. Among other things you do, you transplant organs, and you are such a great surgeon that the organs you transplant always take. At the moment you have five patients who need organs. Two need one lung each, two need a kidney each, and the fifth needs a heart. If they do not get those organs today, they will all die; if you find organs for them today, you can transplant the organs and they will all live. But where to find the lungs, the kidneys, and the heart? The time is almost up when a report is brought to you that a young man who has just come into your clinic for his yearly check-up has exactly the right blood-type, and is in excellent health. Lo, you have a possible donor. All you need do is cut him up and distribute *his* parts among the five who need them. You ask, but he says, "Sorry. I deeply sympathize, but no." Would it be morally permissible for you to operate anyway? Everybody to whom I have put this second hypothetical case says, No, it would not be morally permissible for you to proceed.

Here then is Mrs. Foot's problem: *Why* is it that the trolley driver may turn his trolley, though the surgeon may not remove the young man's lungs, kidneys, and heart?[3] In both cases, one will die if the agent acts, but five will live who would otherwise die—a net saving of four lives. What difference in the other facts of these cases explains the moral difference between them? I fancy that the theorists of tort and criminal law will find this problem as interesting as the moral theorist does.

2. Mrs. Foot's own solution to the problem she drew attention to is simple, straightforward, and very attractive. She would say: Look, the surgeon's choice is between operating, in which case he kills one, and not operating, in which case he lets five die; and killing is surely worse than letting die[4]—indeed, so much worse that we can even say

3. I doubt that anyone would say, with any hope of getting agreement from others, that the surgeon ought to flip a coin. So even if you think that the trolley driver ought to flip a coin, there would remain, for you, an analogue of Mrs. Foot's problem, namely: Why ought the trolley driver flip a coin, whereas the surgeon may not?

4. Mrs. Foot speaks more generally of causing injury and failing to provide aid; and her reason for thinking that the former is worse than the latter is that the negative duty to refrain from causing injury is stricter than the positive duty to provide aid. See Foot, "The Problem of Abortion," pp. 27–29.

(I) Killing one is worse than letting five die.

So the surgeon must refrain from operating. By contrast, the trolley driver's choice is between turning the trolley, in which case he kills one, and not turning the trolley, in which case he does not *let five die*, he positively *kills* them. Now surely we can say

(II) Killing five is worse than killing one.

But then that is why the trolley driver may turn his trolley: He would be doing what is worse if he fails to turn it, since if he fails to turn it he kills five.

I do think that that is an attractive account of the matter. It seems to me that if the surgeon fails to operate, he does not kill his five patients who need parts; he merely lets them die. By contrast, if the driver fails to turn his trolley, he does not merely let the five track workmen die; he drives his trolley into them, and thereby kills them.

But there is good reason to think that this problem is not so easily solved as that.

Let us begin by looking at a case that is in some ways like Mrs. Foot's story of the trolley driver. I will call her case *Trolley Driver*; let us now consider a case I will call *Bystander at the Switch*. In that case you have been strolling by the trolley track, and you can see the situation at a glance: The driver saw the five on the track ahead, he stamped on the brakes, the brakes failed, so he fainted. What to do? Well, here is the switch, which you can throw, thereby turning the trolley yourself. Of course you will kill one if you do. But I should think you may turn it all the same.[5]

Some people may feel a difference between these two cases. In the first place, the trolley driver is, after all, captain of the trolley. He is charged by the trolley company with responsibility for the safety of his passengers and anyone else who might be harmed by the trolley he drives. The bystander at the switch, on the other hand, is a private person who just happens to be there.

Second, the driver would be driving a trolley into the five if he does not turn it, and the bystander would not—the bystander will do the five no harm at all if he does not throw the switch.

I think it right to feel these differences between the cases.

5. A similar case (intended to make a point similar to the one that I shall be making) is discussed in Nancy Davis, "The Priority of Avoiding Harm," in *Killing and Letting Die*, ed. Bonnie Steinbock (Englewood Cliffs, N.J.: Prentice Hall, 1980), pp. 172 and 194–195.

Nevertheless, my own feeling is that an ordinary person, a mere bystander, may intervene in such a case. If you see something, a trolley, a boulder, an avalanche, heading towards five, and you can deflect it onto one, it really does seem that—other things being equal—it would be permissible for you to *take* charge, *take* responsibility, and deflect the thing, whoever you may be. Of course you run a moral risk if you do, for it might be that, unbeknownst to you, other things are not equal. It might be, that is, that there is some relevant difference between the five on the one hand, and the one on the other, which would make it morally preferable that the five be hit by the trolley than that the one be hit by it. That would be so if, for example, the five are not track workmen at all, but Mafia members in workmen's clothing, and they have tied the one workman to the right-hand track in the hope that you would turn the trolley onto him. I won't canvass all the many kinds of possibilities, for in fact the moral risk is the same whether you are the trolley driver, or a bystander at the switch.

Moreover, second, we might well wish to ask ourselves what exactly is the difference between what the driver would be doing if he failed to turn the trolley and what the bystander would be doing if he failed to throw the switch. As I said, the driver would be driving a trolley into the five; but what exactly would his driving the trolley into the five consist in? Why, just sitting there, doing nothing! If the driver does just sit there, doing nothing, then that will have been how come he drove his trolley into the five.

I do not mean to make much of that fact about what the driver's driving his trolley into the five would consist in, for it seems to me to be right to say that if he does not turn the trolley, he does drive his trolley into them, and does thereby kill them. (Though this does seem to me to be right, it is not easy to say exactly what makes it so.) By contrast, if the bystander does not throw the switch, he drives no trolley into anybody, and he kills nobody.

But as I said, my own feeling is that the bystander *may* intervene. Perhaps it will seem to some even less clear that morality requires him to turn the trolley than that morality requires the driver to turn the trolley; perhaps some will feel even more discomfort at the idea of the bystander's turning the trolley than at the idea of the driver's turning the trolley. All the same, I shall take it that he *may*.

If he may, there is serious trouble for Mrs. Foot's thesis (I). It is plain that if the bystander throws the switch, he causes the trolley to hit the one, and thus he kills the one. It is equally plain that if the bystander does not throw the switch, he does not cause the trolley to hit the five, he does not kill the five, he merely fails to save them—he lets them die. His choice therefore is between throwing the switch, in which case he kills one, and not throwing the switch, in which case he lets five die. If thesis (I) were true, it would follow that the bystander may not throw the switch, and I am taking that to be false.

3. I have been arguing that

(I) Killing one is worse than letting five die

is false, and a fortiori that it cannot be appealed to to explain why the surgeon may not operate in the case I shall call *Transplant*.

I think it pays to take note of something interesting which comes out when we pay close attention to

(II) Killing five is worse than killing one.

For let us ask ourselves how we would feel about *Transplant* if we made a certain addition to it. In telling you that story, I did not tell you why the surgeon's patients are in need of parts. Let us imagine that the history of their ailments is as follows. The surgeon was badly overworked last fall—some of his assistants in the clinic were out sick, and the surgeon had to take over their duties dispensing drugs. While feeling particularly tired one day, he became careless, and made the terrible mistake of dispensing chemical X to five of the day's patients. Now chemical X works differently in different people. In some it causes lung failure, in others kidney failure, in others heart failure. So these five patients who now need parts need them because of the surgeon's carelessness. Indeed, if he does not get them the parts they need, so that they die, he will have killed them. Does that make a moral difference? That is, does the fact that he will have killed the five if he does nothing make it permissible for him to cut the young man up and distribute his parts to the five who need them?

We could imagine it to have been worse. Suppose what had happened was this: The surgeon was financially badly overextended last fall, he had known he was named a beneficiary in his five patients' wills, and it swept over him one day to give them chemical X to kill them. Now he repents, and would save them if he could. If he does not save them, he will positively have murdered them. Does *that* fact make it permissible for him to cut the young man up and distribute his parts to the five who need them?

I should think plainly not. The surgeon must not operate on the young man. If he can find no other way of saving his five patients, he will *now* have to let them die—despite the fact that if he now lets them die, he will have killed them.

We tend to forget that some killings themselves include lettings die, and do include them where the act by which the agent kills takes time to cause death—time in which the agent can intervene but does not.

In face of these possibilities, the question arises what we should think of thesis (II), since it *looks* as if it tells us that the surgeon ought to operate, and thus that he may permissibly do so, since if he operates he kills only one instead of five.

There are two ways in which we can go here. First, we can say: (II) does tell us that the surgeon ought to operate, and that shows it is false. Second, we can say: (II) does not tell us that the surgeon ought to operate, and it is true.

For my own part, I prefer the second. If Alfred kills five and Bert kills only one, then questions of motive apart, and other things being equal, what Alfred did *is* worse than what Bert did. If the surgeon does not operate, so that he kills five, then it will later be true that he did something worse than he would have done if he had operated, killing only one—especially if his killing of the five was murder, committed out of a desire for money, and his killing of the one would have been, though misguided and wrongful, nevertheless a well-intentioned effort to save five lives. Taking this line would, of course, require saying that assessments of which acts are worse than which other acts do not by themselves settle the question what it is permissible for an agent to do.

But it might be said that we ought to by-pass (II), for perhaps what Mrs. Foot would have offered us as an explanation of why the driver may turn the trolley in *Trolley Driver* is not (II) itself, but something more complex, such as

> (II') If a person is faced with a choice between doing something *here and now* to five, by the doing of which he will kill them, and doing something else *here and now* to one, by the doing of which he will kill only the one, then (other things being equal) he ought to choose the second alternative rather than the first.

We may presumably take (II') to tell us that the driver ought to, and hence permissibly may, turn the trolley in *Trolley Driver*, for we may presumably view the driver as confronted with a choice between here and now driving his trolley into five, and here and now driving his trolley into one. And at the same time, (II') tells us nothing at all about what the surgeon ought to do in *Transplant*, for he is not confronted with such a choice. If the surgeon operates, he does do something by the doing of which he will kill only one; but if the surgeon does not operate, he does not do something by the doing of which he kills five; he merely fails to do something by the doing of which he would make it be the case that he has not killed five.

I have no objection to this shift in attention from (II) to (II'). But we should not overlook an interesting question that lurks here. As it might be put: *Why* should the present tense matter so much? Why should a person prefer killing one to killing five if the alternatives are wholly in front of him, but not (or anyway, not in every case) where one of them is partly behind him? I shall come back to this question briefly later.

Meanwhile, however, even if (II') can be appealed to in order to explain why the trolley driver may turn his trolley, that would leave it entirely open why the bystander at the switch may turn *his* trolley. For he does not drive a trolley into each of five if he refrains from turning the trolley; he merely lets the trolley drive into each of them.

So I suggest we set *Trolley Driver* aside for the time being. What I shall be concerned with is a first cousin of Mrs. Foot's problem, namely: Why is it that the bystander may turn his trolley, though the surgeon may not remove the young man's lungs, kidneys, and heart? Since *I* find it particularly puzzling that the bystander may turn his trolley, I am inclined to call this The Trolley Problem. Those who find it particularly puzzling that the surgeon may not operate are cordially invited to call it The Transplant Problem instead.

4. It should be clear, I think, that "kill" and "let die" are too blunt to be useful tools for the solving of this problem. We ought to be looking within killings and savings for the ways in which the agents would be carrying them out.

It would be no surprise, I think, if a Kantian idea occurred to us at this point. Kant said: "Act so that you treat humanity, whether in your own person or in that of another, always as an end and never as a means only." It is striking, after all, that the surgeon who proceeds in *Transplant* treats the young man he cuts up "as a means only": He literally uses the young man's body to save his five, and does so without the young man's consent. And perhaps we may say that the agent in *Bystander at the Switch* does not use his victim to save his five, or (more generally) treat his victim as a means only, and that that is why he (unlike the surgeon) may proceed.

But what exactly is it to treat a person as a means only, or to use a person? And why exactly is it wrong to do this? These questions do not have obvious answers.[6]

Suppose an agent is confronted with a choice between doing nothing, in which case five die, or engaging in a certain course of action, in which case the five live, but one dies. Then perhaps we can say: If the agent chooses to engage in the course of action, then he uses the one to save the five only if, had the one gone out of existence just before the agent started, the agent would have been unable to save the five. That is true of the surgeon in *Transplant*. He needs the young man if he is to save his five; if the young man goes wholly out of existence just before the surgeon starts to operate, then the surgeon cannot save his five. By contrast, the agent in *Bystander at the Switch* does not need the one track workman on the right-hand track if he is to save his five; if the one track workman goes wholly out of existence before the bystander starts to turn the trolley, then the bystander *can* all the same save his five. So here anyway is a striking difference between the cases.

It does seem to me right to think that solving this problem requires attending to the means by which the agent would be saving his five if he proceeded. But I am inclined to think that this is an overly simple way of taking account of the agent's means.

One reason for thinking so[7] comes out as follows. You have been thinking of the tracks in *Bystander at the Switch* as not merely diverging, but continuing to diverge, as in the following picture:

Consider now what I shall call "the loop variant" on this case, in

6. For a sensitive discussion of some of the difficulties, see Nancy Davis, "Using Persons and Common Sense," *Ethics* 94 (April 1984), p. 382. Among other things, she argues (I think rightly) that the Kantian idea is not to be identified with the common sense concept of "using a person." See p. 402.

7. For a second reason to think so, see note 13 below.

which the tracks do not continue to diverge—they circle back, as in the following picture:

Let us now imagine that the five on the straight track are thin, but thick enough so that although all five will be killed if the trolley goes straight, the bodies of the five will stop it, and it will therefore not reach the one. On the other hand, the one on the right-hand track is fat, so fat that his body will by itself stop the trolley, and the trolley will therefore not reach the five. May the agent turn the trolley? Some people feel more discomfort at the idea of turning the trolley in the loop variant than in the original *Bystander at the Switch*. But we cannot really suppose that the presence or absence of that extra bit of track makes a major moral difference as to what an agent may do in these cases, and it really does seem right to think (despite the discomfort) that the agent may proceed.

On the other hand, we should notice that the agent here needs the one (fat) track workman on the right-hand track if he is to save his five. If the one goes wholly out of existence just before the agent starts to turn the trolley, then the agent cannot save his five[8]—just as the surgeon in *Transplant* cannot save his five if the young man goes wholly out of existence just before the surgeon starts to operate.

Indeed, I should think that there is no plausible account of what is involved in, or what is necessary for, the application of the notions "treating a person as a means only," or "using one to save five," under which the surgeon would be doing this whereas the agent in this variant of *Bystander at the Switch* would not be. If that is right, then appeals to these notions cannot do the work being required of them here.

5. Suppose the bystander at the switch proceeds: He throws the switch, thereby turning the trolley onto the right-hand track, thereby

8. It is also true that if the five go wholly out of existence just before the agent starts to turn the trolley, then the one will die whatever the agent does. Should we say, then, that the agent uses one to save five if he acts, *and* uses five to save one if he does not act? No: What follows *"and"* is false. If the agent does not act, he uses nobody. (I doubt that it can even be said that if he does not act, he lets them *be used*. For what is the active for which this is passive? Who or what would be using them if he does not act?)

causing the one to be hit by the trolley, thereby killing him—but saving the five on the straight track. There are two facts about what he does which seem to me to explain the moral difference between what he does and what the agent in *Transplant* would be doing if *he* proceeded. In the first place, the bystander saves his five by making something that threatens them threaten the one instead. Second, the bystander does not do that by means which themselves constitute an infringement of any right of the one's.

As is plain, then, my hypothesis as to the source of the moral difference between the cases makes appeal to the concept of a right. My own feeling is that solving this problem requires making appeal to that concept—or to some other concept that does the same kind of work.[9] Indeed, I think it is one of the many reasons why this problem is of such interest to moral theory that it does force us to appeal to that concept; and by the same token, that we learn something from it about that concept.

Let us begin with an idea, held by many friends of rights, which Ronald Dworkin expressed crisply in a metaphor from bridge: Rights "trump" utilities.[10] That is, if one would infringe a right in or by acting, then it is not sufficient justification for acting that one would thereby maximize utility. It seems to me that something like this must be correct.

Consideration of this idea suggests the possibility of a very simple solution to the problem. That is, it might be said (i) The reason why the surgeon may not proceed in *Transplant* is that if he proceeds, he maximizes utility, for he brings about a net saving of four lives, but in so doing he would infringe a right of the young man's.

Which right? Well, we might say: The right the young man has against the surgeon that the surgeon not kill him—thus a right in the cluster of rights that the young man has in having a right to life.

Solving this problem requires being able to explain also why the bystander may proceed in *Bystander at the switch*. So it might be said (ii) The reason why the bystander may proceed is that if he proceeds, he maximizes utility, for he brings about a net saving of four lives, and in so doing he does *not* infringe any right of the one track workman's.

9. I strongly suspect that giving an account of what makes it wrong to *use* a person (see section 4) would also require appeal to the concept of a right.

10. Ronald Dworkin, *Taking Rights Seriously* (Cambridge, Mass.: Harvard University Press, 1977), p. ix.

But I see no way—certainly there is no easy way—of establishing that these ideas are true.

Is it clear that the bystander would infringe no right of the one track workman's if he turned the trolley? Suppose there weren't anybody on the straight track, and the bystander turned the trolley onto the right-hand track, thereby killing the one, but not saving anybody, since nobody was at risk, and thus nobody needed saving. Wouldn't that infringe a right of the one workman's, a right in the cluster of rights that he was in having a right to life?

So should we suppose that the fact that there are five track workmen on the straight track who are in need of saving makes the one lack that right—which he would have had if that had not been a fact?

But then why doesn't the fact that the surgeon has five patients who are in need of saving make the young man also lack that right?

I think some people would say there is good (excellent, conclusive) reason for thinking that the one track workman lacks the right (given there are five on the straight track) lying in the fact that (given there are five on the straight track) it is morally permissible to turn the trolley onto him. But if your reason for thinking the one lacks the right is that it is permissible to turn the trolley onto him, then you can hardly go on to explain its being permissible to turn the trolley onto him by appeal to the fact that he lacks the right. It pays to stress this point: If you want to say, as (ii) does, that the bystander may proceed because he maximizes utility and infringes no right, then you need an independent account of what makes it be the case that he infringes no right—independent, that is, of its being the case that he may proceed.

There is *some* room for maneuver here. Any plausible theory of rights must make room for the possibility of waiving a right, and within that category, for the possibility of failing to have a right by virtue of assumption of risk; and it might be argued that that is what is involved here, i.e., that track workmen know of the risks of the job, and consent to run them when signing on for it.

But that is not really an attractive way of dealing with this difficulty. Track workmen certainly do not explicitly consent to being run down with trolleys when doing so will save five who are on some other track—certainly they are not asked to consent to this at the time of signing on for the job. And I doubt that they consciously assume the risk of it at that or any other time. And in any case, what if the six people involved had not been track workmen? What if they had been young children? What if they had been people who had been shoved out of helicopters? Wouldn't it all the same be permissible to turn the trolley?

So it is not clear what (independent) reason could be given for thinking that the bystander will infringe no right of the one's if he throws the switch.

I think, moreover, that there is *some* reason to think that the bystander will infringe a right of the one if he throws the switch, even though it is permissible for him to do so. What I have in mind issues simply from the fact that if the bystander throws the switch, then he does what will kill the one. Suppose the bystander proceeds, and that the one is now dead. The bystander's motives were, of course, excellent—he acted with a view to saving five. But the one did not volunteer his life so that the five might live; the bystander volunteered it for him. The bystander made him pay with his life for the bystander's saving of the fire. This consideration seems to me to lend some weight to the idea that the bystander did do him a wrong—a wrong it was morally permissible to do him, since five were saved, but a wrong *to him* all the same.

Consider again that lingering feeling of discomfort (which, as I said, some people do feel) about what the bystander does if he turns the trolley. No doubt it is permissible to turn the trolley, but still . . . but still. . . . People who feel this discomfort also think that, although it is permissible to turn the trolley, it is not morally required to do so. My own view is that they are right to feel and think these things. We would be able to explain why this is so if we supposed that if the bystander turns the trolley, then he does do the one track workman a wrong—if we supposed, in particular, that he infringes a right of the one track workman's which is in that cluster of rights which the workman has in having a right to life.[11]

I do not for a moment take myself to have established that (ii) is false. I have wished only to draw attention to the difficulty that lies ahead of a person who thinks (ii) true, and also to suggest that there is some reason to think that the bystander would infringe a right of the one's if he proceeded, and thus some reason to think that (ii) is false. It can easily be seen that if there is some reason to think the

11. Many of the examples discussed by Bernard Williams and Ruth Marcus plainly call out for this kind of treatment. See Bernard Williams, "Ethical Consistency," in *Problems of the Self* (Cambridge: Cambridge University Press, 1973), p. 166; Ruth Marcus, "Moral Dilemmas and Consistency," *Journal of Philosophy*, 77 (March 1980), p. 121.

bystander would infringe a right of the one's, then there is also some reason to think that (i) is false—since if the bystander does infringe a right of the one's if he proceeds, and may nevertheless proceed, then it cannot be the fact that the surgeon infringes a right of the young man's if *he* proceeds which makes it impermissible for *him* to do so.

Perhaps a friend of (i) and (ii) can establish that they are true. I propose that, just in case he can't, we do well to see if there isn't some other way of solving this problem than by appeal to them. In particular, I propose we grant that both the bystander and the surgeon would infringe a right of their ones, a right in the cluster of rights that the ones have in having a right to life, and that we look for some *other* difference between the cases which could be appealed to to explain the moral difference between them.

Notice that accepting this proposal does not commit us to rejecting the idea expressed in that crisp metaphor of Dworkin's. We can still say that rights trump utilities—if we can find a further feature of what the bystander does if he turns the trolley (beyond the fact that he maximizes utility) which itself trumps the right, and thus makes it permissible to proceed.

6. As I said, my own feeling is that the trolley problem can be solved only by appeal to the concept of a right—but not by appeal to it in as simple a way as that discussed in the preceding section. What we were attending to in the preceding section was only the fact that the agents would be killing and saving if they proceeded; what we should be attending to is the means by which they would kill and save.[12] (It is very tempting, because so much simpler, to regard a human act as a solid nugget, without internal structure, and to try to trace its moral value to the shape of its surface, as it were. The trolley problem seems to me to bring home that that will not do.)

I said earlier that there seem to me to be two crucial facts about what the bystander does if he proceeds in *Bystander at the Switch*. In the first place, he saves his five by making something that threatens

12. It may be worth stressing that what I suggest calls for attention is not (as some construals of "double effect" would have it) whether the agent's killing of the one is his means to something, and not (as other construals of "double effect" would have it) whether the death of the one is the agent's means to something, but rather what are the means by which the agent both kills and saves. For a discussion of "the doctrine of double effect," see Foot, "The Problem of Abortion."

them instead threaten the one. And second, he does not do that by means which themselves constitute infringements of any right of the one's.

Let us begin with the first.

If the surgeon proceeds in *Transplant*, he plainly does not save his five by making something that threatens them instead threaten one. It is organ-failure that threatens his five, and it is not *that* which he makes threaten the young man if he proceeds.

Consider another of Mrs. Foot's cases, which I shall call *Hospital*.

> Suppose that there are five patients in a hospital whose lives could be saved by the manufacture of a certain gas, but that this will inevitably release lethal fumes into the room of another patient whom for some reason we are unable to move.[13]

Surely it would not be permissible for us to manufacture the gas.

In *Transplant* and *Hospital*, the five at risk are at risk from their ailments, and this might be thought to make a difference. Let us by-pass it. In a variant on *Hospital*—which I shall call *Hospital'*—all six patients are convalescing. The five at risk are at risk, not from their ailments, but from the ceiling of their room, which is about to fall on them. We can prevent this by pumping on a ceiling-support mechanism; but doing so will inevitably release lethal fumes into the room of the sixth. Here too it is plain we may not proceed.

Contrast a case in which lethal fumes are being released by the heating system in the basement of a building next door to the hospital. They are headed towards the room of five. We can deflect them towards the room of one. Would that be permissible? I should think it would be—the case seems to be in all relevant respects like *Bystander at the Switch*.

In *Bystander at the Switch*, something threatens five, and if the agent proceeds, he saves the five by making that very thing threaten the one instead of the five. That is not true of the agents in *Hospital'* or *Hospital* or *Transplant*. In *Hospital'*, for example, what threatens the five is the ceiling, and the agent does not save them by making *it*

13. Ibid., p. 29. As Mrs. Foot says, we do not *use* the one if we proceed in *Hospital*. Yet the impermissibility of proceeding in *Hospital* seems to have a common source with the impermissibility of operating in *Transplant*, in which the surgeon would be using the one whose parts he takes for the five who need them. This is my second reason for thinking that an appeal to the fact that the surgeon would be using his victim is an over-simple way of taking account of the means he would be employing for the saving of his five. See note 7 above.

threaten the one, he saves them by doing what will make something wholly different (some lethal fumes) threaten the one.

Why is this difference morally important? Other things being equal, to kill a man is to infringe his right to life, and we are therefore morally barred from killing. It is not enough to justify killing a person that if we do so, five others will be saved: To say that if we do so, five others will be saved is merely to say that utility will be maximized if we proceed, and that is not by itself sufficient to justify proceeding. Rights trump utilities. So if that is all that can be said in defense of killing a person, then killing that person is not permissible.

But that five others will be saved is not all that can be said in defense of killing in *Bystander at the Switch*. The bystander who proceeds does not merely minimize the number of deaths which get caused: He minimizes the number of deaths which get caused by something that already threatens people, and that will cause deaths whatever the bystander does.

The bystander who proceeds does not make something be a threat to people which would otherwise not be a threat to anyone; he makes be a threat to fewer what is already a threat to more. We might speak here of a "distributive exemption," which permits arranging that something that will do harm anyway shall be better distributed than it otherwise would be—shall (in *Bystander at the Switch*) do harm to fewer rather than more. Not just any distributive intervention is permissible: It is not in general morally open to us to make one die to save five. But other things being equal, it is not morally required of us that we let a burden descend out of the blue onto five when we can make it instead descend onto one.

I do not find it clear why there should be an exemption for, and only for, making a burden which is descending onto five descend, instead, onto one. That there is seems to me very plausible, however. On the other hand, the agent who acts under this exemption makes be a threat to one something that is *already* a threat to more, and thus something that will do harm *whatever* he does; on the other hand, the exemption seems to allow those acts which intuition tells us are clearly permissible, and to rule out those acts which intuition tells us are clearly impermissible.

7. More precisely, it is not morally required of us that we let a burden descend out of the blue onto five when we can make it instead descend onto one *if* we can make it descend onto the one by means which do not themselves constitute infringements of rights of the one.

Consider a case—which I shall call *Fat Man*—in which you are standing on a footbridge over the trolley track. You can see a trolley hurtling down the track, out of control. You turn around to see where the trolley is headed, and there are five workmen on the track where it exits from under the footbridge. What to do? Being an expert on trolleys, you know of one certain way to stop an out-of-control trolley: Drop a really heavy weight in its path. But where to find one? It just so happens that standing next to you on the footbridge is a fat man, a really fat man. He is leaning over the railing, watching the trolley; all you have to do is to give him a little shove, and over the railing he will go, onto the track in the path of the trolley. Would it be permissible for you to do this? Everybody to whom I have put this case says it would not be. But why?

Suppose the agent proceeds. He shoves the fat man, thereby toppling him off the footbridge into the path of the trolley, thereby causing him to be hit by the trolley, thereby killing him—but saving the five on the straight track. Then it is true of this agent, as it is true of the agent in *Bystander at the Switch,* that he saves his five by making something which threatens them instead threaten one.

But *this* agent does so by means which themselves constitute an infringement of a right of the one's. For shoving a person is infringing a right of his. So also is toppling a person off a footbridge.

I should stress that doing these things is infringing a person's rights even if doing them does not cause his death—even if doing them causes him no harm at all. As I shall put it, shoving a person, toppling a person off a footbridge, are *themselves* infringements of rights of his. A theory of rights ought to give an account of what makes it be the case that doing either of these things is itself an infringement of a right of his. But I think we may take it to be a datum that it is, the job which confronts the theorist of rights being, not to establish that it is, but rather to explain why it is.

Consider by contrast the agent in *Bystander at the Switch.* He too, if he proceeds, saves five by making something that threatens them instead threaten one. But the means he takes to make that be the case are these: Turn the trolley onto the right-hand track. And turning the trolley onto the right-hand track is not *itself* an infringement of a right of anybody's. The agent would do the one no wrong at all if he turned the trolley onto the right-hand track, and by some miracle the trolley did not hit him.

We might of course have imagined it not necessary to shove the fat man. We might have imagined that all you need do to get the trolley to threaten him instead of the five is to wobble the handrail, for the handrail is low, and he is leaning on it, and wobbling it will cause him to fall over and off. Wobbling the handrail would be impermissible, I should think—no less so than shoving. But then there is room for an objection to the idea that the contrast I point to will help explain the moral differences among these cases. For it might be said that if you wobble the handrail, thereby getting the trolley to threaten the one instead of the five, then the means you take to get this to be the case are just these: Wobble the handrail. But doing that is not *itself* an infringement of a right of anybody's. You would do the fat man no wrong at all if you wobbled the handrail and no harm came to him in consequence of your doing so. In his respect, then, your situation seems to be exactly like that of the agent in *Bystander at the Switch*. Just as the means he would be taking to make the trolley threaten one instead of five would not constitute an infringement of a right, so also would the means you would be taking to make the trolley threaten one instead of five not constitute an infringement of a right.

What I had in mind, however, is a rather tighter notion of "means" than shows itself in this objection. By hypothesis, wobbling the handrail will cause the fat man to topple onto the track in the path of the trolley, and thus will cause the trolley to threaten him instead of the five. But the trolley will not threaten him instead of the five unless wobbling the handrail does cause him to topple. Getting the trolley to threaten the fat man instead of the five *requires* getting him into its path. You get the trolley to threaten him instead of them by wobbling the handrail only if, and only because, by wobbling the handrail you topple him into the path of the trolley.

What I had in mind, then, is a notion of "means" which comes out as follows. Suppose you get a trolley to threaten one instead of five by wobbling a handrail. The means you take to get the trolley to threaten the one instead of the five include wobbling the handrail, *and* all those further things that you have to succeed in doing by wobbling the handrail if the trolley is to threaten the one instead of the five.

So the means by which the agent in *Fat Man* gets the trolley to threaten one instead of five include toppling the fat man off the footbridge; and doing that is itself an infringement of a right of the fat man's. By contrast, the means by which the agent in *Bystander at the Switch* gets the trolley to threaten one instead of five include no more than getting the trolley off the straight track onto the right-hand track; and doing that is not itself an infringement of a right of any-body's.

8. It is arguable, however, that what is relevant is not that toppling the fat man off the footbridge is itself an infringement of *a* right of the fat man's but rather that toppling him off the footbridge is itself an infringement of a particularly stringent right of his.

What I have in mind comes out in yet another variant on *Bystander at the Switch*. Here the bystander must cross (without permission) a patch of land that belongs to the one in order to get to the switch; thus in order to get the trolley to threaten the one instead of five, the bystander must infringe a right of the one's. May he proceed?

Or again, in order to get the switch thrown, the bystander must use a sharply pointed tool, and the only available sharply pointed tool is a nailfile that belongs to the one; here too the bystander must infringe a right of the one's in order to get the trolley to threaten the one instead of five. May he proceed?

For my own part, I do not find it obvious that he may. (Remember what the bystander will be doing to the one by throwing that switch.) But others tell me they think it clear the bystander may proceed in such a case. If they are right—and I guess we should agree that they are—then that must surely be because the rights which the bystander would have to infringe here are minor, trivial, nonstringent—prop-erty rights of no great importance. By contrast, the right to not be toppled off a footbridge onto a trolley track is on any view a stringent right. We shall therefore have to recognize that what is at work in these cases is a matter of degree: If the agent must infringe a stringent right of the one's in order to get something that threatens five to threaten the one (as in *Fat Man*), then he may not proceed, whereas if the agent need infringe no right of the one's (as in *Bystander at the Switch*), or only a more or less trivial right of the one's (as in these variants on *Bystander at the Switch*), in order to get something that threatens five to threaten the one, then he may proceed.

Where what is at work is a matter of degree, it should be no surprise that there are borderline cases, on which people disagree. I confess to having been greatly surprised, however, at the fact of disagreement on the following variant on *Bystander at the Switch*:

> The five on the straight track are regular track workmen. The right-hand track is a dead end, unused in ten years. The Mayor, representing the City, has set out picnic tables on it, and invited the convalescents at the nearby City Hospital to have their meals there, guaranteeing them that

no trolleys will ever, for any reason, be turned onto that track. The one on the right-hand track is a convalescent having his lunch there; it would never have occurred to him to do so if the Mayor had not issued his invitation and guarantee. The Mayor was out for a walk; he now stands by the switch.[14]

For the Mayor to get the trolley to threaten the one instead of the five, he must turn the trolley onto the right-hand track; but the one has a right against the Mayor that he not turn the trolley onto the right-hand track—a right generated by an official promise, which was then relied on by the one. (Contrast the original *Bystander at the Switch*, in which the one had no such right.) My own feeling is that it is plain the Mayor may not proceed. To my great surprise, I find that some people think he may. I conclude they think the right less stringent than I do.

In any case, that distributive exemption that I spoke of earlier is very conservative. It permits intervention into the world to get an object that already threatens death to those many to instead threaten death to these few, but only by acts that are not themselves gross impingements on the few. That is, the intervenor must not use means that infringe stringent rights of the few in order to get his distributive intention carried out.

It could of course be argued that the fact that the bystander of the original *Bystander at the Switch* makes threaten the one what already threatens the five, and does so by means that do not themselves constitute infringements of any right of the one's (not even a trivial right of the one's), shows that the bystander in that case infringes no right of the one's at all. That is, it could be argued that we have here that independent ground for saying that the bystander does not infringe the one's right to life which I said (in section 5) would be needed by a friend of (ii). But I see nothing to be gained by taking this line, for I see nothing to be gained by supposing it never permissible to infringe a right; and something is lost by taking this line, namely the possibility of viewing the bystander as doing the one a wrong if he proceeds—albeit a wrong it is permissible to do him.

14. Notice that in this case too the agent does not *use* the one if he proceeds. (This case, along with a number of other cases I have been discussing, comes from Essay 6. Mrs. Thomson seems to me to have been blundering around in the dark in that essay, but the student of this problem may possibly find some of the cases she discusses useful.)

9. What counts as "*an* object which threatens death"? What marks one threat off from another? I have no doubt that ingenious people can construct cases in which we shall be unclear whether to say that if the agent proceeds, he makes threaten the one the very same thing as already threatens the five.

Moreover, which are the interventions in which the agent gets a thing that threatens five to instead threaten one by means that themselves constitute infringements of stringent rights of the one's? I have no doubt that ingenious people can construct cases in which we shall all be unclear whether to say that the agent's means do constitute infringements of stringent rights—and cases also in which we shall be unclear whether to say the agent's means constitute infringements of any rights at all.

But it is surely a mistake to look for precision in the concepts brought to bear to solve this problem: There isn't any to be had. It would be enough if cases in which it seems to us unclear whether to say "same threat," or unclear whether to say "non-right-infringing-means," also seemed to us to be cases in which it is unclear whether the agent may or may not proceed; and if also coming to see a case as one to which these expressions do (or do not) apply involves coming to see the case as one in which the agent may (or may not) proceed.

10. If these ideas are correct, then we have a handle on anyway some of the troublesome cases in which people make threats. Suppose a villain says to us "I will cause a ceiling to fall on five unless you send lethal fumes into the room of one." Most of us think it would not be permissible for us to accede to this threat. Why? We may think of the villain as part of the world around the people involved, a part which is going to drop a burden on the five if we do not act. On this way of thinking of him, nothing *yet* threatens the five (certainly no ceiling as yet threatens them) and a fortiori we cannot save the five by making what (already) threatens them instead threaten the one. Alternatively, we may think of the villain as himself a threat to the five. But sending the fumes in is not making *him* be a threat to the one instead of to the five. The hypothesis I proposed, then, yields what it should: We may not accede.

That is because the hypothesis I proposed says nothing at all about the source of the threat to the five. Whether the threat to the five is, or is caused by, a human being or anything else, it is not permissible to do what will kill one to save the five except by making what threatens the five itself threaten the one.

By contrast, it seems to me very plausible to think that if a villain has started a trolley towards five, we may deflect the trolley towards one—other things being equal, of course. If a trolley is headed towards five, and we can deflect it towards one, we *may*, no matter who or what caused it to head towards the five.

I think that these considerations help us in dealing with a question I drew attention to earlier. Suppose a villain says to us "I will cause a ceiling to fall on five unless you send lethal fumes into the room of one." If we refuse, so that he does what he threatens to do, then he surely does something very much worse than we would be doing if we acceded to his threat and sent the fumes in. If we accede, we do something misguided and wrongful, but not nearly as bad as what he does if we refuse.

It should be stressed: The fact that he will do something worse if we do not send the fumes in does not entail that we ought to send them in, or even that it is permissible for us to do so.

How after all could that entail that we may send the fumes in? The fact that we would be saving five lives by sending the fumes in does not itself make it permissible for us to do so. (Rights trump utilities.) How could adding that the taker of those five lives would be doing what is worse than we would tip the balance? If we may not infringe a right of the one in order to save the five lives, it cannot possibly be thought that we may infringe the right of that one in order, not merely to save the five lives, but to make the villain's moral record better than it otherwise would be.

For my own part, I think that considerations of motives apart, and other things being equal, it does no harm to say that

(II) Killing five is worse than killing one

is, after all, true. *Of course* we shall then have to say that assessments of which acts are worse than which do not by themselves settle the question of what it is permissible for a person to do. For we shall have to say that, despite the truth of (II), it is not the case that we are required to kill one in order that another person shall not kill five, or even that it is everywhere permissible for us to do this.

What is of interest is that what holds interpersonally also holds intrapersonally. I said earlier that we might imagine the surgeon of *Transplant* to have caused the ailments of his five patients. Let us imagine the worst: He gave them chemical X precisely in order to cause their deaths, in order to inherit from them. Now he repents. But the fact that he would be saving five lives by operating on the one does not itself make it permissible for him to operate on the one. (Rights trump utilities.) And if he may not infringe a right of the one in order to save the five lives, it cannot possibly be thought that he may infringe the right of that one in order, not merely to save the five lives, but to make his own moral record better than it otherwise would be.

Another way to put the point is this: Assessments of which acts are worse than which have to be directly relevant to the agent's circumstances if they are to have a bearing on what he may do. If A threatens to kill five unless B kills one, then although killing five is worse than killing one, these are not the alternatives open to B. The alternatives open to B are: Kill one, thereby forestalling the deaths of five (and making A's moral record better than it otherwise would be), or let it be the case that A kills five. And the supposition that it would be worse for B to choose to kill the one is entirely compatible with the supposition that killing five is worse than killing one. Again, the alternatives open to the surgeon are: Operate on the one, thereby saving five (and making the surgeon's own moral record better than it otherwise would be), or let it be the case that he himself will have killed the five. And the supposition that it would be worse for the surgeon to choose to operate is entirely compatible with the supposition that killing five is worse than killing one.

On the other hand, suppose a second surgeon is faced with a choice between here and now giving chemical X to five, thereby kiling them, and operating on, and thereby killing, only one. (It taxes the imagination to invent such a second surgeon, but let that pass. And compare *Trolley Driver*.) Then, other things being equal, it does seem he may choose to operate on the one. Some people would say something stronger, namely that he is required to make this choice. Perhaps they would say that

> (II′) If a person is faced with a choice between doing something *here and now* to five, by the doing of which he will kill them, and doing something else *here and now* to one, by the doing of which he will kill only the one, then (other things being equal) he ought to choose the second alternative rather than the first

is a quite general moral truth. Whether or not the second surgeon is morally required to make this choice—and thus whether or not (II′) is a general moral truth—it does seem to be the case that he may.

But this did seem puzzling. As I put it: Why should the present tense matter so much?

It is plausible to think that the present tense matters because the question for the agent at the time of acting is about the present, namely, "What may I here and now do?," and because that question is the same as the question "Which of the alternatives here and now open to me may I choose?" The alternatives now open to the second surgeon are: kill five or kill one. If killing five is worse than killing one, then perhaps he ought to, but at any rate he may, kill the one.[15]

15. Many people have given me helpful criticism of this essay's many successive reincarnations over the years; I cannot list them all—for want of space, not of gratitude. Most recently, it benefited from criticism by the members of the Yale Law School Civil Liability Workshop and the Legal Theory Workshop, Faculty of Law, University of Toronto.

8 · *The Right to Privacy*

1. Perhaps the most striking thing about the right to privacy is that nobody seems to have any very clear idea what it is. Consider, for example, the familiar proposal that the right to privacy is the right "to be let alone." On the one hand, this doesn't seem to take in enough. The police might say, "We grant we used a special X-ray device on Smith, so as to be able to watch him through the walls of his house; we grant we trained an amplifying device on him so as to be able to hear everything he said; but we let him strictly alone: we didn't touch him, we didn't even go near him—our devices operate at a distance." Anyone who believes there is a right to privacy would presumably believe that it has been violated in Smith's case; yet he would be hard put to explain precisely how, if the right to privacy is the right to be let alone. And on the other hand, this account of the right to privacy lets in far too much. If I hit Jones on the head with a brick I have not let him alone. Yet, while hitting Jones on the head with a brick is surely violating some right of Jones's, doing it should surely not turn out to violate his right to privacy. Else, where is this to end? Is *every* violation of a right a violation of the right to privacy?

It seems best to be less ambitious, to begin with at least. I suggest, then, that we look at some specific, imaginary cases in which people would say, "There, in that case, the right to privacy has been violated," and ask ourselves precisely why this would be said, and what, if anything would justify saying it.

2. But there is a difficulty to be taken note of first. What I have in mind is that there may not be so much agreement on the cases as I implied. Suppose that my husband and I are having a fight, shouting

at each other as loud as we can; and suppose that we have not thought to close the windows, so that we can easily be heard from the street outside. It seems to me that anyone who stops to listen violates no right of ours; stopping to listen is at worst bad, Not Nice, not done by the best people. But now suppose, by contrast, that we are having a quiet fight, behind closed windows, and cannot be heard by the normal person who passes by; and suppose that someone across the street trains an amplifier on our house, by means of which he can hear what we say; and suppose that he does this in order to hear what we say. It seems to me that anyone who does this does violate a right of ours, the right to privacy, I should have thought.

But there is room for disagreement. It might be said that in neither case is there a violation of a right, that both are cases of mere bad behavior—though no doubt worse behavior in the second case than in the first, it being very much naughtier to train amplifiers on people's houses than merely to stop in the street to listen.

Or, alternatively, it might be said that in both cases there is a violation of a right, the right to privacy in fact, but that the violation is less serious in the first case than in the second.

I think that these would both be wrong. I think that we have in these two cases, not merely a difference in degree, but a difference in quality: that the passerby who stops to listen in the first case may act badly, but violates no one's rights, whereas the neighbor who uses an amplifier in the second case does not merely act badly but violates a right, the right to privacy. But I have no argument for this. I take it rather as a datum in this sense: it seems to me there would be a mark against an account of the right to privacy if it did not yield the conclusion that these two cases do differ in the way I say they do, and moreover explain why they do.

But there is one thing perhaps worth drawing attention to here: doing so may perhaps diminish the inclination to think that a right is violated in both cases. What I mean is this. There is a familiar account of rights—I speak now of rights generally, and not just of the right to privacy—according to which a man's having a right that something shall not be done to him just itself consists in its being the case that anyone who does it to him acts badly or wrongly or does what he ought not do. Thus, for example, it is said that to have a right that you shall not be killed or imprisoned just itself consists in its being the case that if anyone does kill or imprison you, he acts badly, wrongly, does what he ought not do. If this account of rights were correct, then my husband and I would have a right that nobody shall stop in the street and listen to our loud fight, since anyone who does stop in the street and listen acts badly, wrongly, does what he ought not do. Just as we have a right that people shall not train amplifiers on the house to listen to our quiet fights.

But this account of rights is just plain wrong. There are many, many things we ought not do to people, things such that if we do them to a person, we act badly, but which are not such that to do them is to violate a right of his. It is bad behavior, for example, to be ungenerous and unkind. Suppose that you dearly love chocolate ice cream but that, for my part, I find that a little of it goes a long way. I have been given some and have eaten a little, enough really, since I don't care for it very much. You then, looking on, ask, "May I have the rest of your ice cream?" It would be bad indeed if I were to reply, "No, I've decided to bury the rest of it in the garden." I ought not do that; I ought to give it to you. But you have no right that I give it to you, and I violate no right of yours if I do bury the stuff.

Indeed, it is possible that an act which is not a violation of a right should be a far worse act than an act which is. If you did not merely want that ice cream but needed it, for your health perhaps, then my burying it would be monstrous, indecent, though still, of course, no violation of a right. By contrast, if you snatch it away, steal it, before I can bury it, then while you violate a right (the ice cream is mine, after all), your act is neither monstrous nor indecent—if it's bad at all, it's anyway not very bad.

From the point of view of conduct, of course, this doesn't really matter: bad behavior is bad behavior, whether it is a violation of a right or not. But if we want to be clear about *why* this or that bit of bad behavior is bad, then these distinctions do have to get made and looked into.

3. To return, then, to the two cases I drew attention to, and which I suggest we take to differ in this way: in one of them a right is violated, in the other not. It isn't I think, the fact that an amplifying device is used in the one case, and not in the other, that is responsible for this difference. On the one hand, consider someone who is deaf: if he passes by while my husband and I are having a loud fight at an open window and turns up his hearing-aid so as to be able to hear

us, it seems to me he no more violates our right to privacy than does one who stops to listen and can hear well enough without a hearing-aid. And on the other hand, suppose that you and I have to talk over some personal matters. It is most convenient to meet in the park, and we do so, taking a bench far from the path since we don't want to be overheard. It strikes a man to want to know what we are saying to each other in that heated fashion, so he creeps around in the bushes behind us and crouches back of the bench to listen. He thereby violates the right to privacy—fully as much as if he had stayed a hundred yards away and used an amplifying device to listen to us.

4. The cases I drew attention to are actually rather difficult to deal with, and I suggest we back away from them for a while and look at something simpler.

Consider a man who owns a pornographic picture. He wants that nobody but him shall ever see that picture—perhaps because he wants that nobody shall know that he owns it, perhaps because he feels that someone else's seeing it would drain it of power to please. So he keeps it locked in his wall-safe, and takes it out to look at only at night or after pulling down the shades and closing the curtains. We have heard about his picture, and we want to see it, so we train our X-ray device on the wall-safe and look in. To do this is, I think, to violate a right of his—the right to privacy, I should think.

No doubt people who worry about violations of the right to privacy are not worried about the possibility that the others will look at their *possessions*. At any rate, this doesn't worry them very much. That it is not nothing, however, comes out when one thinks on the special source of discomfort there is if a burglar doesn't go straight for the TV set and the silver, and then leave, but if he stops for a while just to look at things—at your love letters or at the mound of torn socks on the floor of your closet. The trespass and the theft *might* swamp everything else; but they might not: the burglar's merely looking around in that way might make the episode feel worse than it otherwise would have done.

So I shall suppose that we do violate this man's right to privacy if we use an X-ray device to look at the picture in his wall-safe. And now let us ask how and why.

To own a picture is to have a cluster of rights in respect of it. The cluster includes, for example, the right to sell it to whomever you like, the right to give it away, the right to tear it, the right to look at it. These rights are all "positive rights": rights to do certain things to or in respect of the picture. To own a picture is also to have certain "negative rights" in respect of it, that is, rights that others shall not do certain things to it—thus, for example, the right that others shall not sell it or give it away or tear it.

Does owning a picture also include having the negative right that others shall not look at it? I think it does. If our man's picture is good pornography, it would be pretty mingy of him to keep it permanently hidden so that nobody but him shall ever see it— a nicer person would let his friends have a look at it too. But he is within his rights to hide it. If someone is about to tear his picture, he can snatch it away: it's his, so he has a right that nobody but him shall tear it. If someone is about to look at his picture, he can snatch it away or cover it up: it's his, so he has a right that nobody but him shall look at it.

It is important to stress that he has not merely the right to snatch the picture away in order that nobody shall tear it, he has not merely the right to do everything he can (within limits) to prevent people from tearing it, he has also the right that nobody *shall* tear it. What I have in mind is this. Suppose we desperately want to tear his picture. He locks it in his wall-safe to prevent us from doing so. And suppose we are so eager that we buy a penetrating long-distance picture-tearer: we sit quietly in our apartment across the street, train the device on the picture in the wall-safe, press the button—and lo! we have torn the picture. The fact that he couldn't protect his picture against the action of the device doesn't make it all right that we use it.

Again, suppose that there was a way in which he could have protected his picture against the action of the device: the rays won't pass through platinum, and he could have encased the picture in platinum. But he would have had to sell everything else he owns in order to pay for the platinum. The fact he didn't do this does not make it all right for us to have used the device.

We all have a right to do what we can (within limits) to secure our belongings against theft. I gather, however, that it's practically impossible to secure them against a determined burglar. Perhaps only hiring armed guards or enclosing the house in solid steel will guarantee that our possessions cannot be stolen; and perhaps even these things won't work. The fact (if it's a fact) that we can't guarantee our belongings against theft; the fact (if it's a fact) that though we can, the cost of doing so is wildly out of proportion to the value of the things, and therefore we don't; neither of these makes it all right for the determined burglar to walk off with them.

Now, I said that if a man owns a picture he can snatch it away or he can cover it up to prevent anyone else from *looking* at it. He can also hide it in his wall-safe. But I think he has a right, not merely to do what he can (within limits) to prevent it from being looked at: he has a right that it shall not be looked at—just as he has a right that it shall not be torn or taken away from him. That he has a right that it shall not be looked at comes out, I think, in this way: if he hides it in his wall-safe, and we train our X-ray device on the wall-safe and look in, we have violated a right of his in respect of it, and the right is surely the right that it shall not be looked at. The fact that he couldn't protect his picture against the action of an X-ray device which enables us to look at it doesn't make it all right that we use the X-ray device to look at it—just as the fact that he can't protect his picture against the action of a long-distance picture-tearing device which enables us to tear his picture doesn't make it all right that we use the device to tear it.

Compare, by contrast, a subway map. You have no right to take it off the wall or cover it up: you haven't a right to do whatever you can to prevent it from being looked at. And if you do cover it up, and if anyone looks through the covering with an X-ray device, he violates no right of yours: you do not have a right that nobody but you shall look at it—it's not *yours*, after all.

Looking at a picture doesn't harm it, of course, whereas tearing a picture does. But this doesn't matter. If I use your toothbrush I don't harm it; but you, all the same, have a right that I shall not use it.

However, to have a right isn't always to claim it. Thus, on any view to own a picture is to have (among other rights) the right that others shall not tear it. Yet you might want someone else to do this and therefore (1) invite him to, or (2) get him to whether he wants to or not—for example, by carefully placing it where he'll put his foot through it when he gets out of bed in the morning. Or again, while not positively wanting anyone else to tear the picture, you might not care whether or not it is torn, and therefore you might simply (3) let someone tear it—for example, when, out of laziness, you leave it where it fell amongst the things the children are in process of wrecking. Or again still, you might positively want that nobody shall tear the picture and yet in a fit of absent-mindedness (4) leave it in some place such that another person would have to go to some trouble if he is to avoid tearing it, or (5) leave it in some place such that another person could not reasonably be expected to know that it still belonged to anybody.

Similarly, you might want someone else to look at your picture and therefore (1) invite him to, or (2) get him to whether he wants to or not. Or again, while not positively wanting anyone else to look at the picture, you might not care whether or not it is looked at, and therefore you might simply (3) let it be looked at. Or again still, you might positively want that nobody shall look at the picture, and yet in a fit of absent-mindedness (4) leave it in some place such that another person would have to go to some trouble if he is to avoid looking at it (at least, avert his eyes) or (5) leave it in some place such that another person could not reasonably be expected to know that it still belonged to anybody.

In all of these cases, it is permissible for another person on the one hand to tear the picture, on the other to look at it: no right of the owner's is violated. I think it fair to describe them as cases in which, though the owner had a right that the things not be done, he *waived* the right: in cases (1), (2), and (3) intentionally, in cases (4) and (5) unintentionally. It is not at all easy to say under what conditions a man has waived a right—by what acts of commission or omission and in what circumstances. The conditions vary, according as the right is more or less important; and while custom and convention, on the one hand, and the cost of securing the right, on the other hand, play very important roles, it is not clear precisely what roles. Nevertheless there plainly is such a thing as waiving a right; and once a man has waived his right to a thing, we violate no right of his if we do not accord it to him.

There are other things which may bring about that although a man had a right to a thing, we violate no right of his if we do not accord it to him: he may have transferred the right to another or he may have forfeited the right or he may still have the right, though it is overridden by some other, more stringent right. (This is not meant to be an exhaustive list.) And there are also some circumstances in which it is not clear what should be said. Suppose someone steals your picture and invites some third party (who doesn't know it's yours) to tear or look at it; or suppose someone takes your picture by mistake, thinking it's his, and invites some third party (who doesn't know it's yours) to tear it or look at it; does the *third* party violate a right of yours if he accepts the invitation? A general theory of rights should provide an account of all of these things.

It suffices here, however, to stress one thing about rights: a man may have had a right that we shall not do a thing, he may even still have a right that we shall not do it, consistent with its being the case that we violate no right of his if we go ahead.

If this is correct, we are on the way to what we want. I said earlier that when we trained our X-ray device on that man's wall-safe in order to have a look at his pornographic picture, we violated a right of his, the right to privacy, in fact. It now turns out (if I am right) that we violated a property right of his, specifically the negative right that others shall not look at the picture, this being one of the (many) rights which his owning the picture consists of. I shall come back a little later to the way in which these rights interconnect.

5. We do not, of course, care nearly as much about our possessions as we care about ourselves. We do not want people looking at our torn socks; but it would be much worse to have people watch us make faces at ourselves in the mirror when we thought no one was looking or listen to us while we fight with our families. So you might think I have spent far too much time on that pornographic picture.

But in fact, if what I said about pornographic pictures was correct, then the point about ourselves comes through easily enough. For if we have fairly stringent rights over our property, we have very much more stringent rights over our own persons. None of you came to possess your knee in exactly the way in which you came to possess your shoes or your pornographic pictures: I take it you neither bought nor inherited your left knee. And I suppose you could not very well sell your left knee. But that isn't because it isn't yours to sell—some women used to sell their hair, and some people nowadays sell their blood—but only because who'd buy a used left knee? For if anyone wanted to, you are the only one with a right to sell yours. Again, it's a nasty business to damage a knee; but you've a right to damage yours, and certainly nobody else has—its being your left knee includes your having the right that nobody else but you shall damage it. And, as I think, it also includes your having the right that nobody else shall touch it or look at it. Of course you might invite somebody to touch or look at your left knee; or you might let someone touch or look at it; or again still, you might in a fit of absent-mindedness leave it in some place such that another person would have to go to some trouble if he is to avoid touching or looking at it. In short, you might waive your right that your left knee not be touched or looked at. But that is what doing these things would be: waiving a right.

I suppose there are people who would be deeply distressed to learn that they had absent-mindedly left a knee uncovered, and that some-body was looking at it. Fewer people would be deeply distressed to learn that they had absent-mindedly left their faces uncovered. Most of us wouldn't, but many Moslem women would; and so might a man whose face had been badly disfigured, in a fire, say. Suppose you woke up one morning and found that you had grown fangs or that you no longer had a nose; you might well want to claim a right which most of us so contentedly waive: the right that your face not be looked at. That we have such a right comes out when we notice that if a man comes for some reason or another to want his face not to be looked at, and if he therefore keeps it covered, and if we then use an X-ray device in order to be able to look at it through the covering, we violate a right of his in respect of it, and the right we violate is surely the right that his face shall not be looked at. Compare again, by contrast, a subway map. No matter how much you may want a subway map to not be looked at, if we use an X-ray device in order to be able to look at it through the covering you place over it, we violate no right of yours: you do not have a right that nobody but you shall look at it—it is not *yours*, after all.

Listening, I think, works in the same way as looking. Suppose you are an opera singer, a great one, so that lots of people want to listen to you. You might sell them the right to listen. Or you might invite them to listen or let them listen or absent-mindedly sing where they cannot help but listen. But if you have decided you are no longer willing to be listened to; if you now sing only quietly, behind closed windows and carefully sound-proofed walls; and if somebody trains an amplifier on your house so as to be able to listen, he violates a right, the right to not be listened to.

These rights—the right to not be looked at and the right to not be listened to[1]—are analogous to rights we have over our property. It

1. In "A Definition of Privacy," *Rutgers Law Review*, 27 (1974), p. 281, Richard B. Parker writes: "The definition of privacy defended in this article is that *privacy is control over when and by whom the various parts of us can be sensed by others*. By 'sensed,' is meant simply seen, heard, touched, smelled, or tasted. By 'parts of us,' is meant the parts of our bodies, our voices, and the products of our bodies. 'Parts of us' also includes objects very closely associated with us. By 'closely associated' is meant primarily what is spatially associated. The objects which are 'parts of us' are objects we usually keep with us or locked up in a place accessible only to us."

The right to privacy, then, is presumably the right to this control. But I find this puzzling, on a number of counts. First, why *control*? If my neighbor invents an X-ray device which enables him to look through walls, then I should imagine I thereby lose control over who can look at me: going home and closing the doors no longer suffices sounds funny to say we have such rights. They are not mentioned in lists of rights. When we talk of rights, those that come to mind are the grand ones: the right to life, the right to liberty, the right to not be hurt or harmed, and property rights. Looking at and listening to a man do not harm him, but neither does stroking his left knee harm him, and yet he has a right that it shall not be stroked without permission. Cutting off all a man's hair while he's asleep will not harm him, nor will painting his elbows green; yet he plainly has a right that these things too shall not be done to him. These un-grand rights seem to be closely enough akin to be worth grouping together under one heading. For lack of a better term, I shall simply speak of "the right over the person," a right which I shall take to consist of the un-grand rights I mentioned, and others as well.

When I began, I said that if my husband and I are having a quiet fight behind closed windows and cannot be heard by the normal person who passes by, then if anyone trains an amplifier on us in order to listen he violates a right, the right to privacy, in fact. It now turns out (if I am right) that he violates our right to not be listened to, which is one of the rights included in the right over the person.

I had said earlier that if we use an X-ray device to look at the pornographic picture in a man's wall-safe, we violate his right to privacy. And it then turned out (if I was right) that we violated the right that others shall not look at the picture, which is one of the rights that his owning the picture consists in.

It begins to suggest itself, then, as a simplifying hypothesis, that the right to privacy is itself a cluster of rights, and that it is not a distinct cluster of rights but itself intersects with the cluster of rights which the right over the person consists in and also with the cluster

---

to prevent others from doing so. But my right to privacy is not violated until my neighbor actually does train the device on the wall of my house. It is the actual looking that violates it, not the acquisition of power to look. Second, there *are* other cases. Suppose a more efficient bugging device is invented: instead of tapes, it produces neatly typed transcripts (thereby eliminating the middleman). One who reads those transcripts does not *hear* you, but your right to privacy is violated just as if he does.

On the other hand, this article is the first I have seen which may be taken to imply (correctly, as I think) that there are such rights as the right to not be looked at and the right to not be listened to. And in any case, Parker's interest is legal rather than moral: he is concerned to find a definition which will be useful in legal contexts. (I am incompetent to estimate how successful he is in doing this.)

I am grateful to Charles Fried for drawing my attention to this article.

of rights which owning property consists in. That is, to use an X-ray device to look at the picture is to violate a right (the right that others shall not look at the picture) which is both one of the rights which the right to privacy consists in and also one of the rights which property ownership consists in. Again, to use an amplifying device to listen to us is to violate a right (the right to not be listened to) which is both one of the rights which the right to privacy consists in and also one of the rights which the right over the person consists in.

Some small confirmation for this hypothesis comes from the other listening case. I had said that if my husband and I are having a loud fight, behind open windows, so that we can easily be heard by the normal person who passes by, then if a passerby stops to listen, he violates no right of ours, and so in particular does not violate our right to privacy. Why doesn't he? I think it is because, though he listens to us, we have *let* him listen (whether intentionally or not), we have waived our right to not be listened to—for we took none of the conventional and easily available steps (such as closing the windows and lowering our voices) to prevent listening. But this would only be an explanation if waiving the right to not be listened to were waiving the right to privacy, or if it were at least waiving the only one among the rights which the right to privacy consists in which might plausibly be taken to have been violated by the passerby.

But for further confirmation, we shall have to examine some further violations of the right to privacy.

6. The following cases are similar to the ones we have just been looking at. (a) A deaf spy trains on your house a bugging device which produces, not sounds on tape, but a typed transcript, which he then reads. (See footnote 1.) (b) A blind spy trains on your house an X-ray device which produces, not views of you, but a series of bas-relief panels, which he then feels. The deaf spy doesn't listen to you, the blind spy doesn't look at you, but both violate your right to privacy just as if they did.

It seems to me that in both these cases there is a violation of that same right over the person which is violated by looking at or listening to a person. You have a right, not merely that you not be looked at or listened to but also that you not have your words transcribed, and that you not be modeled in bas-relief. These are rights that the spies violate, and it is these rights in virtue of the violation of which they violate your right to privacy. Of course, one may waive these rights:

a teacher presumably waives the former when he enters the classroom, and a model waives the latter when he enters the studio. So these cases seem to present no new problem.

7. A great many cases turn up in connection with information.

I should say straightaway that it seems to me none of us has a right over any fact to the effect that the fact shall not be known by others. You may violate a man's right to privacy by looking at him or listening to him: there is no such thing as violating a man's right to privacy by simply knowing something about him.

Where our rights in this area do lie is, I think, here: we have a right that certain steps shall not be taken to find out facts, and we have a right that certain uses shall not be made of facts. I shall briefly say a word about each of these.

If we use an X-ray device to look at a man in order to get personal information about him, then we violate his right to privacy. Indeed, we violate his right to privacy whether the information we want is personal or impersonal. We might be spying on him in order to find out what he does all alone in his kitchen at midnight; or we might be spying on him in order to find out how to make puff pastry, which we already know he does in the kitchen all alone at midnight; either way his right to privacy is violated. But in both cases, the simplifying hypothesis seems to hold: in both cases we violate a right (the right to not be looked at) which is both one of the rights that the right to privacy consists in and one of the rights that the right over the person consists in.

What about torturing a man in order to get information? I suppose that if we torture a man in order to find out how to make puff pastry, then though we violate his right to not be hurt or harmed, we do not violate his right to privacy. But what if we torture him to find out what he does in the kitchen all alone at midnight? Presumably in that case we violate both his right to not be hurt or harmed and his right to privacy—the latter, presumably, because it was personal information we tortured him to get. But here too we can maintain the simplifying hypothesis: we can take it that to torture a man in order to find out personal information is to violate a right (the right to not be tortured to get personal information) which is both one of the rights which the right to privacy consists in and one of the rights which the right to not be hurt or harmed consists in.

And so also for extorting information by threat: if the information is not personal, we violate only the victim's right to not be coerced by threat; if it is personal, we presumably also violate his right to privacy—in that we violate his right to not be coerced by threat to give personal information, which is both one of the rights which the right to privacy consists in and one of the rights which the right to not be coerced by threat consists in.

I think it a plausible idea, in fact, that doing something to a man to get personal information from him is violating his right to privacy only if doing that to him is violating some right of his not identical with or included in the right to privacy. Thus writing a man a letter asking him where he was born is no violation of his right to privacy: writing a man a letter is no violation of any right of his. By contrast, spying on a man to get personal information is a violation of the right to privacy, and spying on a man for any reason is a violation of the right over the person, which is not identical with or included in (though it overlaps) the right to privacy. Again, torturing a man to get personal information is presumably a violation of the right to privacy, and torturing a man for any reason is a violation of the right to not be hurt or harmed, which is not identical with or included in (though it overlaps) the right to privacy. If the idea is right, the simplifying hypothesis is trivially true for this range of cases. If a man has a right that we shall not do such and such to him, then he has a right that we shall not do it to him in order to get personal information from him. And his right that we shall not do it to him in order to get personal information from him is included in both his right that we shall not do it to him, and (if doing it to him for this reason is violating his right to privacy) his right to privacy.

I suspect the situation is the same in respect of uses of information. If a man gives us information on the condition we shall not spread it, and we then spread it, we violate his right to confidentiality, whether the information is personal or impersonal. If the information is personal, I suppose we also violate his right to privacy—by virtue of violating a right (the right to confidentiality in respect of personal information) which is both one of the rights which the right to privacy consists in and one of the rights which the right to confidentiality consists in.The point holds whether our motive for spreading the information is malice or profit or anything else.

Again, suppose I find out by entirely legitimate means (e.g. from a third party who breaks no confidence in telling me) that you keep a pornographic picture in your wall-safe; and suppose that, though

I know it will cause you distress, I print the information in a box on the front page of my newspaper, thinking it newsworthy: Professor Jones of State U. Keeps Pornographic Picture in Wall-Safe! Do I violate your right to privacy? I am, myself, inclined to think not. But if anyone thinks I do, he can still have the simplifying hypothesis: he need only take a stand on our having a right that others shall not cause us distress, and then add that what is violated here is the right to not be caused distress by the publication of personal information, which is one of the rights which the right to privacy consists in, and one of the rights which the right to not be caused distress consists in. Distress, after all, is the heart of the wrong (if there is a wrong in such a case): a man who positively wants personal information about himself printed in newspapers, and therefore makes plain he wants it printed, is plainly not wronged when newspapers cater to his want.

My reluctance to go along with this is not due to a feeling that we have no such right as the right to not be caused distress: that we have such a right seems to me a plausible idea. So far as I can see, there is nothing special about physical hurts and harms; mental hurts and harms are hurts and harms too. Indeed, they may be more grave and long-lasting than the physical ones, and it is hard to see why we should be thought to have rights against the one and not against the other. My objection is, rather, that even if there is a right to not be caused distress by the publication of personal information, it is mostly, if not always, overridden by what seems to me a more stringent right, namely the public's right to a press which prints any and all information, personal or impersonal, which it deems newsworthy; and thus that in the case I mentioned no right is violated, and hence, a fortiori, the right to privacy is not violated.[2]

8. The question arises, then, whether or not there are *any* rights in the right-to-privacy cluster which aren't also in some other rights cluster. I suspect there aren't any, and that the right to privacy is everywhere overlapped by other rights. But it's a difficult question. Part of the difficulty is due to its being (to put the best face on it) unclear just what is in this right-to-privacy cluster. I mentioned at the

2. It was Warren and Brandeis, in their now classic article, "The Right to Privacy," *Harvard Law Review* 4 (December 1890), who first argued that the law ought to recognize wrongs that are (they thought) committed in cases such as these. For a superb discussion of this article, see Harry Kalven, Jr., "Privacy in Tort Law—Were Warren and Brandeis Wrong?" *Law and Contemporary Problems* 31 (Spring 1966).

outset that there is disagreement on cases; and the disagreement comes even more stark as we move away from the kinds of cases I've so far been drawing attention to, which seem to me to be the central, core cases.

What should be said, for example, of the following?

(a) The neighbors make a terrible racket every night. Or they cook foul-smelling stews. Do they violate my right to privacy? Some think yes, I think not. But even if they do violate my right to privacy, perhaps all would be well for the simplifying hypothesis since their doing this is presumably a violation of another right of mine, roughly, the right to be free of annoyance in my house.

(b) The city, after a city-wide referendum favoring such a measure, installs loudspeakers to play music in all the buses and subways. Do they violate my right to privacy? Some think yes, I think not. But again perhaps all is well: it is if those of us in the minority have a right to be free of what we (though not the majority) regard as an annoyance in public places.

(c) You are famous, and photographers follow you around, every-where you go, taking pictures of you. Crowds collect and stare at you. Do they violate your right to privacy? Some think yes, I think not: it seems to me that if you do go out in public, you waive your right to not be photographed and looked at. But of course you, like the rest of us, have a right to be free of (what anyone would grant was) annoyance in public places; so in particular, you have a right that the photographers and crowds not press in too closely.

(d) A stranger stops you on the street and asks, "How much do you weigh?" Or an acquaintance, who has heard of the tragedy, says, "How terrible you must have felt when your child was run over by that delivery truck!"[3] Or a cab driver turns around and announces, "My wife is having an affair with my psychoanalyst." Some think that your right to privacy is violated here; I think not. There is an element of coercion in such cases: the speaker is trying to force you into a relationship you do not want, the threat being your own em-barrassment at being impolite if you refuse. But I find it hard to see how we can be thought to have a right against such attempts. Of course the attempt may be an annoyance. Or a sustained series of such attempts may become an annoyance. (Consider, for example, an acquaintance who takes to stopping at your office *every morning*

---

3. Example from Thomas Nagel.

to ask you if you slept well.) If so, I suppose a right *is* violated, namely, the right against annoyances.

(e) Some acquaintances of yours indulge in some very personal gossip about you.[4] Let us imagine that all of the information they share was arrived at without violation of any right of yours, and that none of the participants violates a confidence in telling what he tells. Do they violate a right of yours in sharing the information? If they do, there is trouble for the simplifying hypothesis, for it seems to me there is no right not identical with, or included in, the right-to-privacy cluster which they could be thought to violate. On the other hand, it seems to me they *don't* violate any right of yours. It seems to me we simply do not have rights against others that they shall not gossip about us.

(f) A state legislature makes it illegal to use contraceptives. Do they violate the right to privacy of the citizens of that state? No doubt certain techniques for enforcing the statute (such as peering into bedroom windows) would be obvious violations of the right to privacy; but is there a violation of the right to privacy in the mere enacting of the statute—in addition to the violations which may be involved in enforcing it? I think not. But it doesn't matter for the simplifying hypothesis if it is: making a kind of conduct illegal is infringing on a liberty, and we all of us have a right that our liberties not be infringed in the absence of compelling need to do so.

9. The fact, supposing it a fact, that every right in the right-to-privacy cluster is also in some other rights cluster does not by itself show that the right to privacy is in any plausible sense a "derivative" right. A more important point seems to me to be this: the fact that we have a right to privacy does not explain our having any of the rights in the right to privacy cluster. What I have in mind is this. We have a right to not be tortured. Why? Because we have a right to not be hurt or harmed. I have a right that my pornographic picture shall not be torn. Why? Because it's mine, because I own it. I have a right to do a somersault now. Why? Because I have a right to liberty. I have a right to try to preserve my life. Why? Because I have a right to life. In these cases we explain the having of one right by appeal to the having of another which includes it. But I don't have a right

4. Example from Gilbert Harman.

to not be looked at because I have a right to privacy; I don't have a right that no one shall torture me in order to get personal information about me because I have a right to privacy; one is inclined, rather, to say that it is because I have *these* rights that I have a right to privacy.

This point, supposing it correct, connects with what I mentioned at the outset: that nobody seems to have any very clear idea what the right to privacy is. We are confronted with a cluster of rights—a cluster with disputed boundaries—such that most people think that to violate at least any of the rights in the core of the cluster is to violate the right to privacy; but what have they in common other than their being rights such that to violate them is to violate the right to privacy? To violate these rights is to not let someone alone? To violate these rights is to visit indignity on someone? There are too many acts in the course of which we do not let someone alone, in the course of which we give affront to dignity, but in the performing of which we do not violate anyone's right to privacy. That we feel the need to find something in common to all of the rights in the cluster and, moreover, feel we haven't yet got it in the very fact that they *are* all in the cluster, is a consequence of our feeling that one cannot explain our having any of the rights in the cluster in the words: "Because we have a right to privacy."

But then if, as I take it, every right in the right-to-privacy cluster is also in some other rights cluster, there is no need to find the that-which-is-in-common to all rights in the right-to-privacy cluster and no need to settle disputes about its boundaries. For if I am right, the right to privacy is "derivative" in this sense: it is possible to explain in the case of each right in the cluster how come we have it without ever once mentioning the right to privacy. Indeed, the wrongness of every violation of the right to privacy can be explained without ever once mentioning it. Someone tortures you to get personal information from you? He violates your right to not be tortured to get personal information from you, and you have that right because you have the right to not be hurt or harmed—and it is because you have this right that what he does is wrong. Someone looks at your pornographic picture in your wall-safe? He violates your right that your belongings not be looked at, and you have that right because you have ownership rights—and it is because you have them that what he does is wrong. Someone uses an X-ray device to look at you through the walls of your house? He violates your right to not be looked at, and you have that right because you have rights over your person analogous to the rights you have over your property—and it is because you have these rights that what he does is wrong.

In any case, I suggest it is a useful heuristic device in the case of any purported violation of the right to privacy to ask whether or not the act is a violation of any other right, and if not whether the act *really* violates a right at all.[5] We are still in such deep dark in respect of rights that any simplification at all would be well worth having.[6]

5. Frederick Davis, "What Do We Mean by 'Right to Privacy'?" *South Dakota Law Review* 4 (Spring 1959), concludes, in respect of tort law, that: "If truly fundamental interests are accorded the protection they deserve, no need to champion a right to privacy arises. Invasion of privacy is, in reality, a complex of more fundamental wrongs. Similarly, the individual's interest in privacy itself, however real, is derivative and a state better vouchsafed by protecting more immediate rights . . . Indeed, one can logically argue that the concept of a right to privacy was never required in the first place, and its whole history is an illustration of how well-meaning but impatient academicians can upset the normal development of the law by pushing it too hard." I am incompetent to assess this article's claims against the law, but I take the liberty of warmly recommending it to philosophers who have an interest in looking further into the status and nature of the right to privacy.

6. I am grateful to the members of the Society for Ethical and Legal Philosophy for criticisms of the first draft of the following paper. Alan Sparer made helpful criticisms of a later draft.

9 · *Preferential Hiring*

Many people are inclined to think preferential hiring an obvious injustice. I should have said "feel" rather than "think": it seems to me the matter has not been carefully thought out, and that what is in question, really, is a gut reaction.

I am going to deal with only a very limited range of preferential hirings: that is, I am concerned with cases in which several candidates present themselves for a job, in which the hiring officer finds, on examination, that all are equally qualified to hold that job, and he then straightway declares for the black, or for the woman, because he or she *is* a black or a woman. And I shall talk only of hiring decisions in the universities, partly because I am most familiar with them, partly because it is in the universities that the most vocal and articulate opposition to preferential hiring is now heard—not surprisingly, perhaps, since no one is more vocal and articulate than a university professor who feels deprived of his rights.

I suspect that some people may say, Oh well, in *that* kind of case it's all right, what we object to is preferring the less qualified to the better qualified. Or again, what we object to is refusing even to consider the qualifications of white males. I shall say nothing at all about these things. I think that the argument I shall give for saying that preferential hiring is not unjust in the cases I do concentrate on can also be appealed to to justify it outside that range of cases. But I won't draw any conclusions about cases outside it. Many people do have that gut reaction I mentioned against preferential hiring in *any* degree or form; and it seems to me worthwhile bringing out that there is good reason to think they are wrong to have it. Nothing I say will be in the slightest degree novel or original. It will, I hope, be enough to set the relevant issues out clearly.

   1. But first, something should be said about qualifications.

   I said I would consider only cases in which the several candidates who present themselves for the job are equally qualified to hold it; and there plainly are difficulties in the way of saying precisely how this is to be established, and even what is to be established. Strictly academic qualifications seem at first glance to be relatively straight-forward: the hiring officer must see if the candidates have done equally well in courses (both courses they took, and any they taught), and if they are recommended equally strongly by their teachers, and if the work they submit for consideration is equally good. There is no de-nying that even these things are less easy to establish than first ap-pears: for example, you may have a suspicion that Professor Smith is given to exaggeration, and that his "great student" is in fact less strong than Professor Jones's "good student"—but do you *know* that this is so? But there is a more serious difficulty still: as blacks and women have been saying, strictly academic indicators may themselves be skewed by prejudice. My impression is that women, white and black, may possibly suffer more from this than black males. A black male who is discouraged or downgraded for being black is discour-aged or down-graded out of dislike, repulsion, a desire to avoid con-tact; and I suspect that there are very few teachers nowadays who allow themselves to feel such things, or, if they do feel them, to act on them. A woman who is discouraged or downgraded for being a woman is not discouraged or downgraded out of dislike, but out of a conviction that she is not serious, and I suspect that while there are very few teachers nowadays who allow themselves to feel that women generally are not serious, there are many who allow themselves to feel of the particular individual women students they confront that Ah, this one isn't serious, and in fact that one isn't either, nor is that other one—women generally are, of course, one thing, but these particular women, really they're just girls in search of husbands, are quite another. And I suspect that this will be far harder to root out. A teacher could not face himself in the mirror of a morning if he had downgraded anyone out of dislike, but a teacher can well face himself in the mirror if he downgrades someone out of a conviction that that person is not serious: after all, life is serious, and jobs and work, and who can take the unserious seriously? who pays attention to the dilettante? So the hiring officer must read very very carefully between the lines in the candidates' dossiers even to assess their strictly aca-demic qualifications.

   And then of course there are other qualifications besides the strictly academic ones. Is one of the candidates exceedingly disagreeable? A department is not merely a collection of individuals, but a working unit; and if anyone is going to disrupt that unit and to make its work more difficult, then this counts against him—he may be as well qualified in strictly academic terms, but he is not as well qualified. Again, is one of the candidates incurably sloppy? Is he going to mess up his records, is he going to have to be nagged to get his grades in, and worse, is he going to lose students' papers? This too would count against him: keeping track of students' work, records, and grades, after all, is part of the job.

What seems to me to be questionable, however, is that a candidate's race or sex is itself a qualification. Many people who favor preferential hiring in the universities seem to think it is; in their view, if a group of candidates is equally well qualified in respect of those measures I have already indicated, then if one is of the right race (black) or of the right sex (female), then that being itself a qualification, it tips the balance, and that one is the best qualified. If so, then of course no issue of injustice, or indeed of any other impropriety, is raised if the hiring officer declares for that one of the candidates straightway.

Why does race or sex seem to many to be, itself, a qualification? There seem to be two claims in back of the view that it is. First, there is the claim that blacks learn better from a black, women from a woman. One hears this less often in respect of women; blacks, however, are often said to mistrust the whites who teach them, with the result that they simply do not learn as well, or progress as far, as they would if taught by blacks. Secondly, and this one hears in respect of women as well as blacks, what is wanted is *role models*. The proportion of black and women faculty members in the larger universities (particularly as one moves up the ladder of rank) is very much smaller than the proportion of blacks and women in the society at large—even, in the case of women, than the proportion of them amongst recipients of Ph.D. degrees from those very same universities. Black and women students suffer a constricting of ambition because of this. They need to see members of their race or sex who are accepted, successful, professionals. They need concrete evidence that those of their race or sex *can* become accepted, successful professionals.

And perhaps it is thought that it is precisely by virtue of having a role model right in the classroom that blacks do learn better from a black, women from a woman.

Now it is obviously essential for a university to staff its classrooms with people who can teach, and so from whom its students can learn, and indeed learn as much and as well as possible—teaching, after all, is, if not the whole of the game, then anyway a very large part of it. So if the first claim is true, then race and sex *do* seem to be qualifications. It obviously would not follow that a university should continue to regard them as qualifications indefinitely; I suppose, however, that it would follow that it should regard them as qualifications at least until the proportion of blacks and women on the faculty matches the proportion of blacks and women among the students.

But in the first place, allowing this kind of consideration to have a bearing on a hiring decision might make for trouble of a kind that blacks and women would not be at all happy with. For suppose it could be made out that white males learn better from white males? (I once, years ago, had a student who said he really felt uncomfortable in a class taught by a woman, it was interfering with his work, and did I mind if he switched to another section?) I suppose we would feel that this was due to prejudice, and that it was precisely to be discouraged, certainly not encouraged by establishing hiring ratios. I don't suppose it is true of white males generally that they learn better from white males; I am concerned only with the way in which we should take the fact, if it were a fact, that they did—and if it would be improper to take it to be reason to think being a white male is a qualification in a teacher, then how shall we take its analogue to be reason to think being black, or being a woman, is a qualification in a teacher?

And in the second place, I must confess that, speaking personally, I do not find the claim we are looking at borne out in experience; I do not think that as a student I learned any better, or any more, from the women who taught me than from the men, and I do not think that my own women students now learn any better or any more from me than they do from my male colleagues. Blacks, of course, may have, and may have had, very different experiences, and I don't presume to speak for them—or even for women generally. But my own experience being what it is, it seems to *me* that any defense of preferential hiring in the universities which takes this first claim as premise is so far not an entirely convincing one.

The second claim, however, does seem to me to be plainly true: black and women students do need role models, they do need concrete evidence that individuals of their race or sex can become accepted, successful, professionals—plainly, you won't try to become what you don't believe you can become.

But do they need these role models right there in the classroom? Of course it might be argued that they do: that a black learns better from a black teacher, a woman from a woman teacher. But we have already looked at this. And if they are, though needed, not needed in the classroom, then is it the university's job to provide them?

For it must surely be granted that a college, or university, has not the responsibility—or perhaps, if it is supported out of public funds, even the right—to provide just *any* service to its students which might be good for them, or even which they may need. Sports seem to me plainly a case in point. No doubt it is very good for students to be offered, and perhaps even required to become involved in, a certain amount of physical exercise; but I can see no reason whatever to think that universities should be expected to provide facilities for it, or taxpayers to pay for those facilities. I suspect others may disagree, but my own feeling is that it is the same with medical and psychiatric services: I am sure that at least some students need medical and psychiatric help, but I cannot see why it should be provided for them in the universities, at public expense.

So the further question which would have to be answered is this: granting that black and female students need black and female role models, why should the universities be expected to provide them within their faculties? In the case of publicly supported universities, why should taxpayers be expected to provide them?

I don't say these question can't be answered. But I do think we need to come at them from a quite different direction. So I shall simply sidestep this ground for preferential hiring in the universities. The defense I give will not turn on anyone's supposing that of two otherwise equally well qualified candidates, one may be better qualified for the job by virtue, simply, of being of the right race or sex.

2. I mentioned several times in the preceding section the obvious fact that it is the taxpayers who support public universities. Not that private universities are wholly private: the public contributes to the support of most of them, for example by allowing them tax-free use of land, and of the dividends and capital gains on investments. But it will be the public universities in which the problem appears most starkly: as I shall suggest, it is the fact of public support that makes preferential hiring in the universities problematic.

For it seems to me that—other things being equal—there is no problem about preferential hiring in the case of a wholly private college or university, that is, one which receives no measure of public support at all, and which lives simply on tuition and (non-tax-deductible) contributions.

The principle here seems to me to be this: no perfect stranger has a right to be given a benefit which is yours to dispose of; no perfect stranger even has a right to be given an equal chance at getting a benefit which is yours to dispose of. You not only needn't give the benefit to the first perfect stranger who walks in and asks for it; you needn't even give him a chance at it, as, for example, by tossing a coin.

I should stress that I am here talking about *benefits*, that is, things which people would like to have, which would perhaps not merely please them, but improve their lives, but which they don't actually *need*. (I suspect the same hold true of things people do actually need, but many would disagree, and as it is unnecessary to speak here of needs, I shall not discuss them.) If I have extra apples (they're mine: I grew them, on my own land, from my own trees), or extra money, or extra tickets to a series of lectures I am giving on How to Improve Your Life Through Philosophy, and am prepared to give them away, word of this may get around, and people may present themselves as candidate recipients. I do not have to give to the first, or to proceed by letting them all draw straws; if I really do own the things, I can give to whom I like, on any ground I please, and in so doing, I violate no one's *rights*, I treat no one *unjustly*. None of the candidate recipients has a right to the benefit, or even to a chance at it.

There are four caveats. (1) Some grounds for giving or refraining from giving are less respectable than others. Thus, I might give the apples to the first who asks for them simply because he is the first who asks for them. Or again, I might give the apples to the first who asks for them because he is black, and because I am black and feel an interest in and concern for blacks which I do not feel in and for whites. In either case, not merely do I do what it is within my rights to do, but more, my ground for giving them to that person is a not immoral ground for giving them to him. But I might instead give the apples to the sixth who asks, and this because the first five were black and I hate blacks—or because the first five were white and I hate whites. Here I do what I have a right to do (for the apples are *mine*), and I violate no one's rights in doing it, but my ground for disposing of the apples as I did was a bad one; and it might even, more strongly, be said that I ought not have disposed of the apples in the way I did. But it is important to note that it is perfectly consistent, on the one hand, that a man's ground for acting as he did was a bad one, and even that he ought not have done what he did, and, on the other hand, that he had a right to do what he did, that he violated no one's rights in doing it, and that no one can complain *he* was unjustly treated.

The second caveat (2) is that although I have a right to dispose of my apples as I wish, I have no right to harm, or gratuitously hurt or offend. Thus I am within my rights to refuse to give the apples to the first five because they are black (or because they are white); but I am not within my rights to say to them "I refuse to give you apples because you are black (or white) and because those who are black (or white) are inferior."

And (3) if word of my extra apples, and of my willingness to give them away, got around because I advertised, saying or implying First Come First Served Till Supply Runs Out, then I cannot refuse the first five because they are black, or white. By so advertising I have *given* them a right to a chance at the apples. If they come in one at a time, I must give out apples in order, till the supply runs out; if they come in together, and I have only four apples, then I must either cut up the apples, or give them an equal chance, as, for example, by having them draw straws.

And lastly (4), there may be people who would say that I don't really, or don't fully own these apples, even though I grew them on my own land, from my own trees, and therefore that I don't have a right to give them away as I see fit. For after all, I don't own the police who protected my land while those apples were growing, or the sunlight because of which they grew. Or again, wasn't it just a matter of luck for me that I was born with a green thumb?—and why should I profit from a competence that I didn't deserve to have, that I didn't earn? Or perhaps some other reason might be put forward for saying that I don't own those apples. I don't want to take this up here. It seems to me wrong, but I want to let it pass. If anyone thinks that I don't own the apples, or, more generally, that no one really or fully owns anything, he will regard what I shall say in the remainder of this section, in which I talk about what may be done with what is privately owned, as an idle academic exercise. I'll simply ask that anyone who does think this be patient: we will come to what is publicly owned later.

Now what was in question was a job, not apples; and it may be insisted that to give a man a job is not to give him a benefit, but rather something he needs. Well, I am sure that people do need jobs, that it does not fully satisfy people's needs to supply them only with food, shelter, and medical care. Indeed, I am sure that people need, not merely jobs, but jobs that interest them, and that they can therefore get satisfaction from the doing of. But on the other hand, I am not at all sure that any candidate for a job in a university needs a job in a univeristy. One would very much like it if all graduate students who wish it could find jobs teaching in universities; it is in some measure a tragedy that a person should spend three or four years preparing for a career, and then find there is no job available, and that he has in consequence to take work which is less interesting than he had hoped and prepared for. But one thing seems plain: no one *needs* that work which would interest him most in all the whole world of work. Plenty of people have to make do with work they like less than other work—no economy is rich enough to provide everyone with the work he likes best of all—and I should think that this does not mean they lack something they *need*. We are all of us prepared to tax ourselves so that no one shall be in need; but I should imagine that we are not prepared to tax ourselves (to tax barbers, truck drivers, salesclerks, waitresses, and factory workers) in order that everyone who wants a university job, and is competent to fill it, shall have one made available to him.

All the same, if a university job is a benefit rather than something needed, it is anyway not a "pure" benefit (like an apple), but an "impure" one. To give a man a university job is to give him an opportunity to do work which is interesting and satisfying; but he will only *be* interested and satisfied if he actually does the work he is given an opportunity to do, and does it well.

What this should remind us of is that certain cases of preferential hiring might well be utterly irrational. Suppose we have an eating club, and need a new chef; we have two applicants, a qualified French chef, and a Greek who happens to like to cook, though he doesn't do it very well. We are fools if we say to ourselves "We like the Greeks, and dislike the French, so let's hire the Greek." We simply won't eat as well as we could have, and eating, after all, was the point of the club. On the other hand, it's *our* club, and so *our* jobs. And who shall say it is not within a man's rights to dispose of what really is his in as foolish a way as he likes?

And there is no irrationality, of course, if one imagines that the two applicants are equally qualified French chefs, and one is a cousin of one of our members, the other a perfect stranger. Here if we declare directly for the cousin, we do not act irrationally, we violate no one's rights, and indeed do not have a morally bad ground for making the choice we make. It's not a morally splendid ground, but it isn't a morally bad one either.

Universities differ from eating clubs in one way which is important for present purposes: in an eating club, those who consume what the club serves are the members, and thus the owners of the club themselves—by contrast, even if the university is wholly private, those who consume what it serves are not among the owners. This makes a difference: the owners of the university have a responsibility not merely to themselves (as the owners of an eating club do), but also to those who come to buy what it offers. It could, I suppose, make plain in its advertising that it is prepared to allow the owners' racial or religious or other preferences to outweigh academic qualifications in its teachers. But in the absence of that, it must, in light of what a university is normally expected to be and to aim at, provide the best teachers it can afford. It does not merely act irrationally, but indeed violates the rights of its student-customers if it does not.

On the other hand, this leaves it open to the university that in case of a choice between equally qualified candidates, it violates no one's rights if it declares for the black because he is black, or for the white because he is white. To the wholly *private* university, that is, for that is all I have so far been talking of. Other things being equal—that is, given it has not advertised the job in a manner which would entitle applicants to believe that all who are equally qualified will be given an equal chance at it, and given it does not gratuitously give offense to those whom it rejects—the university may choose as it pleases, and violates no one's rights in doing so. Though no doubt its grounds for choosing may be morally bad ones, and we may even wish to say, more strongly, that it ought not choose as it does.

What will have come out in the preceding is that the issue I am concerned with is a moral, and not a legal one. My understanding is that the law does prevent an employer wholly in the private sector from choosing a white rather than a black on ground of that difference alone—though not from choosing a black rather than a white on ground of that difference alone. Now if, as many people say, legal rights (or perhaps, legal rights in a relatively just society) create moral rights, then even a moral investigation should take the law into account; and indeed, if I am not mistaken as to the law, it would have to be concluded that blacks (but not whites) do have rights of the kind I have been denying. I want to sidestep all this. My question can be restated: would a private employer's choosing a white (or black) rather than a black (or white) on ground of that difference alone be a violation of anyone's rights if there were no law making it illegal? And the answer seems to me to be: it would not.

3. But hardly any college or university in America is purely private. As I said, most enjoy some public support, and the moral issues may be affected by the extent of the burden carried by the public. I shall concentrate on universities which are entirely publicly funded, such as state or city universities, and ignore the complications that might arise in case of partial private funding.

The special problem here, as I see it, is this: where a community pays the bills, the community owns the university.

I said earlier that the members, who are therefore the owners, of a private eating club may declare for whichever chef they wish, even if the man they declare for is not as well qualified for the job as some other; in choosing amongst applicants, they are *not* choosing amongst fellow members of the club who is to get some benefit from the club. But now suppose, by contrast, that two of us who are members arrive at the same time, and there is only one available table. And suppose also that this has never happened before, and that the club has not voted on any policy for handling it when it does happen. What seems to me to be plain is this: the headwaiter cannot indulge in preferential seating, he cannot simply declare for one or the other of us on just any ground he pleases. He must randomize: as it might be, by tossing a coin.

Or again, suppose someone arrives at the dining room with a gift for the club: a large and very splendid apple tart. And suppose that this, too, has never happened before, and that the club has not voted on any policy for handling it when it does happen. What seems to me plain is this: the headwaiter cannot distribute that tart in just any manner, and on any ground he pleases. If the tart won't keep till the next meeting, and it's impossible to convene one now, he must divide the tart amongst us equally.

Consideration of these cases might suggest the following principle: every owner of a jointly owned property has a right to either an equal chance at, or an equal share in, any benefit which that property generates, and which is available for distribution amongst the owners—equal chance rather than equal share if the benefit is indivisible, or for some reason is better left undivided.

Now I have all along been taking it that the members of a club jointly own the club, and therefore jointly own whatever the club owns. It seems to me possible to view a community in the same way: to suppose that its members jointly own it, and therefore jointly own whatever it owns. If a community is properly viewed in this way, and if the principle I set out above is true, then every member of the community is a joint owner of whatever the community owns, and so in particular, a joint owner of its university; and therefore every member of the community has a right to an equal chance at, or equal share in, any benefit which the university generates, which is available for distribution amongst the owners. And that includes university jobs, if, as I argued, a university job is a benefit.

Alternatively, one might view a community as an imaginary Person: one might say that the members of that community are in some sense participants in that Person, but that they do not jointly own what the Person owns. One might in fact say the same of a club: that its members do not jointly own the club or anything which the club owns, but only in some sense participate in the Person which owns the things. And then the cases I mentioned might suggest an analogous principle: every "participant" in a Person (Community-Person, Club-Person) has a right to either an equal chance at, or an equal share in, any benefit which is generated by a property which that Person owns, which is available for distribution amongst the "participants."

On the other hand, if we accept any of this, we have to remember that there are cases in which a member may, without the slightest impropriety, be deprived of this equal chance or equal share. For it is plainly not required that the university's hiring officer decide who gets the available job by randomizing amongst *all* the community members, however well- or ill-qualified, who want it. The university's student-customers, after all, have rights too; and their rights to good teaching are surely more stringent than each member's right (if each has such a right) to an equal chance at the job. I think we do best to reserve the term "violation of a right" for cases in which a man is unjustly deprived of something he has a right to, and speak rather of "overriding a right" in cases in which, though a man is deprived of something he has a right to, it is not unjust to deprive him of it. So here the members' rights to an equal chance (if they have them) would be, not violated, but merely overridden.

It could of course be said that these principles hold only of benefits of a kind I pointed to earlier, and called "pure" benefits (such as apples and apple tarts), and that we should find some other, weaker, principle to cover "impure" benefits (such as jobs).

Or it could be said that a university job is not a benefit which is available for distribution amongst the community members—that although a university job is a benefit, it is, in light of the rights of the students, available for distribution only amongst those members of the community who are best qualified to hold it. And therefore that they alone have a right to an equal chance at it.

It is important to notice, however, that unless *some* such principle as I have set out is true of the publicly owned university, there is no real problem about preferential hiring in it. Unless the white male applicant who is turned away had a right that this should not be done, doing so is quite certainly not violating any of his rights. Perhaps being joint owner of the university (on the first model) or being joint participant in the Person which owns the university (on the second model), do not give him a right to an equal chance at the job; perhaps he is neither owner nor joint participant (some third model is preferable), and it is something else which gives him his right to an equal chance at the job. Or perhaps he hasn't a right to an equal chance at the job, but has instead some other right which is violated by declaring for the equally qualified black or woman straightway. Here is where it emerges most clearly that opponents of preferential hiring are merely expressing a gut reaction against it, for they have not asked themselves precisely what right is in question, and what it issues from.

Perhaps lurking in the background there is some sense that everyone has a right to "equal treatment," and that it is this which is violated by preferential hiring. But what on earth right is this? Mary surely does not have to decide between Tom and Dick by toss of a coin, if what is in question is marrying. Nor even, as I said earlier, if what is in question is giving out apples, which she grew on her own land, on her own trees.

It could, of course, be argued that declaring for the black or woman straightway isn't a violation of the white male applicant's rights, but is all the same wrong, bad, something which ought not be done. As I said, it is perfectly consistent that one ought not do something which it is, nevertheless, no violation of anyone's rights to do. So perhaps opponents of preferential hiring might say that rights are not in question, and still argue against it on other grounds. I say they *might*, but I think they plainly do better not to. If the white male applicant has no rights which would be violated, and appointing the black or woman indirectly benefits other blacks or women (remember that need for role models), and thereby still more indirectly benefits us all (by widening the available pool of talent), then it is very hard to see how it could come out to be morally objectionable to declare for the black or woman straightway.

I think we should do the best we can for those who oppose preferential hiring: I think we should grant that the white male applicant has a right to an equal chance at the job, and see what happens for preferential hiring if we do. I shall simply leave open whether this right issues from considerations of the kind I drew attention to, and so also whether or not every member of the community, however well- or ill-qualified for the job, has the same right to an equal chance at it.

Now it is, I think, widely believed that we may, without injustice, refuse to grant a man what he has a right to only if *either* someone else has a conflicting and more stringent right, *or* there is some very great benefit to be obtained by doing so—perhaps that a disaster of some kind is thereby averted. If so, then there really is trouble for preferential hiring. For what more stringent right could be thought to override the right of the white male applicant for an equal chance? What great benefit obtained, what disaster averted, by declaring for the black or the woman straightway? I suggested that benefits are obtained, and they are not small ones. But are they large enough to override a right? If these questions canot be satisfactorily answered, then it looks as if the hiring officer does act unjustly, and does violate the rights of the white males, if he declares for the black or woman straightway.

But in fact there are two other ways in which a right may be overridden. Let's go back to that eating club again. Suppose that now it has happened that two of us arrive at the same time when there is only one available table, we think we had better decide on some policy for handling it when it happens. And suppose that we have of late had reason to be especially grateful to one of the members, whom I'll call Smith: Smith has done a series of very great favors for the club. It seems to me we might, out of gratitude to Smith, adopt the following policy: for the next six months, if two members arrive at the time, and there is only one available table, then Smith gets in first, if he's one of the two; whereas if he's not, then the headwaiter shall toss a coin.

We might even vote that for the next year, if he wants apple tart, he gets more of it than the rest of us.

It seems to me that there would be no impropriety in our taking these actions—by which I mean to include that there would be no injustice in our taking them. Suppose another member, Jones, votes No. Suppose he says "Look. I admit we all benefited from what Smith did for us. But still, I'm a member, and a member in as good standing as Smith is. So I have a right to an equal chance (and equal share), and I demand what I have a right to." I think we may rightly feel that Jones merely shows insensitivity: he does not adequately appreciate what Smith did for us. Jones, like all of us, has a right to an equal chance at such benefits as the club has available for distribution to the members; but there is no injustice in a majority's refusing to grant the members this equal chance, in the name of a debt of gratitude to Smith.

It is worth noticing an important difference between a debt of gratitude and debts owed to a creditor. Suppose the club had borrowed $1,000 from Dickenson, and then was left as a legacy a painting appraised at $1,000. If the club has no other saleable assets, and if no member is willing to buy the painting, then I take it that justice would precisely require *not* randomizing amongst the members who is to get that painting, but would instead require our offering it to Dickenson. Jones could not complain that to offer it to Dickenson is to treat him, Jones, unjustly: Dickenson has a right to be paid back, and that right is more stringent than any member's right to an equal chance at the panting. Now Smith, by contrast, did not have a right to be given anything, he did not have a right to our adopting a policy of preferential seating in his favor. If we fail to do anything for Smith, we do *him* no injustice—our failing is, not injustice, but ingratitude. There is no harm in speaking of debts of gratitude and in saying that they are owed to a benefactor, by analogy with debts owed to a creditor; but it is important to remember that a creditor has, and a benefactor does not have, a right to repayment.

To move now from clubs to more serious matters, suppose two candidates for a civil service job have equally good test scores, but there is only one job available. We could decide between them by coin-tossing. But in fact we do allow for declaring for A straightway, where A is a veteran, and B is not.[1] It may be that B is a nonveteran

1. To the best of my knowledge, the analogy between veterans' preference and the preferential hiring of blacks has been mentioned in print only by Edward T. Chase, in a Letter to the Editor, *Commentary* (February 1973), pp. 12 and 16.

through no fault of his own: perhaps he was refused induction for flat feet, or a heart murmur. That is, those things in virtue of which B is a nonveteran may be things which it was no more in his power to control or change than it is in anyone's power to control or change the color of his skin. Yet the fact is that B is not a veteran and A is. On the assumption that the veteran has served his country,[2] the country owes him something. And it seems plain that giving him preference is a not unjust way in which part of that debt of gratitude can be paid.

And now, finally, we should turn to those debts which are incurred by one who wrongs another. It is here we find what seems to me the most powerful argument for the conclusion that the preferential hiring of blacks and women is not unjust.

I obviously cannot claim any novelty for this argument: it's a very familiar one. Indeed, not merely is it familiar, but so is a battery of objections to it. It may be granted that if we have wronged A, we owe him something: we should make amends, we should compensate him for the wrong done him. It may even be granted that if we have wronged A, we must make amends, that justice requires it, and that a failure to make amends is not merely callousness, but injustice. But (a) are the young blacks and women who are amongst the current applicants for university jobs amongst the blacks and women who were wronged? To turn to particular cases, it might happen that the black applicant is middle class, son of professionals, and has had the very best in private schooling; or that the woman applicant is plainly the product of feminist upbringing and encouragement. Is it proper, much less required, that the black or woman be given preference over a white male who grew up in poverty, and has to make his own way and earn his encouragements? Again, (b), did we, the current members of the community, wrong any blacks or women? Lots of people once did; but then isn't it for them to do the compensating? That is, if they're still alive, for presumably nobody now alive owned any slaves and perhaps nobody now alive voted against women's suffrage. And (c) what if the white male applicant for the job has never in any degree wronged any blacks or women? If so, *he* doesn't owe any debts to them, so why should *he* make amends to them?

These objections seem to me quite wrong-headed.

2. Many people would reject this assumption, or perhaps accept it only selectively, for veterans of this or that particular war. I ignore this. What interests me is what follows if we make the assumption—as, of course, many other people do, more, it seems, than do not.

Obviously the situation for blacks and women is better than it was a hundred and fifty, fifty, twenty-five years ago. But it is absurd to suppose that the young blacks and women now of an age to apply for jobs have not been wronged. Large-scale, blatant, overt wrongs have presumably disappeared; but it is only within the last twenty-five years (perhaps the last ten years in the case of women) that it has become at all widely agreed in this country that blacks and women must be recognized as having, not merely this or that particular right normally recognized as belonging to white males, but all of the rights and respect which go with full membership in the community. Even young blacks and women have lived through downgrading for being black or female: they have not merely not been given that very equal chance at the benefits generated by what the community owns which is so firmly insisted on for white males, they have not until lately even been felt to have a right to it.

And even those who were not themselves downgraded for being black or female have suffered the consequences of the downgrading of other blacks and women: lack of self-confidence, and lack of self-respect. For where a community accepts that a person's being black, or being a woman, are right and proper grounds for denying that person full membership in the community, it can hardly be supposed that any but the most extraordinarily independent black or woman will escape self-doubt. All but the most extraordinarily independent of them have had to work harder—if only against self-doubt—than all but the most deprived white males, in the competition for a place amongst the best qualified.

If any black or woman has been unjustly deprived of what he or she has a right to, then of course justice does call for making amends. But what of the blacks and women who haven't actually been deprived of what they have a right to, but only made to suffer the consequences of injustice to other blacks and women? *Perhaps* justice doesn't require making amends to them as well; but common decency certainly does. To fail, at the very least, to make what counts as public apology to all, and to take positive steps to show that it is sincerely meant, is, if not injustice, then anyway a fault at least as serious as ingratitude.

Opting for a policy of preferential hiring may of course mean that some black or woman is preferred to some white male who in fact has had a harder life than the black or woman. But so may opting for a policy of veterans' preference mean that a healthy, unscarred, middle class veteran is preferred to a poor, struggling, scarred non-veteran. Indeed, opting or a policy of settling who gets the job by having all equally qualified candidates draw straws may also mean that in a given case the candidate with the hardest life loses out. Opting for any policy other than hard-life preference may have this result.

I have no objection to anyone's arguing that it is precisely hard-life preference that we ought to opt for. If all, or anyway all of the equally qualified, have a right to an equal chance, then the argument would have to draw attention to something sufficiently powerful to override that right. But perhaps this could be done along the lines I followed in the case of blacks and women: perhaps it could be successfully argued that we have wronged those who have had hard lives, and therefore owe it to them to make amends. And then we should have in more extreme form a difficulty already present: how are these preferences to be ranked? shall we place the hard-lifers ahead of blacks? both ahead of women? and what about veterans? I leave these questions aside. My concern has been only to show that the white male applicant's right to an equal chance does not make it unjust to opt for a policy under which blacks and women are given preference. That a white male with a specially hard history may lose out under this policy cannot possibly be any objection to it, in the absence of a showing that hard-life preference is not unjust, and, more important, takes priority over preference for blacks and women.

Lastly, it should be stressed that to opt for such a policy is not to make the young white male applicants themselves make amends for any wrongs done to blacks and women. Under such a policy, no one is asked to give up a job which is already his; the job for which the white male competes isn't his, but is the community's, and it is the hiring officer who gives it to the black or woman in the community's name. Of course the white male is asked to give up his equal chance at the job. But that is not something he pays to the black or woman by by way of making amends; it is something the community takes away from him in order that *it* may make amends.

Still, the community does impose a burden on him: it is able to make amends for its wrongs only by taking something away from him, something which, after all, we are supposing he has a right to. And why should *he* pay the cost of the community's amends-making?

If there were some appropriate way in which the community could make amends to its blacks and women, some way which did not require depriving anyone of anything he has a right to, then that would be the best course of action for it to take. Or if there were anyway some way in which the costs could be shared by everyone, and not imposed entirely on the young white male job applicants, then that would be, if not best, then anyway better than opting for a policy of preferential hiring. But in fact the nature of the wrongs done is such as to make jobs the best and most suitable form of compensation. What blacks and women were denied was full membership in the community; and nothing can more appropriately make amends for that wrong than precisely what will make them feel they now finally have it. And that means jobs. Financial compensation (the cost of which could be shared equally) slips through the fingers; having a job, and discovering you do it well, yield—perhaps better than anything else—that very self-respect which blacks and women have had to do without.

But of course choosing this way of making amends means that the costs are imposed on the young white male applicants who are turned away. And so it should be noticed that it is not entirely inappropriate that those applicants should pay the costs. No doubt few, if any, have themselves, individually, done any wrongs to blacks and women. But they have profited from the wrongs the community did. Many may actually have been direct beneficiaries of policies which excluded or downgraded blacks and women—perhaps in school admissions, perhaps in access to financial aid, perhaps elsewhere; and even those who did not directly benefit in this way had, at any rate, the advantage in the competition which comes of confidence in one's full membership, and of one's rights being recognized as a matter of course.

Of course it isn't only the young white male applicant for a university job who has benefited from the exclusion of blacks and women: the older white male, now comfortably tenured, also benefited, and many defenders of preferential hiring feel that he should be asked to share the costs. Well, presumably we can't demand that he give up his job, or share it. But it seems to me in place to expect the occupants of comfortable professorial chairs to contribute in some way, to make some form of return to the young white male who bears the cost and is turned away. It will have been plain that I find the outcry now heard against preferential hiring in the universities objectionable; it would also be objectionable that those of us who are now securely situated should placidly defend it, with no more than a sigh of regret for the young white male who pays for it.

4. One final word: "discrimination." I am inclined to think we so use it that if anyone is convicted of discriminating against blacks, women, white males, or what have you, then he is thereby convicted of acting unjustly. If so, and if I am right in thinking that preferential hiring in the restricted range of cases we have been looking at is *not* unjust, then we have two options: (a) we can simply reply that to opt for a policy of preferential hiring in those cases is not to opt for a policy of discriminating against white males, or (b) we can hope to get usage changed—by trying to get people to allow that there is discriminating against and discriminating against, and that some is unjust, but some is not.

Best of all, however, would be for that phrase to be avoided altogether. It's at best a blunt tool: there are all sorts of nice moral discriminations *(sic)* which one is unable to make while occupied with it. And that bluntness itself is apt to do harm: blacks and women are hardly likely to see through to what precisely is owed them while they are being accused of welcoming what is unjust.[3]

3. This essay is an expanded version of a talk given at the Conference on the Liberation of Female Persons, held at North Carolina State University at Raleigh, on March 26–28, 1973, under a grant from the S & H Foundation. I am indebted to James Thomson and the members of the Society for Ethical and Legal Philosophy for criticism of an earlier draft.

10 · *Some Questions About Government Regulation of Behavior*

Government has always been, and must continue to be, in the business of regulating behavior. The question before us is not whether it should be in this business at all, but only which behavior it should, or even may, regulate.

For example, it is illegal in this, and in every other civilized society, for one private citizen to kill another for pleasure or profit. Government declares such behavior impermissible and attaches severe penalties to it. There is an interesting theoretical question *why* government may do this; but it is a datum *that* it may.

Killing someone is causing him a serious physical harm. And we may, more generally, accept as a given that government may make it illegal for one private citizen, A, to cause another, B, a serious physical harm, intending to cause that harm, and having no further intention in causing that harm than pleasure or profit. This formula is not without its difficulties, but its difficulties are not important for present purposes.[1]

What interests us here are the harms that A can cause B *without* intending to cause them. It is when one turns to unintentionally harmful behavior that government regulation begins to seem problematic.

The issues are complex; I hope merely to sort out some considerations relevant to the settling of them.

1. Suppose you manufacture bread, and that you sell me a loaf. I eat a piece, and am thereby caused a harm. You did not intend that harm; you did not intend to cause me any harm at all. Is it permissible

1. What about harms to which one consents? For the most part I ignore them—but see concluding section.

for government to have had, in advance and already 'on the books, a law under which your conduct was illegal? There obviously is no saying. Different answers are in place according as further details are filled in one way or another.

Let us attend first to the question why eating that bread caused me a harm. And let us suppose first that it caused me a harm because it was made in unsanitary or unsafe conditions—for example, it contained rat droppings. Here we are inclined to say "Yes." Government may make it illegal to cause harms by negligence as well as by intention.

But *may* it? Why not merely say that the manufacturer who does not wish to spend resources on keeping his factory clean and safe must print on his labels: "Eat at your own risk—we do not guarantee that the conditions under which this particular loaf of bread was made were both clean and safe"? I shall come back to printed warnings later.

Meanwhile, however, it does seem plain that government may make it illegal to cause harms by negligence in the absence of warnings of the possibility of those harms. If the tiles on my roof are loose, and I am too lazy to fix them, and if one falls off onto a passerby, I am, as things stand, legally liable for the harm caused that person, and rightly so.

It should go without saying that government regulates in other ways than by legislation and executive order—that it regulates also via the common law. When I spoke of government having had, in advance and already "on the books," law under which this or that conduct is illegal, I put the words "on the books" in scare-quotes, for I meant to include case-books as well as lists of statutes.

That government regulates via tort law is surely plain. Government regulates behavior primarily by attaching penalties. A statute (I shall use this term to cover both legislation and executive order) may say: "Penalty for letting it be the case that your roof tiles are loose: $50." Tort law, however, does not attach a penalty to anything so simple and straightforward as allowing your roof tiles to be loose. It says, for example: "If the tiles on your roof are loose due to your own negligence, and if one falls off onto a passerby, causing harm, then you must pay damages"; *that is,* it says: "Penalty for letting it be the case that your roof tiles are loose due to your own negligence, and that one falls off onto a passerby, causing harm: Payment of damages." So it too attaches penalties.

There is a morally important difference between these two samples of government regulation that I conceal by using the same term "penalty" in both cases. The statutory penalty of $50 that I invented is a fine, paid to the government; the tort penalty I invented is not a fine, and is paid, not to government, but to a private person, the victim of the harm.

This difference connects with another morally important difference, namely that the tort penalty is attached to actually causing a harm, whereas the statutory penalty is attached to imposing a risk of harm. We should examine all this more closely.

2. Suppose that in a certain country the only law concerning roof tiles is tort law, and that all tort law in that country says concerning them is this:

(T) Penalty for letting it be the case that your roof tiles are loose due to your own negligence, and that one falls off onto a passerby and causes harm: Payment of damages.

Is there any injustice in there being such a law? I take it to be a datum that there is not. If one causes a harm by one's negligence, it is entirely just that one pay damages for it.

For quite some time (we may imagine) all goes well: homeowners in that country mostly keep their roof tiles tight, out of a moral concern to avoid causing harm, or out of fear of having to pay damages, or out of some mix of both.

But alas, all does not go well indefinitely. One after the other, there now begin to occur an increasing number of harms done by flying roof tiles, and the harms are increasingly serious. Many homeowners are no longer moved by the moral and prudential considerations that moved the earlier generation of homeowners. What should be done?

One possible answer is that nothing should be done because nothing will work on homeowners of the kind I am asking you to imagine.

What is of more interest is that there is in the wings an argument to the effect that nothing need be done. No doubt increasing numbers of people are being more seriously harmed by flying roof tiles; but as things stand, all victims of harm can sue for damages for the harm done them. Let us be clear: they can sue for reimbursement for *all* of their costs, including not merely medical and legal costs, but also the pay they forfeit while convalescing and even a sum in return for the pain they suffer. All of this is plausibly included under the heading of "damages." And if it is—if, that is, the tort law already in force does require the negligent homeowner to pay all of this to the victim—then the victim is reimbursed. Homeowner and victim have then squared their accounts. And who are we, or what is government, to ask homeowners that they do more than settle equitably with their victims?

One reply is that those who bring suit do not always win. Thus a passerby might in fact be harmed by a homeowner's negligence, and yet be unable to establish this fact to the court's satisfaction. This worry may be real, but I do not think it theoretically interesting. Whether a homeowner will have to pay the tort law penalty turns on whether the plaintiff wins the suit; but similarly, whether a homeowner would have to pay a statutory penalty would turn on whether the government "won *its* suit"—in other words, on whether the government's agents were able to establish that the statute was violated.

The theoretically interesting reply seems to me to come out as follows.

It may have been noticed that I have so far used only the term "damages"; I wanted (for the space of this essay) to reserve the term "compensation" for something special.

Let us say that A causes B a compensable harm if and only if A causes B a harm, and there exists a sum of money for which B did, or would have been willing to, sell A the right to cause B that harm for that sum of money. If you destroy some of my property, you cause me a harm. So suppose you smash my paperweight. The harm you thereby cause me is a compensable harm, for there is a sum of money for which you could have bought from me the right to cause me that harm—$50 would certainly do it. By contrast, if you cause me to go blind, then you cause me an *in*compensable harm, for there is no sum of money whatever for which I would have sold you the right to cause me to go blind.

If by your negligence you cause me to go blind, then I shall sue you for damages; some would say, "for compensation." Though I will certainly take what I can get, no sum of money would compensate me for the loss of my eyesight: I not only will not, I cannot, win in the courts a sum of money for which I would have sold you the right to cause me to go blind—for no such sum of money exists. I sue for damages all the same, but only because being blind and rich is preferable to being blind and poor.

My example of a compensable harm was a harm to me caused by a harm to my property; my example of an incompensable harm was a physical injury. But there are compensable harms that are physical injuries. Thus, for example, $100,000 would easily buy you the right to cause me a case of twenty-four-hour flu (if I can be sure that's the worst harm your injection will do me). And there are incompensable harms that are caused by harms to property. Thus it might be that there is no sum of money that would buy you the right to smash the teacups I inherited from my great-grandmother.

No doubt there are also borderline cases. No sum of money would buy you the right to cut off my little finger. Is there a sum of money for which I would sell you the right to break it under anaesthetic? I don't know.

Now if you cause me an incompensable harm, you cause me a harm for which (by definition) no amount of money in damages will compensate me. There is no way in which you can reimburse me, or make full restitution, for causing me an incompensable harm.

Let us even suppose, then, that the judicial system in the country I have envisioned is maximally fair and efficient. I said we are to suppose that increasing numbers of people are being caused increasingly serious harm by flying roof tiles; and let us suppose that these harms are not merely serious, but incompensable. Then the argument to the effect that nothing need be done—the argument whose premise is that the existing tort law ensures that negligent homeowners make full restitution to their victims—does not succeed. For however fair and efficient the judicial system may be, homeowners who cause incompensable harms by their negligence *cannot* square accounts with their victims.

Homeowners who cause compensable harms by their negligence *can* square accounts with their victims. But will they? In every case? There are a number of reasons for thinking that they will not.

If you cause me a harm so serious that it would have cost you a great deal of money to buy from me the right to cause me that harm, I will sue. And I *may* get what I sue for. But I may not. In the first place, the court may not assess my costs exactly as I do. (You have torn my autographed photograph of John Wayne; the court may not agree with me in valuing that photograph at $100,000.) In the second place, other considerations will weigh on a court in setting damages than simply the cost to the plaintiff of the defendant's act.

If you cause me a harm so superficial that it would have cost you only a small sum of money to buy from me the right to cause me that harm, I will not sue—the cost to me (in time and effort) is more than

I will get back in damages. Even a maximally fair and efficient judicial system cannot (indeed, should not) be made costless to those who bring suit. And if it were imagined that a successful plaintiff is to get back, in damages, a sum that includes a fair assessment of the costs (in time and effort) of bringing suit (an inefficient policy, in that it encourages suits), even then, the court again may not value my loss (now in time and effort) exactly as I do, and has other considerations in mind when setting damages than simply my own costs.

So the argument claiming that nothing need be done—on the premise that the existing tort law in our imaginary country ensures that negligent homeowners square accounts with their victims—does not succeed. In the case of incompensable harms, they cannot square accounts with their victims; in the case of compensable harms, they very often will not.

What can be done? Well, what do the people in that country *want* to do? They want to get homeowners to keep their roof tiles tight, with a view to cutting down on the number of harms done by flying roof tiles. They can try to do this in one of two ways. In the first place, they can try to "indirectly coerce" homeowners into keeping their roof tiles tight by increasing the penalty for causing harms by flying roof tiles. In the second place, they can try to "directly coerce" homeowners into keeping their roof tiles tight by instituting a (new) penalty for allowing one's roof tiles to be loose.

How might the attempt at indirect coercion proceed? The simplest way is for a statute to be passed that says:

(S_1) Penalty for letting it be the case that your roof tiles are loose due to your own negligence, and that one falls off onto a passerby and causes harm: $1,000.

A more complicated statute might have attached different penalties according to whether the harm is compensable or incompensable—for example, $100 for a compensable harm, $5,000 for an incompensable harm. But I shall ignore this. Our concern is not the fairness of the particular penalty attached to the conduct described in the statute; our concern is only why is it permissible to adopt *any* increase in the penalty.

Again, they might have thought to attach a different penalty: not $1,000, but (as it might be) ten days in jail. Wiser legislators would have prevailed, however. People who are sitting in jail are not out on their roofs, tightening their roof tiles. I mention the possibility, not because I think it a good idea, but to stress that the additional penalty they contemplate attaching constitutes, not damages, but punishment. The $1,000 penalty (assuming they choose that) will be, not damages, not even "punitive damages" (which would be paid to the victim), but *mere* punishment—a fine, to be paid to goverenment.

To avoid complaints of ex post facto law, we may imagine that people are given advance warning: the statute is to go into effect only six months after date of passage.

Let us suppose that the small print in the statute tells us that the rules of the game are to be as follows: If A's roof tiles are loose, and B is thereby caused a harm, B may proceed to bring civil suit against A. If B does so, and actually wins the case, B is awarded damages, under existing tort law (T). A then must pay damages to B. In addition, A must pay a fine of $1,000 to the Government Collector-of-Fines. Thus, the penalty for the conduct described in the statute is increased: from mere payment of damages to B, it is increased to payment of damages to B plus a fine to government.

I take it to be a datum that they may adopt this new policy. Why is it permissible for them to do so? It is not at all easy to say. Utilitarian arguments are notoriously overblunt: we know in advance that they permit, and may even prescribe, violations of rights. On the other hand, it is not at all plain that there is any natural right to punish, where punishing involves extracting more from an aggressor than fair damages to the victim.

I should think that the answer lies in the right to self-defense. But what the content of that right is, and how it is to be brought to bear here, are not at all easy to say.

Let us begin with harms. There is a kind of harm that, when inflicted by one person on another, does *not* infringe a right. I have in mind what might be called "market harms." Suppose, for example, that you make lace and now have a cupboardful ready to bring to market tomorrow. This afternoon, I invent a way of making lace cheaply, by machine, which only an expert can tell from handmade lace like yours. I thereby cause you a market harm: I cause a drop in the value of your lace. I do this without damaging your lace or dirtying it, without in any way touching it. It seems plain enough that I infringe no right of yours in doing so.

As we all know, it is not at all clear what precisely counts as a harm. So might it be argued that a market harm is not really a harm at all? I think not. Notice how we react when *government* causes what

I am calling market harms. If I have (at considerable expense) turned parts of my house into rental units, and have done this compatibly with existing law, and if then, the local zoning board passes a new ordinance under which no more than one family unit may live in any one house, it will have caused me a serious market harm—and we shall all feel that I am owed damages.

Market harms are compensable harms, of course. So what I think we may say is this: if A causes B an incompensable harm, then A infringes a right of B's; if A causes B a compensable harm that is not a market harm, then A infringes a right of B's.

Now the relevant thesis about self-defense seems to me to be this: no one has a right that we shall *let* him infringe our rights. No one has a right that we shall not prevent him from infringing our rights.

Let us distinguish between "direct prevention" and "indirect prevention." I directly prevent you from engaging in an activity if I prevent you from engaging in it by force—for example, I break your arm, or lock you up. I indirectly prevent you from engaging in an activity if I do so by attaching a penalty to your engaging in it—I make it be the case (and let you know I made it be the case) that if you engage in it, you will suffer this or that penalty.

It seems to me a plausible idea that if B *knows* that A will infringe a right of B's unless B prevents A from infringing that right, then B is at liberty as regards A to prevent A from doing so—even directly, in other words, by force. A has no right against B that B not do this.[2]

Such knowledge is rare, however. (This explains our views on "preventive detention.") And without such knowledge, B may not directly prevent A from infringing B's right—even if, in fact. A has every intention of infringing the right, and will do so unless prevented from doing so. B is at liberty to protect himself, however: B is at liberty as regards A to *indirectly* prevent A from infringing his right—by attaching a penalty to infringing it. A has no right against B that B not do this.

Each of us has this liberty in regard to *all* others. So we are all at liberty as regards all of ourselves to jointly attach penalties to right-infringing conduct.

Now to say that B is at liberty as regards A to do such and such is *not* to say that it is morally permissible for B to do it. Thus, B may be at liberty as regards A to defend his rights by force, yet it may be

---

2. Readers familiar with Hohfeldian terminology will recognize it here.

morally impermissible for B to do this because too great a degree of force would be required, or the force would have to be used on an innocent bystander. If A propopses to smash B's favorite concrete garden gnome, B is at liberty as regards A to use force to prevent A from doing so—and it would be morally permissible for B to knock A down. But if preventing A requires killing A, or killing an innocent bystander, it would not be morally permisible for B to act.

I concluded, above, that we are all at liberty as regards all of ourselves to jointly attach penalties to right-infringing conduct. Is it morally permissible for us to do so? Presumably yes—so long as the penalties to be attached are not disproportionate to the stringency of the rights infringed.

This, in brief, and in very rough, is how I think the argument to the permissibility of punishing those who engage in right-infringing behavior should go. Something *like* it must surely be right.

If so, the citizens of our imaginary country may pass statute (S_1)—for we are supposing that increasing numbers of incompensable harms are being caused by flying roof tiles, and we may also suppose that none of the compensable harms so caused is a mere market harm.

But perhaps it will be thought that I have gone on too long about this, since increasing the penalty for actually causing harms does not trouble most opponents of government regulation. What they *really* find irksome is, rather, adopting (new) penalties for imposing risks of harms. It is that to which we must now turn.

3. Let us suppose that passing (S_1) turns out to be ineffective: homeowners who were not moved to keep their roof tiles tight by the fact that tort law (T) was in force are not moved to do so by the fact that statute (S_1) is in force. The lazy, who were prepared to risk having to pay damages for harm done, are equally prepared to risk having to pay damages plus $1,000 for harms done.

Now direct coercion seems to be called for, and the legislature considers passing the following additional statute:

(S_2) Penalty for letting it be the case that your roof tiles are loose: $100.

How should (S_2) be administered? One way is to leave it to the citizenry to report seeing loose tiles on their neighbors' roofs—and to the Government-Collector-of-Fines to present an additional bill for $100 to a defendant homeowner who loses a suit under (T). But the legislators do not expect that to be particularly effective. So they consider declaring also that homeowners are to permit monthly inspection of their roof tiles by the Government's Roof-Tile Inspector, who is then to decide whether the penalty set out in (S$_2$) is to be imposed on a homeowner, ensuring that this inspection will be permitted by also passing:

(S$_3$) Penalty for refusing entry to Government Roof-Tile Inspector: $125.

We may (but need not) also imagine that the government's Roof-Tile Expert has found that there is only one way in which one can be absolutely certain of tight roof tiles; so the legislators consider prescribing it by passing also the following:

(S$_4$) Penalty for failing to keep roof tiles tight by use of two-inch stainless steel nails, hammered in three to a tile, in a triangular pattern, apex down, and so forth: $50.

It seems right to imagine the penalty in (S$_2$) to be smaller than the penalty in (S$_1$). Why this seems right is a good question, but I shall not pursue it. It is first cousin to the good question why it seems right that mere attempts at murder should be penalized less heavily than murder itself.

What we must consider, however, is why it would be permissible for the legislature to pass (S$_2$). I take it to be a datum *that* it may, and that our question is only why it may.

Permitting your roof tiles to be loose imposes a risk of harm—indeed, as we are supposing, incompensable harm—on the neighbors. All would be well if we could say that people have a right not to have imposed on them a risk of incompensable harm. An argument exactly like that of the preceding section would show it to be permissible to attach a penalty to permitting one's roof tiles to be loose. Unfortunately it does not seem obvious that people do have a right not to have a risk of incompensable harm imposed on them.

Suppose I play Russian roulette on you. (Gun with six chambers, one bullet) And suppose that nothing happens: the bullet was not under the firing pin when I fired. Suppose that I did this without your knowledge, so that you were caused no fear. Did I infringe a right of yours? It does not seem obvious that I did.

There is an argument to the effect that I did which I think it worth our while to look at. If you break my little finger, you harm me; but if I have to choose, I would prefer your breaking my little finger to your playing Russian roulette on me. If you cut off my little finger, you harm me; but if I have to choose, I would prefer your cutting off my little finger to your playing Russian roulette on me. And does this not suggest that your playing Russian roulette on me *is* harming me—harming me more seriously in fact than your breaking my little finger, or even cutting it off? And do we not assume that to harm a person—where the harm is not a market harm—*is* to infringe a right of that person's?

This argument has *some* merit. Which would I prefer you to give me, a plum or a ticket in the state lottery? Well, I like plums, but not all that much; I'd prefer the lottery ticket. If you give me the ticket, you give me something I'd like to have (indeed, I'd have paid a certain amount for it myself); and even if it turns out I lose, can't you later say that you gave me a benefit—that you benefited me? Why not similarly say, on similar grounds, that if you play Russian roulette on me then you harm me—even if no bullet is under the firing pin when you fire?

Some people think you *do* benefit me by giving me a lottery ticket, even if I do not win the lottery. If they are right, we have to make a choice. We can say (1) harm and benefit are asymmetrical. You benefit me by giving me a chance to win a lot of money, but do not harm me by giving me a chance at death. Or we can say (2) harm and benefit are symmetrical. You benefit me by giving me a chance to win a lot of money, and harm me by giving me a chance at death.

It seems to me that (1) is preferable, for the following reasons.

If we choose (2), we must relinquish the link we assume exists between harm and rights. Suppose I like concrete garden gnomes, but *hate* plastic garden geese. I own a concrete garden gnome, and if you smash it, you harm me, for you destroy a piece of my property. The fact is, however, that if I have to choose, I would prefer your smashing my concrete garden gnome to your installing plastic garden geese on your lawn. If we take this to show that your installing plastic garden geese on your lawn is harming me—harming me more seriously in fact than your smashing my concrete garden gnome—then we can no longer say that if A causes B a (nonmarket) harm, then A infringes a right of B's. For your installing plastic garden geese on your lawn is no infringement of any right of mine.

Why not say that your installing plastic garden geese on your lawn *is* harming me, and therefore *is* an infringement of a right of mine? (I cannot imagine who would wish to say this, but let us see the argument through.) If we do say this, we must give up the link we assume exists between rights and damages. It is a very plausible idea that if A infringes a right of B's, then A owes damages to B. No doubt this is at best a rough-and-ready rule of thumb. (What if A kills B? To whom does A then owe damages? Again, suppose A breaks an appointment with B without warning; must A *pay* B something? Mightn't an apology be quite enough? I leave these worries aside. There is always a presumption that *something* is owing when a right is infringed.) But you plainly owe me nothing at all in damages (or anything else) if, loving plastic garden geese as you do, you install them on your lawn.

If we wish to retain both the link between harm and rights, and the link between rights and damages, we must choose (1)—in other words, we must say that harm and benefit are asymmetrical. If this makes the concept of harm seem puzzling, well and good—it *is* puzzling.

To return to Russian roulette. It is preferable to say (as I suggested) that if I play Russian roulette on you, and there is no bullet under the firing pin when I fire, then I do not harm you. So we do not have available the fact that my doing so is my harming you as ground for thinking that I infringe a right of yours when I do so—for there is no such fact.

Indeed, we have available to us now a ground for thinking that I do not infringe a right of yours when I do so. For consider that rule of thumb again: if A infringes a right of B's, then A owes damages to B. If I play Russian roulette on you, and there is no bullet under the firing pin when I fire, do I owe you damages? *No doubt* I ought not have done what I did; but do I *owe* you anything for doing it? I am inclined to think I do not.

So I think we do well to see if there is not some ground for thinking it permissible for our people to pass statute (S_2) that does *not* rest on the supposition that imposing a risk of harm on someone thereby infringes a right of that person's.

4. Considerations of self-defense help here too. If I am about to play Russian roulette on you, you do not have to sit back and accept my doing so, even if I will have infringed no right of yours if no bullet

is under the firing pin when I fire. You may defend yourslf. You may prevent me from going ahead—directly, if necessary. That is, if stopping me requires breaking my arm, it is morally permissible for you to break my arm. If stopping me requires killing me, it is morally permissible for you to kill me.

I don't say that it would be morally permissible for you to do absolutely anything necessary to prevent me from playing Russian roulette on you. It would not be permissible for you to kill three innocent bystanders in order to stop me. But I should think it permissible for you to use *on me* any degree of force whatever which is necessary to stop me.

If it would be permissible for you to use any degree of force on me whatever (direct prevention), if that were necessary, then I should think it would be permissible, *a fortiori*, for you to attach a penalty (indirect prevention), if that were necessary—for example, arrange that I will be charged $100 if I go ahead, and let me know that you have arranged for that.

But what if you don't *know* that I am about to play Russian roulette on you? What if you think I may be about to do this, but cannot be certain of it? Then it would not be permissible for you to kill me, even if in fact that were necessary to prevent me from doing so. Perhaps there is some degree of force that it would be permissible for you to use on me, even if you were in doubt; but not just any degree at all.

What if you think—indeed, are fairly certain—that *somebody* is about to play Russian roulette on you, but haven't the least idea who? Then I should think it would not be permissible for you to use any degree of force on anyone to prevent that person from doing so. But you surely do not have to sit back and allow it to happen. You are entitled to try to protect yourself by trying indirect prevention.

So it seems to me we are not confronted with a quite general problem about risk imposition. There are cases of risk imposition in which it is plainly permissible (on grounds of self-defense) to arrange for later punishment of the risk imposer—even when it is not known who the risk imposer will be.

What we are confronted with is, rather, a narrower question: *which* risk impositions fall into this category?

Two things seem to come together in cases in which it is plainly permissible to arrange for later punishment of the risk imposer. First, the risk imposed is relatively high. (How high is that? I cannot say. But I think we recognize the extremes when we meet them.) If A plays Russian roulette on B, then A imposes a one-in-six risk of death on B, and that is a relatively high risk of death.

I said "the risk imposed," and not "the risk A imposes." Consider people who play what I'll call Polish roulette. (Gun with thirty-six chambers, one bullet.) Each imposes only a one-in-thirty-six risk of death; but if six Polish-roulette players are planning to play *their* little game on B, they jointly impose the same risk of death on B as one Russian-roulette player does.

There is a second thing at work in these cases that I find considerably less clear. If I buy a gas lawn mower to mow my lawn with, I shall be imposing a risk of death on you—for that gas lawn mower just *might* explode, not only destroying you and me, but many others as well. Of course the risk of that is very small indeed. (Note that if it were relatively high—for example, one in six—you would do well to go to court to get an injunction; and you'd probably get one.) What's the risk? One in 50,000? One in 250,000? But it isn't just the fact that the risk is small that disinclines us to think you may prevent me, even indirectly, from using my new gas lawn mower. For however many chambers there are in my gun (50,000; 250,000), you may still, nevertheless, try indirect prevention on me, and probably use some degree of force as well, if that is necessary to prevent me from firing my gun at your head.

What is this additional feature that is present in the gun-roulette cases and absent in the lawn mower case? Though I have no clear idea, I *suspect* that it has to do with this: We think it morally bad to impose a risk of death on another for the sheer pleasure of doing so, however many chambers in one's gun; we do not think it morally bad to impose a (tiny) risk of death on another while using a gas lawn mower to mow one's lawn. But why we think this is not obvious.

In any case, both of these features are surely present in the case of the negligent homeowners. By hypothesis, there have been increasing numbers of incompensable harms caused by flying roof tiles; perhaps no one homeowner, alone, imposes a relatively high risk of an incompensable harm on anyone, but the risk they jointly impose is relatively high. And if it is morally bad to impose a risk of an incompensable harm for the sheer fun of doing so, it is also morally bad (not *as* bad, no doubt, but all the same morally bad) to impose such a risk out of negligence.

So I should imagine that something approximating the self-defense argument for the propriety of adopting (S₁) should be available to support the propriety of adopting (S_2); and (S_3), if policing is really required; and perhaps even (S_4), if that is really required.

5. The harms caused by flying roof tiles in our hypothetical country are harms caused, not by intention, but by negligence. Three further ways in which A can cause harms to B should be briefly mentioned.

Suppose that (1) eating your bread caused me to go blind, not because you were negligent in making it, but rather because you used a new preservative, not knowing (let us suppose that at the time of your using it, *nobody* knew) that the preservative would cause blindness.

Had the preservative been appropriately tested? And, on the basis of the tests, had it been found to be harmless? Suppose that (1a) it had been. Under a system of strict product liability you would be found liable all the same. Is that fair? I should imagine that a variant of the self-defense argument would show that it is, though I shall not examine it.

Suppose instead that (1b) the preservative had not been tested at all, and this was why nobody knew it was harmful. What is regarded as negligence varies with information. (Compare the nineteenth-century doctor who thought his hands were sufficiently clean when he had merely brushed the mud off.) Nowadays the use of a new preservative, without appropriate testing, would be regarded as gross negligence, and therefore the risk imposed would be considered as similar to the risk imposed by the negligent homeowners of the preceding sections.

Suppose that (2) eating a pint of your ice cream caused my death, not because there was any negligence in your production of it, but rather because I am a diabetic. I should think it would be grossly unfair to hold you legally liable for my death, whether or not I knew I was a diabetic. If a product is labeled "ice cream," and is not also labeled "sugar-free," it is (quite properly) assumed that everyone knows it contains sugar. It is also assumed (equally properly, I think) that people have the responsibility of finding out for themselves the known risks to which they are especially susceptible (due to their own individual characteristics), and thereafter of avoiding activities that increase them. A child, of course, is not expected to know these things, but parents are.

By contrast, nobody is expected to know about the harmful effects of a preservative that has been tested and found harmless; and that,

I think, explains the difference between cases (1a) and (2)—in other words in (2), but not in (1a), the consumer is thought to have accepted the risk.

Suppose that (3) drinking a can of your diet soda caused my death, not because there was anything faulty in your method of making it, but rather because it contained saccharin, and saccharin is (let us suppose) carcinogenic.

Is this just another case like (2)? Carcinogens do not cause cancer in everyone; and if B and C both eat saccharin, but only B gets cancer, there must be some physical difference between them to account for this. But we do not know what this difference is, and therefore nobody is expected to know who is among the especially prone, and therefore who must take special care to avoid saccharin.

If saccharin is known to be carcinogenic, and you do not print a warning on your labels, then your behavior is faulty, and it is right to hold you liable for any deaths you cause. But why not merely require that you print a warning (e.g., "Warning: The Surgeon General Has Determined That Saccharin is Dangerous to Your Health—and this product contains saccharin")? We shall turn to printed warnings in the following section.

6. If I let my roof tiles be loose, or play Russian roulette on you without your permission, I *impose* a risk on you. If I offer you, for purchase, products that are defective, or that for some other reason are dangerous, then I do not impose a risk—I merely *offer* one, for you do not have to buy what I offer for purchase.

Let us set aside cases in which the seller commits fraud—either by commission (explicitly denying known risks) or by omission (failing to mention known risks). Let us suppose the seller's labels plainly display what the known risks are.

The crucial distinction here is between products people merely want, as opposed to products people need. Having said that, I regret having to admit that (like everybody else) I have no very clear idea how to make this distinction. We do recognize extremes easily enough, however. For example, I *want* well-cut clothing, but do not need it; I *need* food. So what I propose we do is attend only to extremes. In the case of things needed, that will mean attending to a hypothetical, rather than a real case. (The real, in this area, is full of noise, foreground as well as background.) And that is unfortunate because the real, in this area, is very much more interesting.

In respect of products that people merely want (cigarettes, diet soda containing saccharin, gin, heavy cream), it is plain that there may not be an outright ban—people must be allowed to run whatever risks they think are worth the payoff in satisfaction. The two major problems here are familiar: on the one hand, there is the possibility of the seduction of children by advertising; on the other, is the fact that, as things stand, society will largely be responsible for paying the costs of medical care for those who are run down by their risks. It is plain, however, that these matters can be dealt with at lower cost in infringements of freedom than by an outright ban of the risky products. (Though I do not say that working out a formula here is easy.)

Of considerably more interest are the products that people need. Consider the following story: The people of a certain country need food; but the only food they need to eat is bread. Moreover, bread is the only food they want to, or even can, eat. So bread is the only food that is produced. Now they have discovered two ways of making bread: one yields safe bread, but is very expensive; the other is cheap, but it yields risky bread. They call the products Safe Bread and Risky Bread.

What are the risks you run when you eat Risky Bread? The main risk is twenty-four hours of very severe stomach cramps. That does not happen often; but it happens often enough to be worrisome. From time to time, the stomach cramps are accompanied by fever, which leaves blindness in its wake; this rarely happens, but it does happen. The country's chemists believe it quite possible that Risky Bread will one day cause death; but so far no one has died of it.

Who would eat Risky Bread, then? Well, Safe Bread is very expensive. Let us single out a class, which I'll call the Very Poor. You are a member of the Very Poor just in case, however hard you work, however carefully you manage your finances, you will starve unless you either (1) eat at least *some* Risky Bread, or (2) break the law (for example, by stealing Safe Bread).

Indeed, we may make (2) into an unrealistic alternative: We may imagine that the police in that country are very efficient and that prison inmates are fed only Risky Bread.

We might imagine that some who are not members of the Very Poor also eat Risky Bread. For example, a man who could afford to live wholly on Safe Bread might prefer to eat a little (or a lot) of Risky Bread with a view to saving up for a four-speaker stereo set.

Here we are, the legislators of that country; and the question arises what, if anything, we should do about this state of affairs.

We can (a), do nothing at all, in the hope that, technology being what it is, someone, someday, will invent a procedure for making safe bread cheaply.

Alternatively, we can (b), ban the production and sale of Risky Bread and do nothing else. This would be outrageous. We would thereby cause the Very Poor to starve to death. (And all prison sentences would essentially be death sentences.)

A better option is (c), to ban the production and sale of Risky Bread, and provide a subsidy to the Very Poor sufficient to enable them to eat Safe Bread.

But a still better option is (d), to permit the production and sale of Risky Bread, while providing a subsidy to the Very Poor sufficient to enable them to eat Safe Bread. I think (d) is preferable to (c): the same end is reached in respect of the Very Poor (for they will be able to eat Safe Bread), and those who wish to eat Risky Bread for the sake of four-speaker stereo sets (compare cigarettes, saccharin, gin, and heavy cream) may continue to do so.

Now choosing (c), or better still, (d), would not be costless, obviously. If there are producers of Risky Bread with large supplies on their hands, or specialized equipment not easily converted to the production of Safe Bread, they would be caused a market harm; and if they are to be paid damages for it, or helped to convert to the production of Safe Bread, or both, that too would have to be paid for, ultimately by taxation.

On the other hand, choosing (a) would be unacceptable in even an only moderately well-off society.

I have no doubt that a beginning student of economics could easily give reason to think that the story I imagined could not, in fact, really, be true of any country. But I see no logical impossibility in it; and the question is, what if it *were* true?

I take a rather hard line, myself, on what people have a right to. For my part, if a stranger is starving, and I can easily give him food, he all the same does not have a right against me that I give it to him. (But I shall not even try to defend this here.) What does seem plain to me, however, is that if a stranger is starving, and I can easily provide food, I *ought* to. If we can, jointly among ourselves, provide for the starving among us at no great cost to ourselves, then it is morally indecent to fail to do so—dividing the costs fairly among ourselves. These are matters of degree, of course. But even an only moderately well-off society can, at no very great cost to itself, provide for its starving.

And similarly for those who are faced with a choice between starving on the one hand, and running a risk of an incompensable harm on the other. It is morally indecent that anyone in a moderately well-off society should be faced with such a choice.

Where things really needed are concerned, then, printed warnings are by no means adequate. How government should regulate is presumably a matter for case-by-case consideration; but that it should regulate seems plain.

7. A man who offers to hire me to work in his plastics factory, or his coal mine, is in some ways like a man who offers to sell me Risky Bread. He does not impose any risks on me; he merely offers one.

How great are the risks? What kind of harm is risked? Is the pay higher than in safe employment, so that I get a return for the risks I run if I accept? (Compare construction work.) I need a job; do I need *that* job? What social cost would be imposed by this or that variety of regulation? How large an increment of safety would be bought by how much cost in safety-devices,and so on? (The noise of the real is deafening.)

I draw no conclusions whatever about government regulation of conditions of employment—other than this: to the extent to which we see the risks as both high and serious, and the prospective employee as having no realistic alternative to accepting the job, we shall, rightly, think that some form of government regulation is, not merely permissible, but required.

11 · *Imposing Risks*

1. I think it pays to distinguish three kinds of case. In the first kind, an agent causes an unwanted outcome by his act, or by each of a series of acts. In the second kind, the agent causes an unwanted outcome, and imposes a risk of a further unwanted outcome. I shall call cases of the second kind cases of "impure risk imposition." In the third kind of case, each time the agent acts he imposes a risk of an unwanted outcome, and it may be that he never at any time actually causes an unwanted outcome. I shall call cases of the third kind cases of "pure risk imposition."

2. B owns some tomatoes; A steals one; A thereby causes an outcome unwanted by B, namely, loss-of-tomato. B also owns some carrots; A steals one; A thereby causes another outcome unwanted by B: loss-of-carrot. Each time A steals a vegetable from B, he causes an outcome unwanted by B. This is a case of the first kind.

I shall leave the limits of "unwanted outcome" dark. I mean to include in the range of unwanted outcomes various kinds of harms to persons or their property, a harm being a more or less long-lasting injury. (I include death itself among the harms.) I also include pain and some cases of discomfort. (If you pinch a man's nose, you may cause him pain, but no harm, there being no injury caused him.) I also include some cases of fear. I also include some cases of nuisance. Thus if I open a glue factory in my house, I thereby cause my neighbor an unwanted outcome in the sense of this essay. By contrast, if I decorate my front lawn with concrete gnomes and plastic geese, I certainly do something my neighbor wishes I had not done, but I do not cause an unwanted outcome in the sense of this essay.[1] Perhaps the difference lies in the pervasiveness of the nuisance in the first case. That is, my neighbor can escape the smell of my factory only with difficulty, and at considerable cost to himself, whereas my neighbor can escape the sight of my gnomes and geese more easily, for example, by averting his eyes as he goes in and out, planting shrubs between our lawns, etc. Or perhaps something more or else is involved. We do think of a dislike of certain kinds of sights as a matter of taste; we do not think of a dislike of certain kinds of smell as a mere matter of taste. It is an interesting question why, but I simply pass it by. I shall make no attempt to give a precise characterization of what counts for present purposes as an unwanted outcome. It may help, however, to say that what I have in mind is *very roughly* characterizable as follows: other things being equal, to cause a person an outcome of the kind I mean is to infringe a right of his.

A particularly interesting subclass of the cases of the first kind is the subclass of cases which involve "threshold effects." Suppose I put a cupful of poison in your pond—not enough to kill the fish, but enough to cause the water to turn muddy-looking. So I have caused you a harm. Now I again put a cupful of poison in your pond. Still the fish live, but now the water smells bad, another harm. I put the same amount of poison in the third time, and lo, the fish all die, a very serious harm to you. Each act in the series causes a harm; the last act causes a far more serious harm than the preceding members, but would not have caused that far more serious harm if it had not been preceded by the earlier members of the series. Cases of the kind I have in mind here, then, are cases in which earlier members of the series each cause a harm, and the cumulative effect of those harms is such that a later member of the series causes a far more grave harm, in the circumstances, than it would otherwise have caused.

I think this subclass of cases of particular interest since I suspect that anyway *some* of the cases of pollution which concern people are cases of acts, or series of acts, which fall into this subclass.

In any event, it is worth taking note of the fact that the cases we have been looking at so far raise no worry about imposition of risk. Each act in every series of acts which falls into the first kind of case is an act which itself causes a harm, and is the harm it actually causes

1. In Cambridge recently, a man brought charges against his neighbor on ground of public nuisance: the neighbor had not mowed his lawn in fourteen years. Plaintiff lost.

which gives the victim his ground for complaint against the agent. Insofar as risk is involved, the risk is that the agent will continue to act, that is, go on causing harm, and eventually perhaps cross a threshold, causing a major harm. The risk, as it were, lies between agent and act, not between act and harm. No special moral considerations raised by imposing risks on people need be attended to in order to settle whether it is morally permissible for the agent to proceed.

3. Cases of the second kind are mixed. Suppose A shoots B in the stomach. Then A causes B a very serious harm; but he also imposes a risk of a still more serious harm, namely death. That is, before the shot, B's chances of dying within the week were (let us suppose) very small, since (let us suppose) B is young, in good health, and so on. After the shot, B's chances of dying within the week are high because the stomach wound may cause shock, may become infected, and so on. B has a twofold complaint against A: he has ground for complaint against A in that A caused him a serious harm, and he has yet another ground for complaint against A in that A has imposed a high risk of death on him.

Series of acts may fall into this class too. Each time I smoke a cigarette in the office, I cause Jones discomfort: runny eyes and nose, throat irritation, and so on. (He also hates the smell.) But if I also, each time, impose a risk on him of lung disorder, and even death, then he has two grounds for complaint against me each time I smoke in the office: the unwanted outcome my smoking does in fact cause him, and the risk of serious harm I thereby impose on him.

Perhaps there are threshold effects here too. It might be that after I have been smoking in the office over a period of time, my next act of cigarette-smoking imposes a considerably greater risk of harm on Jones, in the circumstances, than it would have done had it occurred earlier in the series.

Where the unwanted outcome actually caused is relatively trivial by comparison with the unwanted outcome risked, the outcome actually caused may drop out as appearing to be morally insignificant. The case may then seem to fall into the third kind. That is because the ground for complaint lying in the risk imposed is so much more grave than the ground for complaint lying in the unwanted outcome actually caused.

4. Cases of the third kind are pure. Suppose A played Russian roulette on B. B has ground for complaint against A even if B was caused no harm (no bullet was under the firing pin when A fired), and even if B was unaware of what happened, so that he was caused no fear or discomfort. The ground for complaint lies in the fact that A imposed a risk of death on B.

If A *pours* poison into B's fishpond, A causes B a harm. Suppose, instead, that A's smokestacks emit sulfur dioxide, which then combines with water so that acid rain may or may not fall into B's fishpond. In the latter case, A may or may not cause B the harm which he causes in the former case; in the latter case, then, A's acts *may* merely have imposed a risk of harm.

I shall concentrate on cases of this kind, since they are the ones in which the role of the imposition of risk in moral assessment of action is clearest.

The central problem which pure risk-imposition raises for moral theory is this: which instances of pure risk-imposition are wrongful, and which are not. The central problem which pure risk-imposition raises for political theory is this: which kinds of pure risk-imposition should be made illegal, and which should not. I am able to do no more than make some remarks about one of the difficulties which I think gets in the way of an attempt to solve the central problem which pure risk-imposition raises for moral theory.

5. Suppose that if A does such and such now, he will thereby impose a risk of harm on B. (I shall from here on use the term "harm" to cover all of the unwanted outcomes.) Is it permissible for him to do so? Or would it, instead, be true to say to him "You ought not"?

I should perhaps say straightway that I shall throughout use "It is permissible for so and so to do such and such" as an equivalent of "It is not the case that so and so ought not do such and such."

Some such cases seem to be easy to deal with. If the circumstances are such that A would be justified in causing B that harm, then surely A would be justified in imposing a risk of that harm on B—that is, it would not be true to say to him "You ought not." Suppose, for example, that B is coming at A with a knife, obviously meaning to kill him, and suppose that A has no other way of preserving his life than by killing B. Then, other things being equal, it is permissible for A to cause B's death. It seems to follow that it would be permissible for A, in those circumstances, to impose a risk of death on B.

I said that some of these cases seem to be easy to deal with, but I do not for a moment mean to imply that it is easy to say under what conditions it is permissible for one person to cause a harm to another. Cases of self-defense are relatively easy (but only relatively easy); but in other cases the matter is much less clear. For example, aren't there cases in which it is permissible for A to cause a harm H to B in that doing so is the only way in which A can save C and D from suffering a considerably graver harm G? But which cases are they? The question what in general are the conditions in which causing such and such a harm is permissible is one of the central and most difficult questions in moral theory. My point here is only this: other things being equal, it is permissible for A to do something his doing of which will impose a risk of harm H on B *if* it is permissible for A to cause B harm H. That, I think, seems plausible enough.

If we could also say "only if" with equal plausibility, then it would be plausible to think that risk-imposition generates no independent problem for moral theory. Any question as to whether it is permissible to impose a risk of harm would be reducible to the question whether it is permissible to cause that harm. And we would be free to ignore risk-imposition, and concentrate on the (exceedingly difficult) question under what conditions it is permissible to cause this or that harm.

But there unfortunately is what looks like good reason to think we cannot also say "only if." For example, my neighbor is not now coming at me with a knife. (It is early morning, and he is still asleep.) Nor is there anybody whose life or limb I can save by causing my neighbor a harm. It certainly seems plausible to think that the circumstances which now obtain just are not circumstances in which it would be permissible for me to cause my neighbor any harm at all— a fortiori, it seems plausible to think that if anyone said to me now,

(1) You ought not cause your neighbor's death,

he would be speaking truly. So far so good. In fact I want some coffee now, and must turn my stove on if I am to have some. If I turn my stove on, I impose a risk of death on my neighbor—it is a gas stove, and my turning it on *may* cause gas to leak into his apartment, or it *may* cause an explosion, etc. Feeling a surge of moral anxiety, I ask your advice. You say: Absurd. That's a fine stove, in mint condition, and the risk is utterly trivial. So it's *not* the case that you ought not turn your stove on; that is,

(2) It is permissible for you to turn your stove on.

It is very plausible to think that (1) and (2) are both true; but if they are, we cannot say "only if." For my turning my stove on will impose a risk of death on my neighbor, and if (2) is true it is permissible for me to turn my stove on, but if (1) is true it is not permissible for me to cause my neighbor's death.

But perhaps this example sailed by too quickly. *Is* (2) true?

Suppose that, feeling reassured, I turn my stove on. Lo—astonishingly, amazingly—my doing so causes an explosion in my neighbor's apartment, and thereby causes his death. Question: does this show that you spoke falsely when you said (2)? That seems to me to be a very hard question to answer.

We know what G. E. Moore would say. He would say that—astonishingly, amazingly—it has turned out that you spoke falsely when you said (2). He would say that I am not to blame for my neighbor's death, or for anything else for that matter, for I had every reason to think the risk trivial, and I did not turn the stove on with a view to causing my neighbor's death, or even in the belief that I would cause his death—I turned the stove on only to make coffee, as I do every morning, in perfect safety. And Moore would also say that you are also not to blame for anything, and that you were justified in saying what you said. For, as he would remind us:

> We may be justified in saying many things, which we do not know to be true, and which in fact are not so, provided there is a strong probability that they are.[2]

It could even be added—though Moore does not add it—that, not merely am I not to blame for anything, but more, the act which consisted in my turning the stove on was not a morally bad act: for I had every reason to think the risk trivial, and I did not turn the stove on with a view to causing my neighbor's death, or even in the belief etc. etc., as above.

One who takes Moore's line does not thereby commit himself to the view that risk-imposition generates no independent problem for moral theory; but it is not obvious what independent problem it does generate if Moore's line is correct.

I think we all of us feel *some* inclination to take Moore's line. Surely what a person ought or ought not do, what it is permissible or im-

2. G. E. Moore, *Ethics* (Oxford: Oxford University Press, 1912), p. 121.

permissible for him to do, does not turn on what he thinks is or will be the case, or even on what he with the best will in the world thinks is or will be the case, but instead on what *is* the case.

Some people would say that these things are true only of one of the two (or more?) senses of the word "ought"—the objective sense of "ought." And they would contrast it with a (putative) subjective sense of "ought." Presumably the latter (if there is such a thing) is parasitic on the former—that is, presumably "He (subjective) ought" means "If all his beliefs of fact were true, then it would be the case that he (objective) ought," or perhaps, more strongly "If *all* his beliefs were true, then it would be the case that he (objective) ought." But I greatly doubt that there is such a subjective sense of "ought." On those rare occasions on which someone conceives the idea of asking for my advice on a moral matter, I do not take my field work to be limited to a study of what he believes is the case: I take it to be incumbent on me to find out what *is* the case. And if both of us have the facts wrong, and I therefore advise him to do what turns out a disaster, I do not insist that in one sense my moral advice was all the same true, though in another sense it was false.

But does rejecting the idea that "ought" has a subjective sense require us to agree with Moore in saying that you spoke falsely when you said (2)?

Why might one think that you spoke falsely when you said (2)? Well, here is one possible route to that conclusion. At the time when you spoke there were two possibilities.

(a) If she turns her stove on, she will thereby cause her neighbor's death;

and

(b) If she turns her stove on, she will not thereby cause her neighbor's death.

You thought (a) highly improbable, and that is why you said (2). But suppose we make an assumption, namely that if a proposition says that something will happen, and it does happen, then it always was the case that the something would happen—that is, it always was the case that the proposition was *true*. In particular, then, we would be assuming that since I did turn the stove on and caused my neighbor's death by doing so, (a) was true at the time at which you said (2).

A modest assumption, one would surely think. One who makes it is not committed to supposing that (a) was highly probable at the time at which you said (2), much less that (a) was certain in the sense of having probability 1. I shall have nothing at all to say about what probability is in these remarks; but I shall take it throughout that our assuming that (a) was true at the time at which you said (2) is compatible with your having been right to think at that time that (a) was highly improbable, and indeed with (a)'s having *been* highly improbable.

But aren't we now on the road to Moore's view of the case? For shouldn't we agree that if a person will in fact cause his neighbor's death by turning his stove on, then he ought not turn his stove on?— unless, of course, the circumstances are such that it is permissible for him then to cause his neighbor's death. So shouldn't we conclude, with Moore, that though you were entirely justified in saying (2), you spoke falsely in saying it?

I think it pays to spell this reasoning out in detail. What lies behind it is a very plausible-looking principle, namely,

(IP₁) If A ought not cause B's death, then if it is the case that if A verb-phrases, he will thereby cause B's death, then A ought not verb-phrase.

I call the principle "(IP₁)" since it is the first of three "inheritance principles" I shall draw attention to—"inheritance principle" since it says that verb-phrasing inherits impermissibility from causing B's death. I do think this a plausible-looking principle. If you may not cause a man's death, then surely you may not do that which you would cause his death *by* doing. Here is another sample inheritance principle:

(IP₂) If A ought not kill B, then if it is the case that if A verb-phrases, he will thereby kill B, then A ought not verb-phrase.

Also plausible. If you may not kill a man, then surely you may not do that which you would kill him *by* doing. So far so good. Now we were supposing that if anyone had said to me just before I turned the stove on,

(1) You ought not cause your neighbor's death,

he would have spoken truly. The modest assumption tells us that the outcome of my turning the stove on shows that

(a) If she turns her stove on, she will thereby cause her neighbor's
     death

was then true. So if (IP_1) is true, then you spoke falsely when you
said:

(2) It is permissible for you to turn your stove on.

But perhaps this conclusion will not now seem objectionable: perhaps it now seems right to take Moore's line.

That was a case in which a person imposes a low, indeed an utterly
trivial, risk of harm on another. What of cases in which a person
imposes a high risk of harm on another?

What counts as a low or high risk of this or that harm is presumably
a function not merely of the probability of the harm, but also of the
nature of the harm. (Just as the question in what conditions it is all
right to cause a harm turns not merely on the conditions, but on the
nature of the harm.) Thus a low risk of a bruise might well be a high
risk of death. I simply sidestep the hard question what risk of what
harm is low or high.

A one in six chance of death on the spot is on any view a high risk
of death. So let us imagine A is about to play Russian roulette on B—
six chambers, one bullet. For a reason which will come out, I am
going to suppose that the specially made "roulette gun" with which
A is about to play the game works like this: you aim the gun, you
press a button on the handle, that starts the cylinder spinning, and
if there is a bullet under the firing pin when the cylinder stops spinning, it is fired in the direction of aim. B, let us suppose, is asleep;
he is no threat to anyone, and there is no great good which might be
accomplished by his death. So we say to A:

(3) You ought not press that button.

Let us suppose that A cares nothing for that, and proceeds to press
the button. The cylinder spins; and when it stops spinning, the bullet
is not under the firing pin, so the bullet is not fired. B is not killed;
he is in no way harmed; let us suppose he is not even awakened by
the small click which the cylinder made when it stopped spinning.
Does that show that we spoke falsely when we said (3)?

One is surely inclined to say no. I said in section 4 above:

Suppose A played Russian roulette on B. B has ground for complaint
against A even if B was caused no harm (no bullet was under the firing

pin when A fired), and even if B was unaware of what happened so
that he was caused no fear or discomfort. The ground for complaint lies
in the fact that A imposed a risk of death on B.

Surely it was true to say that A ought not press the button, despite
the fact that no harm of any kind came to B.

What if, not only did no harm come of A's pressing the button,
but some good came of it? It is not easy to imagine a good which
might have come of it, but suppose a small good did come of it. Even
so, one is surely inclined to say that that makes no difference: even
so, we spoke truly when we said to A that he ought not press that
button.

Moore is not in fact committed to saying that our inclination to say
this is a mistake. Moore's utilitarianism commits him to saying that
it was permissible for A to press the button only if there was no other
course of action open to A at the time which would have better
consequences than those which his pressing the button actually did
and will have. And it might well have been the case that there were
courses of action open to A at the time which would have had better
consequences. But if we suppose (no doubt *per impossible*) that the
only other course of action open to A at the time was standing still,
with eyes closed, and counting to ten by twos, then on the usual
assumption about what engaging in that course of action causes, it
was permissible for A to press the button; and if A's pressing the
button caused some good, however small, then pressing the button
was something A quite positively ought to do.

Is there anything to be said for taking Moore's line *here*? Not much,
no doubt; but not nothing.

Why did A press the button on his roulette gun? People who play
Russian roulette on others presumably do so in order to get the fun
of imposing a high risk of death on those others; and let us suppose
that that was the point in it for A. A bad intention, if there ever was
one. And so Moore would say: that shows that although A's pressing
the button was not impermissible, and perhaps was even something
he ought to do, he is all the same to blame for doing it.

As I implied earlier, there is something more that could be said,
although Moore does not in fact say it: that A's act of pressing the
button was a morally bad act. (Compare the possibility of saying that,
not merely am I not to blame for my neighbor's death, but also, my
act of turning the stove on was not a morally bad act.)

And it pays to notice that there is a further possibility. It could also be said—the outcome of the button-pressing having been what it was—that although we spoke falsely when we said

(3) You ought not press that button,

we would have been speaking truly if we had said

(4) You ought not press that button in order to get the fun of imposing a high risk of death on B.

I think that the idea that the falsehood of (3) is compatible with the truth of (4) is one which we have good reason to want to make room for in any case. The point in fact is a familiar one. Here is a more familiar kind of example. Jones has a certain stuff that happens to be a medicine which Smith needs for life. Jones, however, thinks the stuff is a deadly poison, and in that he wants Smith dead, if he gives the stuff to Smith he will give it to Smith only in order to cause Smith's death. The fact that he has that belief and desire surely does not make

(3') Jones ought not give the stuff to Smith

true. Indeed, other things being equal, (3') is false. (That is, given it is not the case that Jones stole the stuff from Dickenson, who also needs it for life; given Jones has not promised to give it to Bloggs, whose child needs it for life; and so on.) What is true is, rather,

(4') Jones ought not give the stuff to Smith to cause Smith's death.

It is plausible to view (4') as true no matter what the consequences of Jones's doing what *it* says he ought not do may turn out to be; and the truth of (4') is surely compatible with the falsehood of (3'). As I said, the point is a familiar one: it is that "ought" attaches, not to acts, but to activities or act-kinds. Hence one who says that we spoke falsely when we said (3), and would have spoken truly if we had said (4), is not thereby convicted of inconsistency.

So can it be said that the reason why we feel that we spoke truly when we said (3) is that we are swamped by the thought that A was to blame for acting as he did, and by the fact that his act of pressing the button was a bad one, and by the fact that there was *something* he did which he ought not have done, namely, press the button in order to get the fun of imposing a high risk of death on B? And, in addition, by the fact that we were so patently justified in saying (3) to him at the time?

Compare Bloggs. Bloggs is in his kitchen, about to press the button on his electric toaster. Why? To make toast, of course; that is his only aim, as it always is, every morning. We are an electrician examining the wiring in the basement. What a weird thing we discover! The wire from the toaster circuit has been attached (by some villain, no doubt) to a roulette gun trained on Dickenson, Bloggs's neighbor, who sleeps late. We come tearing up the back stairs, knowing of the breakfast Bloggs always eats; we call out "You ought not press that button!"

Notice in passing, that we do not call out "It is perfectly all right for you to press that button *now*; but we have some information such that after we have given it to you, it will *then* be the case that you ought not press that button." We do not suppose that what a man ought or ought not do turns on what *he* thinks is the case.

Alas, too late. Bloggs has already pressed the button. Fortunately all went well for Dickenson: no harm came to him. Did we speak truly when we said (3), despite the happy outcome of the episode? "Thank goodness," we say, "what luck!" Do we mean "What luck: although you did something you ought not do, no harm came of your doing it"? Or do we mean "What luck: as things turned out, you did nothing you ought not do"? Is it supposed to be obvious that the former is the preferable interpretation? I do not think that is obvious.

What comes out, I think, is that A's belief and bad intention do play a role in generating our thought that we spoke truly when we said (3) to A. For in the case of Bloggs—who differs from A only in belief and intention—it is not obvious that we spoke truly when we said (3) to him. And is it right to assign belief and intention that role? The case of Jones suggests it is not. For the fact that if Jones gives Smith the stuff he will give Smith the stuff in order to cause Smith's death should surely not be taken to warrant saying that Jones ought not give Smith the stuff.

Perhaps it would be helpful at this point to bring these cases together with the case of me and my stove, and list the options.

First option: We can take Moore's line on all of them. Thus we can say the unhappy outcome of my turning the stove on shows that you spoke falsely when you said

(2) It is permissible for you to turn your stove on,

and that the happy outcome in the cases of A and Bloggs shows that we spoke falsely when we said to them

(3) You ought not press that button.

I have been defending Moore's line because I am inclined to think that people have not sufficiently appreciated what can be said for it, and how difficult finding a plausible alternative turns out to be. On the other hand, I do think we had better try. It *is* counterintuitive to say that it was not permissible for me to turn on the stove, and that it was permissible for A to press the button. It is much less counterintuitive to say that it was permissible for Bloggs to press the button; but perhaps we really should agree that it was true to say to him, as we did, that he ought not press it.

People sometimes wonder whether it is all right for them to take a chance; and we often feel it is, even if, in the event, things turn out badly. Here are five, who are starving. They can be saved if and only if Jiggs saves them; but Jiggs will save them if and only if I cause Smith's death by dropping a very heavy weight on his head. Most people are inclined to think I may not do so. But now here are another five, who are also starving. They can be saved if and only if I fly out in my plane and drop them a food parcel. If I drop the parcel, I impose a risk of death on Smith, for Smith is out in a nearby meadow, tending his sheep, and a sudden gust of wind just might, conceivably, blow the falling food parcel onto Smith's head. Is it permissible for me to take that chance? Of course. The risk is utterly trivial. And I think we do feel inclined to go on saying it was permissible for me to take that chance even if, in the event, a sudden gust of wind does blow the food parcel onto Smith's head. We do not think that the permissibility of acting under uncertainty is to be settled only later, when uncertainty has yielded to certainty.

If these ideas are right—and it really does seem that they are—then risk-imposition does generate an independent problem for moral theory. For there is a further question which then arises, beyond the question what harms we may or may not cause in what circumstances, namely, the question what risks of what harms we may or may not impose in what circumstances.

So we need an alternative to Moore's line. And what should it be?

A few pages back I spelled out a bit of reasoning which issued in Moore's conclusion about the case of me and my stove. It issued, that is, in the conclusion that you spoke falsely when you said:

(2) It is permissible for you to turn your stove on.

Which of the premises of that bit of reasoning should be given up?

Second option: I mention first, only to dismiss it, the possibility that we should give up the modest assumption, and in particular, the assumption that the outcome of my turning the stove on shows that

(a) If she turns her stove on, she will thereby cause her neighbor's death

was true at the time at which you said (2). Giving that up strikes me as a dismal idea, and I suggest we pass it by.

Third option: A more interesting idea is to give up the inheritance principle

(IP_1) If A ought not cause B's death, then if it is the case that if A verb-phrases, he will thereby cause B's death, then A ought not verb-phrase.

Abstract principles in moral theory are always suspect; perhaps it was wrong to think this one so plausible? Perhaps we should say that although it was then true that I ought not cause my neighbor's death, it was nevertheless permissible for me to turn the stove on—despite the fact that if I turned it on I would cause my neighbor's death by turning it on?

But one can't just give up (IP_1) and wash one's hands of the question what light (or dark) doing so sheds on the rest of moral theory. One can't just say: I get out of my trouble if I reject (IP_1), so I reject (IP_1). For example, are we to say that all inheritance principles of the same form as (IP_1), namely,

If A ought not VP_1, then if it is the case that if a VP_2s, he will thereby VP_1, then A ought not VP_2,

are false? Or only some subset of them? And if all of them are false, are there any inheritance principles of any other form which are true? Is there no "nesting" of impermissibilities? Does every set of ascriptions of impermissibility such that no one of them entails any other form a mere concatenation—each requiring independent justification?

Fourth option: I think it pays to take note of the remaining possibility—though it is probably no more than a mere possibility—namely that we should retain (IP_1), and instead say that you would have spoken falsely if you had then said

(1) You ought not cause your neighbor's death.

It sounds a very odd idea, in light of the fact that there was nothing in the circumstances in which I was then placed which would have justified my causing my neighbor's death; but I think it worth taking note of.

Suppose we were to say, quite generally, that it just never is true to say of anyone, whatever the circumstances, that he ought not cause another person's death. Suppose we were to say that what is true is at most that a person ought not impose a high risk of death on another.

Consider the following inheritance principle:

(IP$_3$) If A ought not impose a high risk of death on B, then if it is the case that if A verb-phrases, he will thereby impose a high risk of death on B, then A ought not verb-phrase.

This principle will not generate an argument for the conclusion that you spoke falsely when you said it was permissible for me to turn the stove on; for it was not true that if I turned the stove on, I would impose a high risk of death on my neighbor by doing so—I have been supposing that you were right to think it highly improbable that I would cause his death by turning the stove on. By contrast, it will generate an argument for the conclusion that we spoke truly when we said to A—and to Bloggs—"You ought not press that button." For of both it was true that they would impose a high risk of death on a person by pressing the button.

Notice that while taking this line requires giving up some of the objectivity of "ought," it does not require that all be given up. For if we take this line, we are not committed to supposing that what counts is what the agent thinks on the matter. Thus, in particular, it allows us to say that it not only was permissible for me to turn the stove on, it would have been permissible for me to do so even if I had thought (falsely) that doing so would impose a high risk of death on my neighbor. For my doing so would not in fact have imposed a high risk of death on him. I should think that at least that degree of objectivity must be retained whatever line we take on these matters.

But perhaps it really is too counterintuitive to say that it just never is true to say of anyone, whatever the circumstances, that he ought not cause a person's death. Moreover, I think that if we took this line, we should also have to say that it never is true to say of anyone, whatever the circumstances, that he ought not kill a person; and that is, if possible, even more counterintuitive. But I think that we would have to say this further thing. For didn't I kill my neighbor by turning my stove on?—given that my turning the stove on caused an explosion in his apartment, and he died because he was in the apartment at the time? Presumably we could still have it that a person ought not shoot a man in the head, or strangle him, and so on, for doing these things imposes a high risk of death on the victim. But we should be unable to say that a person ought not actually kill another; and that sounds quite unacceptable.

So the third option is probably the best. But I leave the matter open, not having any clear idea how to answer the questions I raised in discussing it.

6. I have been assuming throughout that B does not consent to A's imposing the risk of harm on him—for if he does consent to this, if he wittingly and freely consents to it, then it seems plausible to think that no problem arises: A may impose the risk.

There are notorious difficulties which arise about consent; but there is one which I think has not been much attended to—I do no more than draw attention to it here.

Richard Posner (for purposes which are not relevant here) said the following in a recent article:

> I contend, I hope uncontroversially, that if you buy a lottery ticket and lose the lottery, then, so long as there is no question of fraud or duress, you have consented to the loss.[3]

Vain hope!—his contention was objected to, indeed sneered at, by Jules Coleman and Ronald Dworkin in their commentaries on Posner's article.[4] But what exactly is their objection? I think that what Dworkin had in mind is the same as what Coleman had in mind in saying:

> If I buy the lottery ticket and lose my loss may be a fair or legitimate one, one that it may be appropriate to pin on me. It would be fair because I had willingly taken a risk by consenting to or voluntarily joining an enterprise that was risky in the relevant way. But it would hardly follow that I had consented to the loss.[5]

3. Richard Posner, "The Ethical and Political Basis of the Efficiency Norm in Common Law Adjudication," *Hofstra Law Review* 8 (Spring 1980), p. 492.

4. Jules Coleman, "Efficiency, Utility, and Wealth Maximization," and Ronald Dworkin, "Why Efficiency?," in *Hofstra Law Review*, note 3 above.

5. Coleman, ibid., pp. 534–535.

And what *did* Coleman have in mind in writing those sentences? I hazard a guess it is the following. Suppose that A offers B an $n ticket in a lottery A is running. B buys it. Then the following is true:

(1) B has consented to its being the case that (If A does not draw B's name on ticket-drawing day, then B loses his $n).

Alas for B, the following turns out to be true:

(2) A does not draw B's name on ticket-drawing day.

I hazard a guess that Coleman's and Dworkin's point is this: it does not follow that

(3) B has consented to its being the case that B loses his $n

is true. That is, the conjunction of (1) and (2) does not entail (3).

If that is their point, then I should think they are right. Modal principles of the form

If [M (if p then q) and p] then Mq

have always to be watched; and the modal principle which results from writing "B has consented to its being the case that" in for "M" really does look suspect.

But if that is their point, then why the sneering? What if Posner had instead written:

I contend, I hope uncontroversially, that if you buy a lottery ticket and lose the lottery, then, so long as there is no question of fraud or duress, you have no ground for complaint about your losing.

That contention looks much more plausible. And so far as I can see, nothing Dworkin says makes any trouble for it at all. (Of course, whether my version would have served Posner's purposes as well as his own is quite another matter. I think it would have, but that has no bearing on our present concerns.)

But something Coleman says makes trouble for the hope of obtaining an easy generalization from it; that is, Coleman has a further point (I do not think he sees it is a further point) and that is what raises the interesting difficulty about consent. What I have in mind comes out in the following example, which was suggested by Coleman's own example.[6] Suppose there are two ways in which I can get

6. Ibid., pp. 536–537, fn. 45.

home from the station at the end of the day. The first is pleasant, passes through a brightly lit middle-class shopping area, is quite safe, but is long. The second way is unpleasant, passes through an ill-lit area of warehouses, is unsafe, but is short. Nobody has ever been mugged while walking along Pleasant Way; people have from time to time been mugged on Unpleasant way. Here I am, at the station; I am tired; I think "The hell, I'll chance it, I'll go home via Unpleasant Way." I then promptly get mugged. I surely have ground for complaint!—at least against the mugger, and perhaps also against the city.

Perhaps it was foolish to walk through Unpleasant Way at night. (But the more tired I was, and the less risky Unpleasant Way is, the less foolish it was.) And my friends can later say "Well, it would be out of place for you to feel *surprised* at the fact that you got mugged." But that is different from "Well, it would be out of place for you to feel *wronged*." That comment would itself be out of place.

But didn't I consent to the *risk* of being mugged? And there was no fraud, no misperception of any kind: I knew perfectly well what the risk was. And there was no duress, no coercion or compulsion: I was not under pressure from any person to choose that route home. Of course I chose that route because I was tired. But my fatigue no more coerced or compelled me than any person did.

It *is* plausible to think that one who loses in a nonfradulent lottery, which he entered without duress, has no ground for complaint when he loses. Why is it that I have ground for complaint when I get mugged on Unpleasant Way? I think it a nice problem.

I think that finding an answer requires looking into the content of the consent. More generally, that it is important not merely to look at whether a person's consent is witting and free (that is where most of the attention has been focused), but also at what exactly he consented to. (We talk altogether too glibly of consenting to a risk.) It was easy enough to say what B had consented to when he accepted A's offer of a lottery ticket—see (1) above. What did I consent to in the story I just told?

In the first place, and obviously, there plainly is no person such that I consented to his mugging me.

Second, there is no person or persons such that I consented to his or their imposing a risk of being mugged on me. (In any case, nobody did impose that risk on me. Compare Unpleasant Way with a part of the city in which people indulge in playing Russian roulette on passersby. If I had walked through there, and somebody had played Russian roulette on me, somebody would have imposed a risk on me. But not by my consent.)

Third, I did not consent to Unpleasant Way's being dangerous to walk through at night, or to its being the case that one who walks through it at night is at risk of being mugged. So in particular, I did not consent to its being the case that if I walk through Unpleasant Way at night, then I get mugged—or even to its being the case that if I walk through Unpleasant Way at night, then I am at risk of being mugged.

I am inclined to think that the most that can be said is this: knowing that Unpleasant Way is dangerous to walk through at night, knowing that one who walks through it at night is at risk of being mugged, I consented to its being the case that I walk through Unpleasant Way at night. (Compare the workman in a risky factory. I am inclined to think that the most that can be said of him is this: knowing the factory is risky, he consents to work in it.) And I am inclined to think also that if that is the most that can be said, then my consent goes no way at all towards removing my ground for complaint about what happened to me on Unpleasant Way.

But those ideas call for more, and closer, attention than I can give them now; and it *may* be that there is no future in them in any case.[7]

---

7. I am indebted to all of the participants at the Conference on Risk and Consent, sponsored by the Center for Philosophy and Public Policy at the University of Maryland, for their criticisms of an earlier draft of the present paper, but in particular, to Mary Gibson and Douglas MacLean.

12 · *Remarks on Causation and Liability*

1. Under traditional tort law, a plaintiff had to show three things in order to win his case: that he suffered a harm or loss, that an act or omission of the defendant's caused that harm or loss, and that the defendant was at fault in so acting or refraining from acting. It is widely known by nonlawyers that liability may nowadays be imposed in many kinds of cases in which there is no showing that the third requirement is met. Strict product liability is one example. Thus if you buy a lawn mower, and are harmed when you use it, then (other things being equal) you win your suit against the manufacturer if you show that you suffered a harm when you used it, and that the harm you suffered was caused by a defect in the lawn mower—as it might be, a missing bolt. You do not need also to show the manufacturer was at fault for the defect; it is enough that the lawn mower was defective when it left his hands, and that the defect caused your harm.

What may be less widely known by nonlawyers is that there have been some recent cases which were won without plaintiff's having shown that the second requirement was met, namely, that of causation. Perhaps the most often discussed nowadays is *Sindell v. Abbott Laboratories*,[1] which was decided by the California Supreme Court in 1980. Plaintiff Sindell had brought an action against eleven drug companies that had manufactured, promoted, and marketed diethylstilbesterol (DES) between 1941 and 1971. The plaintiff's mother took DES to prevent miscarriage. The plaintiff alleged that the defendants knew or should have known that DES was ineffective as a miscarriage-preventive, and that it would cause cancer in the daughters of the

1. 26 Cal. 3d 588, 163 Cal. Rptr. 132, 607 P. 2d 924 (1980).

mothers who took it, and that they nevertheless continued to market the drug as a miscarriage-preventive. The plaintiff also alleged that she developed cancer as a result of the DES taken by her mother. Due to the passage of time, and to the fact that the drug was often sold under its generic name, the plaintiff was unable to identify the particular company which had manufactured the DES taken by her mother; and the trial court therefore dismissed the case. The California Supreme Court reversed. It held that if the plaintiff "joins in the action the manufacturers of a substantial share of the DES which her mother might have taken," then she need not carry the burden of showing which manufactured the quantity of DES that her mother took; rather the burden shifts to them to show they could not have manufactured it.[2] And it held also that if damages are awarded her, they should be apportioned among the defendants who cannot make such a showing in accordance with their percentage of "the appropriate market" in DES.

In short, then, the plaintiff need not show about any defendant company that it caused the harm in order to win her suit.

Was the Court's decision in *Sindell* fair? I think most people will be inclined to think it was. On the other hand, it is not easy to give principled reasons why it should be thought fair, for some strong moral intuitions get in the way of quick generalization. What I want to do is to bring out some of the sources of worry.

But the case is in fact extremely complicated, so I suggest we begin with a simpler case, *Summers v. Tice*,[3] which the same court had decided in 1948, and which the plaintiff in *Sindell* offered as a precedent.

2. Plaintiff Summers had gone quail hunting with the two defendants, Tice and Simonson. A quail was flushed, and the defendants fired negligently in the plaintiff's direction; one shot struck the plaintiff in the eye. The defendants were equally distant from the plaintiff, and both had an unobstructed view of him. Both were using the same kind of gun and the same kind of birdshot; and it was not possible to determine which gun the pellet in the plaintiff's eye had come from. The trial court found in the plaintiff's favor, and held both defendants "jointly and severally liable." That is, it declared the

2. One defendant had already been dismissed from the action on the ground that it had not manufactured DES until after the plaintiff was born.
3. 33 Cal. 2d 80, 199 P. 2d I (1948).

plaintiff entitled to collect damages from whichever defendant he chose. The defendants appealed, and their appeals were consolidated. The California Supreme Court affirmed the judgment.

Was the Court's decision in *Summers* fair? There are two questions to be addressed. First, why should either defendant be held liable for any of the costs? And second, why should each defendant be held liable for all of the costs—that is, why should the plaintiff be entitled to collect all of the costs from either?

Why should either defendant be held liable for any of the costs? The facts suggest that in the case of each defendant, it was only .5 probable that he caused the injury; normally, however, a plaintiff must show that it is more likely than not, and thus more than .5 probable, that the defendant caused the harm complained of if he is to win his case.

The Court's reply is this:

> When we consider the relative position of the parties and the results that would flow if plaintiff was required to pin the injury on one of the defendants only, a requirement that the burden of proof on that subject be shifted to defendants becomes manifest. They are both wrongdoers—both negligent toward plaintiff. They brought about a situation where the negligence of one of them injured the plaintiff, hence it should rest with them each to absolve himself if he can. The injured party has been placed by defendants in the unfair position of pointing to which defendant caused the harm. If one can escape the other may also and plaintiff is remediless.

The Court's argument seems to me to go as follows. The plaintiff cannot determine which defendant caused the harm. If the plaintiff has the burden of determining which defendant caused the harm, he will therefore be without remedy. But both defendants acted negligently "toward plaintiff," and the negligence of one of them caused the harm. Therefore the plaintiff should not be without remedy. Therefore it is manifest that the burden should shift to each defendant to show that he did not cause the injury; and, if neither can carry that burden, then both should be held liable.

The argument does not say merely that both defendants are wrongdoers, or that both defendants acted negligently: it says that both defendants acted negligently "toward plaintiff"—that is, both were in breach of a duty of care that they owed to the plaintiff. Suppose, for example, that the plaintiff had brought suit, not against the two hunters who were out quail hunting with him, but against three people: the two hunters, and Jones, who was driving negligently in New York that afternoon. All three members of that class of defendants were wrongdoers, all three acted negligently, and indeed one of the three caused the harm, though it is not possible to tell which. But it could hardly be thought fair for all of them, and so a fortiori for Jones, to have to carry the burden of showing that *his* negligence did not cause the harm. Perhaps he could carry that burden easily; but it would not be fair to require that he do so on pain of liability for the harm. The argument excludes Jones, however, for although he was negligent, he was not negligent toward the plaintiff.

And even that qualification is not enough—we must suppose a further qualification to lie in the background of the argument. Consider Smith, who was driving negligently in California that day, and who in fact nearly ran the plaintiff down as the plaintiff was on his way to go quail hunting. And suppose that the plaintiff had brought his suit against the following three people: the two hunters and Smith. All three were wrongdoers, all three acted negligently, and indeed negligently toward the plaintiff, and one of the three caused the harm, though it is not possible to tell which. But it could hardly be thought fair for all of them, and so a fortiori for Smith, to have to carry the burden of showing that *his* negligence did not cause the harm. As it stands, the argument does not exclude Smith, for he *was* negligent toward the plaintiff. So we must suppose that the Court had in mind not merely that all the defendants were negligent toward the plaintiff, but also that their negligent acts were in a measure likely to have caused the harm for which the plaintiff sought compensation.

There lurks behind these considerations what I take to be a deep and difficult question, namely: Why does it matter to us whose negligent act caused the harm in deciding who is to compensate the victim?

3. It will help to focus on a hypothetical variant of the case, which I shall call *Summers II*. Same plaintiff, same defendants, same negligence, same injury as in *Summers;* but *Summers II* differs in that during the course of the trial, evidence suddenly becomes available which makes it as certain as empirical matters ever get to be, that the pellet lodged in plaintiff Summers' eye came from defendant Tice's gun. Tort law being what it is, defendant Simonson is straightway dismissed from the case. And isn't that the right outcome? Don't we feel

that Tice alone should be held liable in *Summers II*? We do not feel that Simonson should be dismissed with a blessing: he acted very badly indeed. So did Tice act badly. But Tice also caused the harm, and (other things being equal) fairness requires that he pay for it.[4] But why? After all, both defendants acted equally negligently toward Summers in shooting as they did; and it was simple good luck for Simonson that, as things turned out, he did not cause the harm to Summers.

It is arguable that there is no principled stopping place other than Tice.[5] Consider, for example, a rule which says: Liability is to be shared among the actual harm-causer and anyone else (if there is anyone else) who acted as negligently toward the victim, and who nearly caused him a harm of the same kind as the actual harm-causer did. Under this rule, liability should presumably be shared between Tice and Simonson in *Summers II*. But only presumably, since what, after all, counts for these purposes as a "harm of the same kind"? (Compare Smith of the preceding section.) And by what principle should liability be shared only among those who acted negligently toward the victim? (Compare Jones of the preceding section.)

Moreover, even if there is no principled stopping place *other than* Tice, it would remain to be answered what is the principle behind a rule which stops liability *at* Tice.

It pays to begin by asking: What if Tice has an insurance policy that covers him for the costs of harms he causes? We would not feel it unfair for the insurance company to pay Summers off for Tice.

Nor do we feel there would be any unfairness if a friendly philanthropist paid Summers off for Tice.

But the insurance company could simply be living up to its contract with Tice to pay what Tice would have had to pay if he had had no such contract; and the philanthropist would simply be making a gift to Tice—paying a debt for Tice which Tice would otherwise have had to pay himself.

Nevertheless these considerations do bring out that paying Summers' costs is not something we wish to impose on Tice by way of

4. Some people feel that Summers himself should share in the costs, in the thought that Summers assumed a risk in going out quail hunting with Tice and Simonson. I do not myself share that intuition. Anyone who does is invited to imagine, instead, that Summers is a farmer, who was passing by, on his way to market.

5. See Wex S. Malone, "Ruminations on Cause-In-Fact," *Stanford Law Review* 9 (December 1956), p. 66.

retribution or punishment for his act. If imposing this were a punishment, we would not regard it as acceptable that a third party (insurance company, friendly philanthropist) suffer it as a surrogate for Tice.[6]

What we are concerned with here is not blame, but only who is to be out of pocket for the costs. More precisely, why it is Tice who is to be out of pocket for the costs. It pays to take note of what lies on the other side of this coin. You and your neighbor work equally hard, and equally imaginatively, on a cure for the common cold. Nature then smiles on you: a sudden gust of wind blows your test tubes together, and rattles your chemicals, and lo, there you have it. Both of you acted well; but who is to be in pocket for the profits? You are. Why? That is as deep and difficult a question as the one we are attending to. I think that the considerations I shall appeal to for an answer to our question could also be helpfully appealed to for an answer to this one, but I shall not try to show how.

There is something quite general at work here. "B is responsible for the damage to A's fence; so B should repair it." "The mess on A's floor is B's fault; so B should clean it up." Or anyway, B should have the fence repaired, the mess cleaned up. The step is common, familiar, entirely natural. But what warrants taking it?

It is a plausible first idea that the answer lies in the concept "enrichment." Suppose I steal your coffee mug. I am thereby enriched, and at your expense. Fairness calls for return of the good: I must return the coffee mug.

That model is oversimple, of course: it cannot be brought to bear directly. For only I can return the coffee mug, whereas by contrast, anyone can pay the costs of having the fence repaired or the mess cleaned up, either in his own time and effort, or in whatever it takes to get someone else to do these things.

Well, fairness needn't call for the return of the very coffee mug I took, and surely can't call for this if I have now smashed it. Replacement costs might do just as well. Or perhaps something more than replacement costs, to cover your misery while thinking you'd lost your mug. In any case, anyone can pay those costs. But I must pay them to you because I was the person enriched by the theft of the mug, and at your expense. So similarly, perhaps we can say that B

6. A number of people have drawn attention to the general point at work here. See, for example, Jules Coleman, "On the Moral Argument for the Fault System," *The Journal of Philosophy* 71 (August 1974).

must pay the costs of having the fence repaired because B was the person who enriched himself, and at A's expense, by the doing of whatever it was he did by the doing of which he damaged the fence.

Enrichment? Perhaps so: B might literally have made a profit by doing whatever it was he did by the doing of which he made a mess on A's floor. (E.g., mudpie-making for profit.) Or anyway, he might have greatly enjoyed himself. (E.g., mudpie-making for fun.) Perhaps he made the mess out of negligence? Then he at least made a saving: he saved the expense in time or effort or whatever he would have had to expend to take due care. And he made that saving at A's expense.

But this cannot really be the answer—it certainly cannot be the whole answer. For consider Tice and Simonson again. They fired their guns negligently in Summers' direction, and Tice's bullet hit Summers. Why should Tice pay Summers' costs? Are we to say that that is because Tice enriched himself at Summers' expense? Or anyway, that Tice made a saving at Summers' expense—a saving in time or effort or whatever he would have had to expend to take due care? Well, Simonson saved the same as Tice did, for they acted equally negligently.[7] It would have to be said "Ah, but Tice's saving was a saving *at Summers' expense*—and Simonson's was not." But what made Tice's saving *be* a saving at Summers' expense? Plainly not the fact that his negligence was negligence 'toward' Summers, for as the Court said, Tice and Simonson were both "negligent toward plaintiff." It if is said that what made Tice's saving be a saving at Summers' expense is the fact that it was Tice's negligence that caused Summers' injury, then we are back where we were: for what we began with was why that fact should make the difference.

Drawing attention to cases in which two are equally enriched also brings out more clearly a problem which is already present when only one is. Why is it B who must pay the costs of having the mess on A's floor cleaned up, when it is B who caused it to be there? Because in doing what he did which caused it to be there he enriched himself (or made a saving) at A's expense. But if what made the enrichment be *at A's expense* is the fact that his act caused the mess to be there, then the question has not been answered: we have merely been offered new language in which to ask it.

7. The general point I illustrate here was made by Jules Coleman in "Corrective Justice and Wrongful Gain," *The Journal of Legal Studies* 2 (June 1982).

Perhaps it pays to set aside the concept 'enrichment' and attend, instead, to what we have in mind when we characterize a person as "responsible." Consider again: "B is responsible for the damage to A's fence; so B should repair it." Doesn't the responsible *person* pay the costs of damage he or she is responsible *for*? And don't we place a high value on being a responsible person?

Similarly, the responsible person pays the costs of damage which is his or her fault.

This is surely right; but what lies behind it? *Why* do we think it a good trait in a man that he pays the costs of damage he is responsible for? Why do we expect him to?

I hazard a guess that the, or anyway an, answer may be found in the value we place on freedom of action, by which I mean to include freedom to plan on action in the future, for such ends as one chooses for oneself. We take it that people are entitled to a certain "moral space" in which to assess possible ends, make choices, and then work for the means to reach those ends. Freedom of action is obviously not the only thing we value; but let us attend only to considerations of freedom of action, and bring out how they bear on the question in hand.

If A is injured, his planning is disrupted: he will have to take assets he meant to devote to such and such chosen purpose, and use them to pay the costs of his injury. Or that is so unless he is entitled to call on the assets of another, or others, to pay the costs for him. His moral space would be considerably larger if he were entitled to have such costs paid for him.

But who is to pay A's costs? On whose assets is it to be thought he is entitled to call? Whose plans may *he* disrupt?

A might say to the rest of us, "Look, you share my costs with me now, and I'll share with you when you are injured later." And we might then agree to adopt a cost-spreading arrangement under which the costs of all (or some) of our injuries are shared; indeed, we might the better secure freedom of action for all of us if we did agree to such an arrangement. The question which needs answering, however, is whether A may call on this or that person's assets in the absence of agreement.

One thing A is not entitled to do is to choose a person X at random, and call on X's assets to pay his costs. That seems right; but I think it is not easy to say exactly why. That is, it will not suffice to say that if all we know about X is that X is a person chosen at random, then we know of no reason to think that a world in which X pays A's costs is better than a world in which A pays A's costs. That is surely true. But by the same token, if all we know about X is that X is a person chosen at random, then we know of no reason to think that a world in which A pays A's costs is better than a world in which X pays A's costs. So far, it looks as if flipping a coin would be in order.

What I think we should do is to look at A's situation *before* any costs have been incurred. A has been injured. Now he wants to be "made whole": he wants the world changed in such a way as to make him be as nearly as possible what he would have been had he not been injured. That is what he needs money for. But the freedom of action of other people lends weight to the following: If A wants the world changed in that (or any other) way, then—other things being equal— A has to pay the costs, in money, time, energy, whatever is needed, unless he can get the voluntary agreement of those others to contribute to those costs. Again, A's wanting the world changed in that (or any other) way is not by itself a reason to think he may call on another person to supply him with what he needs to change it. It follows that A is not entitled to call on a person unless that person has a feature other than just that of being a person, which marks *his* pockets as open to A. A cannot, then, choose a person X at random, and call on X to pay the costs—on pain of infringing X's freedom of action.

And it could hardly be thought that while A is not entitled to call on X's assets before A has spent anything, A becomes entitled to call on X's assets the moment he has.

So A is not entitled to choose a person X at random, and call on X's assets to pay his costs.

Well, here is B, who is considerably richer than A. Perhaps some people will feel that that does entitle A to call on B. I want to set this aside. As I said, freedom of action is not the only thing we value, but I want to bring out *its* bearing on the question in hand; so I shall sidestep this issue by inviting you to imagine that no one is any richer than anyone else.

A is injured. Let us supply his injury with a certain history. Suppose, first, that A himself caused it—freely and wittingly, for purposes of his own. And suppose, second, that it is not also true of any other person X that X caused it, or even that X in any way causally contributed to it. Thus:

(1)   A caused A's injury, freely, wittingly, for purposes of his own; and no one other than A caused it, or even causally contributed to it.

We can easily construct examples of injuries which consist in loss or damage to property which have histories of this kind—for example, A might have broken up one of his chairs, to use as kindling to light a fire to get the pleasure of looking at a fire. It is harder to construct examples of injuries which consist in physical harm which have histories of this kind. But it is possible—for example, A might have cut off a gangrenous toe to save his life. A might have cut off his nose to spite his face.

Suppose now that having caused himself the injury, A wants for one or another reason to be made whole again. That will cost him something. Here is B. Since (1) is true of A's injury, B's freedom of action protects him against A: A is not entitled to call on B's assets for the purpose—A is not entitled to disrupt B's planning to reverse an outcome wholly of his own planning which he now finds unsatisfactory.

That seems right. And it seems right whatever we imagine true of B. B may be vicious or virtuous, fat or thin, tall or short; none of this gives A a right to call on B's assets. Again, B might have been acting very badly indeed contemporaneously with A's taking the steps he took to cause his own injury: B might even have been imposing risks of very serious injuries on A concurrently with A's act—for example, B might have been playing Russian roulette on A, or throwing bricks at him. No matter: if A's injury has the history I described in (1), then B's freedom of action protects him against the costs of it.

If that is right, then the answer to our question falls out easily enough. Let us suppose that A is injured, and that B did not cause the injury, indeed, that he in no way causally contributed to A's injury. Then whatever did in fact cause A's injury—whether it was A himself who caused his injury, or whether his injury was due entirely to natural causes, or whether C or D caused it—there is nothing true of B which rules out that A's injury had the history described in (1), and therefore nothing true of B which rules out that A should bear his own costs. Everything true of B is compatible with its being the case that A's costs should lie where they fell. So there is no feature of B which marks his pockets as open to A—A is no more entitled to call on B than he is entitled to call on any person X chosen at random.

Causality matters to us, then, because if B did not cause (or even causally contribute to) A's injury, then B's freedom of action protects him against liability for A's costs. And in particular, it is Simonson's freedom of action which protects him against liability for Summers' costs in *Summers II*, for in that case it was discovered that Tice had caused the injury.

I have been saying that freedom of action is not the only thing we value, and that is certainly true. But if I am right that it is freedom of action which lies behind our inclination to think causality matters— and in particular, our inclination to think it right that Simonson be dismissed once it has been discovered that he did not cause Summers' injury—then these considerations by themselves show we place a very high value on it, for those inclinations are very strong.

Since the question we began with was the question why causality matters to us, we could acceptably stop here. But I think it pays to press on, to see how far attention to freedom of action will carry us.

For as we know, however much causality matters to us in assessing liability, it is on no plausible view sufficient for liability. The fact that Tice caused Summers' injury does not by itself yield the conclusion that he is properly to be held liable for it; what yields this conclusion is the conjunction of the fact that Tice caused the injury *and* the relevant facts about Tice's fault—that he was negligent, that the injury was of a kind such that Tice's act was negligent in that he did not exercise the care which is called for precisely in order to avoid causing an injury of that kind, and so on. Suppose A's injury was caused by B as in

(2) B caused A's injury by some freak accident—by doing something which he took all due care in the doing of, and which he could not have been expected to foresee would lead to harm.

Then alas for A, it seems right that A's costs lie where they fell: the fact that B caused the injury does not suffice for imposing liability on him. When fault is added to causality, however, things look very different to us. If A's injury was caused by B as in

(3) B caused A's injury wrongfully—by intention, or out of negligence

then B must plainly pay.

Why this difference between (2) and (3)? It might be thought we could say this. In (3), B caused A's injury by doing what it was a wrong in him to do, and freedom of action has its limits: one is not free to act wrongly. By contrast, in (2), there was nothing B did which it was a wrong in him to do, no constraint of morality that he violated; so it is his freedom of action that protects him against liability for A's costs in (2).

But I think this account of (2) and (3) is oversimple. In the first place, I think we *are* free to act wrongly—so long, that is, as we cause no harm to others (more generally, infringe no right of theirs) in doing so. It is not the fact that B acted wrongly in (3) that makes him liable for A's costs in (3): B can have been acting as wrongfully as you like concurrently with the coming about of A's injury and is all the same not liable for A's costs if A caused his own injury—as in (1). What makes B liable for A's costs in (3) is rather that in (3) he wrongfully caused A's injury. It is *that* which fixes that his freedom of action does not protect him against liability for A's costs in (3).

Second, it is not the fact that B did not act wrongly in (2) that protects him against liability for A's costs in (2). For what if A's injury had a history of the following kind:

(4) B caused A's injury, and did so freely and wittingly, but did so to save himself from a very much greater injury, and was justified in so acting.

B did not act wrongly in (4), and is all the same properly held liable for A's costs in (4). A case of the kind I have in mind, which comes from the legal literature, is *Vincent v. Lake Erie Transportation Co.*[8] in which a ship's captain tied his ship to a dock to protect it from the risk of being sunk in a storm. The dockowner's dock was damaged by the ship's banging against it in the storm, and he sued the ship-owner. The court declared that the ship's captain had acted properly and well; but it (surely rightly) awarded damages to the plaintiff. A second case of the kind I have in mind, which comes from the literature of moral theory, is Joel Feinberg's story of a hiker, lost in a sudden mountain storm, who broke into an empty cabin and burned the furniture to keep warm; the hiker was plainly justified in so acting,

8. 10 Minn. 456, 124 NW 221 (1910).

but he owes the cabinowner compensation for the damage he did.[9]

Why is B protected against liability for A's costs in (2), but not in (4)? B acts wrongly in neither case, and it is not at all easy to see the source of the difference.

Richard A. Epstein offers the following justification for the imposition of liability on the defendant in *Vincent:*

> Had the Lake Erie Transportation Company owned both the dock and the ship, there could have been no lawsuit as a result of the incident. The Transportation Company, now the sole party involved, would, when faced with the storm, apply some form of cost-benefit analysis in order to decide whether to sacrifice its ship or its dock to the elements. Regardless of the choice made, it would bear the consequences and would have no recourse against anyone else. There is no reason why the company as a defendant in a lawsuit should be able to shift the loss in question because the dock belonged to someone else. The action in tort in effect enables the injured party to require the defendant to treat the loss he has inflicted on another as though it were his own. If the Transportation Company must bear all the costs in those cases in which it damages its own property, then it should bear those costs when it damages the property of another.[10]

These seem to me to be very helpful remarks. Suppose the name of the man who actually owns the dock is Jones. What Epstein points to is this: If the dock had belonged, not to Jones, but to the Lake Erie Transportation Company, then the Company would not have been entitled to call on Jones's assets for funds to repair it. Why not? Consider again

(1) A caused A's injury, freely, wittingly, for purposes of his own; and no one other than A caused it, or even causally contributed to it.

If the dock had belonged to the Lake Erie Transportation Company, then the Company would have caused itself an injury (by causing an injury to its own dock); so the history of its injury would have been as described in (1), and the Company would not have been entitled to call on Jones's assets for the costs.

9. Joel Feinberg, "Voluntary Euthanasia and the Inalienable Right to Life," *Philosophy and Public Affairs* 7 (Winter 1978).

10. Richard A. Epstein, "A Theory of Strict Liability," *The Journal of Legal Studies* 2 (January 1973), p. 158.

So far so good. But all of that is counterfactual. The dock in fact belongs to Jones, not to the Lake Erie Transportation Company, and how do we get from the counterfactual remarks about what would have been the case if the Company had owned the dock to what Jones is entitled to, given Jones does own the dock? Perhaps Epstein's thought is that the step is warranted by what is said in the final sentence of the passage I quoted above: "If the Transportation Company must bear all the costs in those cases in which it damages its own property, then it should bear those costs when it damages the property of another." Thus: since (or: just as?) the Company has to bear the costs of repair when it damages its own property, the Company has to bear the costs of repair when it damages the property of another.

But that is unfortunately overstrong. If B has to pay the costs of any injury of A's which B causes (as B has to pay the costs of any injury of his own which he causes), then B may properly be held liable, not merely in

(4) B caused A's injury, and did so freely and wittingly, but did so to save himself from a very much greater injury, and was justified in so acting.

but also in

(2) B caused A's injury by some freak accident—by doing something which he took all due care in the doing of, and which he could not have been expected to foresee would lead to harm.

Doesn't B have to pay the costs of any injury of his own which he causes himself by accident? But it really does seem wrong to hold B liable in (2).

I suppose it is arguable that what makes it seem wrong to hold B liable in (2) is not any considerations of fairness to B, and in particular, that it is not B's own freedom of action that protects him against liability in (2). For it is arguable that what blocks shifting A's costs to B in (2) is a rule-utilitarian argument issuing from our concern for freedom of action for all of us—that is, from our desire to be able to count on being free of costs for harms which we cause others, but which we could not, or anyway, morally speaking need not have foreseen and planned for.[11] (Such an argument would have to make out, more strongly, that we prefer being free of costs for harms which we cause others in this way to being free of costs for harms which we are caused by others in this way.) If that is the ground for leaving A's costs to lie where they fell in (2), then Epstein's point could be restated as follows: *in general* B must pay the costs of any injury of A's which B causes—but that is not so where utility is maximized by the adoption of a rule which relieves B of liability, and utility *is* maximized by the adoption of a rule which relieves B of liability in (2), but not so in (4).

But I fancy that there is more to be said about (4) than Epstein says. Let us look, not at what B's actions caused, but at the content of B's planning before he acts. In a case that will later be describable by (4), B has an end in view that he wants to reach, and he figures he will be able to reach it if he does something which he is aware will cause A a harm, and thereby impose costs on A. I stress: B is aware of the fact that his acting will cause A a harm. In a case that will later be describable by (2), B is not aware of the fact that his acting will cause A a harm, and has no moral duty to find out whether it will. Considerations of freedom of action (namely, A's), however, suggest that if B is aware that his acting will cause A a harm, then—other things being equal—B must buy from A the right to cause A that harm, and must do this before acting. In *Vincent*, the dockowner was not there to be bargained with. (So also was the cabinowner not there to be bargained with in Feinberg's story of the hiker.) So other things were

11. Compare Hart's rule-utilitarian argument for restricting punishment to voluntary acts:

> [Restricting punishment in that way] increases the power of individuals to identify beforehand periods when the law's punishments will not interfere with them and to plan their lives accordingly . . . Where punishment is not so restricted individuals will be liable to have their plans frustrated by punishments for what they do unintentionally, in ignorance, by accident or mistake . . . [Failing to restrict punishment in that way] would diminish the individual's power to identify beforehand particular periods during which he will be free from them. This is so because we can have very little ground for confidence that during a particular period we will not do something unintentionally, accidentally, etc.; whereas from their own knowledge of themselves many can say with justified confidence that for some period ahead they are not likely to engage intentionally in crime and can plan their lives from point to point in confidence that they will be left free during that period.

H. L. A. Hart, "Prolegomenon to the Principles of Punishment," in his *Punishment and Responsibility: Essays in the Philosophy of Law* (Oxford: Oxford University Press, 1968), pp. 23–24.

not equal in *Vincent*. But surely the fact that a right-holder is not there to be bargained with for possession of the right cannot be thought to entitle the one who wants it to have it free.

These remarks are far too brief: the differences between (2) and (4) call for far closer attention than they can be given here. But I have in any case wanted only to suggest that considerations of freedom of action will take us a long way—not merely into the question why causality matters, but also into the question when and where it does.

4. Let us return now from *Summers II* to *Summers*, in the course of which it was not discovered who had caused the harm. I said earlier that we must suppose the Court had in mind not merely that all the defendants were negligent toward the plaintiff, but also that their negligent acts were in a measure likely to have caused the harm for which the plaintiff sought compensation. Only those who were likely to have caused the harm should be among the candidates for liability, and that, it seems clear, in the thought that liability should ideally only be imposed on those who did cause the harm, whatever the degree of fault in others.

Ideally. But here was a case in which there was no way of knowing who caused the harm.

Isn't it unfair to the defendants not to dismiss them both?

Why might one feel that fairness to them requires dismissing them both?

Perhaps simply the fact that it is not known about either that he caused the harm. But the standard of proof of causation in tort generally is not evidence sufficient for a claim to knowledge: tort law does not require evidence which makes it be beyond a reasonable doubt that the defendant caused the harm complained of. What is required of the evidence is merely that it make it be more probable than not that the defendant caused the harm complained of.

Is it to be argued that the "more probable than not" standard is unfair to civil defendants generally? The stricter standard of proof is required in criminal cases; is it fair that a more relaxed standard be employed in civil suits? If you lose in a criminal case, the outcome is punishment, which expresses a moral conclusion about you. Saying that the defendant in a civil suit was negligent also expresses a moral conclusion about him; but the imposition of liability on him is not a punishment of him. It has to be remembered that the question in a civil suit is merely who is to be out of pocket for the costs of the harm, the plaintiff or the defendant. If the defendant caused the harm, then (other things being equal) it is right that he be out of pocket for the costs. What if it is establishable only that it is more probable than not that the defendant caused the harm? I am inclined to think we do think it not unfair to him that he be out of pocket for the costs in so far as we think its being more probable than not that he caused the harm entitles us to conclude that he *did* cause it. I shall come back to this dark saying in Section 8 below.

One might have a stronger ground for thinking it unfair to the defendants in *Summers* to hold them liable than the fact that it is not known about either that he caused the harm, namely, the fact that it is only .5 probable in the case of each that he caused the harm, and thus not even more probable than not in the case of each that he caused the harm.

It seems to me that there really is a measure of unfairness to the defendants issuing from this consideration. And doesn't it increase as we consider a hypothetical *Summers III* in which there are ten shooters, and only a .1 probability in respect of each that he caused the harm?

I suspect that the *Summers* Court itself felt this unfairness. The Court said of the defendants: "They are both wrongdoers—both negligent toward the plaintiff." So far so good. But then it went on to say: "They brought about a situation where the negligence of one of them injured the plaintiff, hence. . . ." The implication of that sentence is one I did not mention in my summary of the Court's argument above: the implication of that sentence is that the defendants *jointly* brought about a situation in which the plaintiff would be injured, and thus hints that they were acting in concert. Stronger still is the implication of the Court's next sentence: "The injured party has been placed by defendants in the unfair position of pointing to which defendant caused the harm." That implies, not merely that they acted in concert, but also that they jointly acted in such a way as to make the plaintiff be unable to point to which defendant caused the harm. (Compare a possible case in which a pair of defendants jointly destroy evidence which would have made it possible for the plaintiff to identify which is the actual harm-causer.) If we thought that even the weaker of these two implications were true, then we would feel no unfairness at all in the Court's holding both defendants liable. If they had been acting in concert, if, for example, they had had a plot, Simonson to shoot at Summers first, and Tice to shoot immediately thereafter if he thinks Simonson missed, then it would not matter from the point of view of liability *whose* shot in fact caused the injury: both should be held liable. I shall be assuming throughout, not merely in *Summers*, but in all the variants on it which we shall look at, that the shooters were independent agents, not acting in concert. And I think the *Summers* Court made this assumption too. It did not actually *assert* these things which it implied, and I do not think that they played a part in its reasoning; I therefore did not include them in my summary of its argument. My point here is merely that the fact that the Court chose those words suggests the presence of a certain discomfort.

On the other hand, whether or not one feels that holding both defendants liable is in a measure unfair to them, that feeling is certainly swamped by the feeling of unfairness which is generated by the thought of the plaintiff's being without remedy from either of them. That is the Court's point; and that is why, at a minimum *on balance* fairly, it affirmed that liability should be imposed on both.

5. I had asked: Was the Court's decision in *Summers* fair? And I said that there were two questions to be addressed. First, why should either defendant be held liable for any of the costs? Let us now turn to the second: Why should the plaintiff be entitled to collect all of his costs from either?

Fairness does seem to allow of, indeed require, holding both defendants liable; but doesn't it require, if both are to be held liable, that they pay in proportion to the probability that they caused the harm, and thus that the plaintiff be entitled to collect only half of the costs from each?

Or perhaps fairness requires that, since each was .5 probably the harm-causer, each should be given a .5 probability of paying all of the costs. But if the defendants are risk-neutral, it must be all the same to them whether each pays half of the costs, or each is given a .5 probability of paying all, and I shall therefore ignore this idea.

So why did the Court decide as it did?

The Court's only real argument for thinking that the plaintiff should be entitled to collect all of the costs from either defendant, as he chooses, appears within a passage which it quotes from Wigmore, *Select Cases on the Law of Torts:*

> The real reason for the rule that each joint tortfeasor is responsible for the whole damage is the practical unfairness of denying the injured redress simply because he cannot prove how much damage each did,

when it is certain that between them they did all; let them be the ones to apportion it among themselves. Since, then, the difficulty of proof is the reason, the rule should apply whenever the harm has plural causes, and not merely when they acted in conscious concert.

I think that the way in which that passage is supposed to support the Court's decision is this: there is a rule to the effect that if two or more people are acting in concert (joint tortfeasors) and between them cause a harm, then each is responsible for the whole damage—that is, the plaintiff may collect his entire costs from any one of them. What is the reason for this rule? It would be unfair to deny the injured redress simply because he cannot prove how much damage each of the defendants did, when it is certain that between them they did it all;[12] therefore they should have the burden of apportioning the costs among themselves. The premise of that argument does not advert to the fact that the defendants are acting in concert, and since the argument succeeds when the defendants are acting in concert, it succeeds also when they are not acting in concert but are both independent causes of the injury ("plural causes")—as, for instance, where two motorcyclists both make loud noises, frightening the plaintiff's horse, the sound made by each being sufficient to frighten the horse.[13] So far, Wigmore. Now the premise of the argument no more adverts to the defendants' being, both of them, causes of the injury than it adverts to their acting in concert; and it would be no surprise if the *Summers* court therefore thought the argument succeeds when the defendants are not "plural causes" but "alternative causes"—that is, where one or the other of them (though not both) caused the injury. So, the *Summers* court concludes: "The wrongdoers should be left to work out between themselves any apportionment."

Collecting from a defendant may be hard. If it is open to one defendant to sue another for a contribution to the costs—and in most states this is a possible proceeding—then isn't it fairer to the plaintiff that he not have the double burden of collecting half of his costs from each? Shouldn't each of them have the following conditional burden: If the plaintiff fastens on me for the whole of his costs, then I collect half from the other defendant?

In any case, if the events take place in a state that allows suits for

12. I doubt that that can be the (sole) reason for the rule, for it must surely sometimes be possible for the plaintiff to prove how much damage each of the joint tortfeasors did.

13. Compare *Corey v. Havener*, 182 Mass. 250, 65 N.E. 69 (1902).

contribution, the outcome of holding both defendants jointly and severally liable is likely to be roughly equivalent to what strikes one intuitively as the fair outcome, namely, holding each defendant liable for that fraction of the costs which is the probability of his having caused the harm. Only "likely," because the suit for contribution might not succeed, and only "roughly" because of the costs of such a suit, but perhaps close enough so as to warrant no concern on the ground of fairness. After all, both of the defendants acted negligently, and one of them caused the plaintiff's injury.

6. The *Sindell* court did not hold that the defendants should be held jointly and severally liable: it held that damages should be apportioned in accordance with the defendants' percentages of "the appropriate market" in DES. Why?

But there is a prior question. The *Sindell* court in fact rejected the plaintiff's claim that she should prevail on the rationale which generated the decision in *Summers*, and we should first ask about its grounds for doing so. The Court said: "There [i.e., in *Summers*], all the parties who were or could have been responsible for the harm to the plaintiff were joined as defendants. Here, by contrast, there are approximately 200 drug companies which made DES, any one of which might have manufactured the injury-producing drug." Thus in *Summers* there were two who could have caused the harm, and both were defendants, whereas by contrast in *Sindell*, there were two hundred who could have caused the harm, but only ten of them were among the defendants.

Why did she not join all two hundred in her action? Presumably because they were not all reachable. Even the defendants she joined in her action granted that not all two hundred were reachable—the Court says: "As defendants candidly admit, there is little likelihood that all the manufacturers who made DES at the time in question are still in business or that they are subject to the jurisdiction of the California courts."

Moreover, she alleged that six or seven of the companies who were among her defendants produced 90% of the DES which was marketed.

In any case, the Court said she could prevail on an "adaptation" or "modification" of the rule in *Summers*. In particular, it said that if she "joins in the action the manufacturers of a substantial share of the DES which her mother might have taken," then the burden should shift to them to show they could not have manufactured the DES which her mother took. What counts as a substantial share? Presumably 90% would count. The Court considered that possibility of requiring 75% to 80% and rejected that idea: it said "we hold only that a substantial percentage is required," and surely 90% is a substantial percentage.

Consider a hypothetical *Summers IV*. Ten shooters; all fired negligently, and all are equally likely to have caused the harm; one has quit the country, so Summers sues the remaining nine. The trial court dismisses. The appeals court says that if Summers joins in his action those who imposed a substantial share of the risk—for example, 90% of it—then the burden should shift to the defendants to show that they could not have caused the harm. Would that be fair?

I should think that anyone who takes it to be fair for liability to have been imposed on Tice and Simonson in *Summers* will take it to be fair for liability to be imposed—in some way and in some measure—on the defendant shooters in *Summers IV*. But in what way and what measure?

Here are two possibilities. First:

(a) Each defendant x is to pay $.n$ of Summers' costs, where $.n =$ the probability that x caused the harm.

Thus if Summers sues all nine reachable defendants, each pays .1 of Summers' costs (since each was .1 probably the harm-causer); and Summers collects only .9—thus 90%—of his costs. The second possibility is more complex:

(b) Each defendant x is to pay $.n/.m$ of Summers' costs, where $.n =$ the probability that x caused the harm, and $.m =$ the probability that the harm-causer is among the defendants.

Thus if Summers sues all nine reachable defendants, each pays .1/.9 of Summers' costs (since each was .1 probably the harm-causer, and the probability that the harm-causer was among the nine was .9); and Summers collects .9/.9—thus 100%—of his costs.

I think that intuitively (a) does strike one as fairer, for under (a) each defendant pays only that fraction of the costs of the harm which is the probability that his negligence caused it.

But if the hypothetical appeals court in *Summers IV* had had (a) in mind, why would it have placed the following condition on the action: that Summers must join in his action those who imposed a substantial share of the risk? If no shooter would be held liable for more than that fraction of the costs of the harm which is the probability that his negligence caused it, why not leave it to Summers to sue as many as he can reach, *or as few as he wishes*?

A number of commentators on *Sindell* have asked why it should matter whether or not Sindell's defendants manufactured a substantial share of the DES which her mother might have taken—for didn't the Court go on to say that damages should be apportioned in accordance with percentage of "the appropriate market" in DES?[14] Suppose that Sindell sues nine drug companies, who among them sold 90% of the DES which her mother might have taken; if no drug company is to pay a larger share of her costs than its percentage of the market, then surely the Court must have had in mind

(a') Each defendant x is to pay $.n$ of Sindell's costs, where $.n =$ x's share of the DES her mother might have taken,

under which she recovers less than her costs, rather than

(b') Each defendant x is to pay $.n/.m$ of Sindell's costs, where $.n = x$'s share of the DES her mother might have taken, and $.m =$ the defendants' joint share of the DES her mother might have taken,

under which she recovers 100% of her costs. But if the Court did have (a') in mind, why require that Sindell sue a defendant group which manufactured a substantial share of the DES that her mother might have taken? She would be a fool to sue fewer than she could reach; but why impose the requirement?

The question is not merely theoretical, that is, not merely a question as to the rationale of the decision. Suppose a person is harmed by a drug manufactured by two hundred companies, and a hundred and ninety-five of them have now gone out of business, and the remaining five manufactured only 40% of the drug then sold. (Or is 40% a substantial share? If so, choose an appropriate smaller percentage.) It might be worth suing for 40% of one's costs if one's costs were heavy; but the rule in *Sindell* would not allow of success in such a suit.

The Court seemed to think it would not be fair for the plaintiff to win if her defendants did not, among themselves, manufacture a substantial share of the then available supply of the drug which caused

14. For a very helpful discussion of this and other issues raised by *Sindell* and similar cases, see Glen O. Robinson, "Multiple Causation in Tort Law: Reflections on the DES Cases," *Virginia Law Review* 68 (April 1982).

her harm, and this because if she does win, and they do not manufacture a substantial share of the drug, then there will be a substantial likelihood that "the responsible manufacturer, not named in the action, will escape liability." But if *any* manufacturer is excluded from the class of defendants, then there is some likelihood that the responsible manufacturer will escape liability, the smaller the market share of the excluded manufacturer, the smaller the likelihood that the responsible manufacturer will escape liability, but some likelihood all the same. Why does it matter whether the likelihood of escape is small or large, given that no defendant will be held liable for more than that fraction which is its share of the market?

Perhaps what was at work in the Court was simply the familiar fact that it should be the causer of the harm who pays the costs of the harm; and the less likely it is that the defendants caused the harm, the more likely it is that the causer of the harm will escape liability.

Perhaps what was at work in the Court was a concern about fairness in distribution of liability. If the plaintiff sues only those who manufactured (as it might be) 40% of the drug, and they lose, then admittedly they pay only 40% of the plaintiff's costs; but the others who manufactured the remaining 60% of the drug have no liability imposed on them at all. All imposed a risk; is it fair that only some be required to pay their share, while a great many are not required to pay theirs? (Compare bringing criminal charges against Jones, and not bringing them against Smith, though Smith and Jones did exactly the same thing.)

But I think that what was at work in the Court was something different and simpler. For the fact is that I have merely been pretending that it is clear how the Court wishes the plaintiff's damages to be apportioned among the defendants. What exactly did the Court have in mind by "the appropriate market" in DES? All of the DES which was then on the market, and which Sindell's mother might have taken? Or: all of the DES which was marketed by the defendants against whom she brings suit? The decision is ambiguous. If the former, the Court had (a') in mind, if the latter, the Court had (b') in mind; and it does not explicitly say which.

What is nowadays commonly called "the *Sindell* rule" is (a'); but I hazard a guess that it was (b') that the Court had in mind. My first reason is textual. The Court says: "Once plaintiff has met her burden of joining the required defendants [i.e., manufacturers of a substantial share of the DES which her mother might have taken], they in turn may cross-complaint against other DES manufacturers, not joined in the action, which they can allege might have supplied the injury-causing product." What would be the point of a manufacturer's doing that, if he were going to have to pay at most that fraction of her costs which is his share of the DES which her mother might have taken?

More interesting, second, it is only if the Court had (b') in mind that fairness really would require that the companies joined in the action have manufactured a substantial share of the DES Sindell's mother might have taken. If all of her costs are to be paid by a group which does not include all who might have caused her harm, then fairness would require (at a minimum) that they, among themselves, have imposed a substantial share of the risk.

In short, it is because the Court had (b') in mind that it imposed the requirement that Sindell join in her action the manufacturers of a substantial share of the DES which her mother might have taken.

7. *At a minimum.* For would it really be fair to impose all of Sindell's costs on a group which does not include all who might have caused her harm?

I said in discussing *Summers IV* that damage rule

(a) Each defendant x is to pay $.n$ of Summers' costs, where $.n =$ the probability that x caused the harm

strikes one intuitively as fairer than damage rule

(b) Each defendant x is to pay $.n/.m$ of Summers' costs, where $.n =$ the probability that x caused the harm, and $.m =$ the probability that the harm-causer is among the defendants,

for under (a) each defendant pays only that fraction of the costs of the harm which is the probability that his negligence caused it. Summers was an entirely innocent victim; all the same, it seems unfair for a defendant to have to pay more than he is assigned by (a).

I have throughout been sidestepping considerations of efficiency, but it does just barely pay to mention the further fact that (a) is more easily generalizable than (b) is. Anyone who thinks (b) a fair choice can think this only insofar as he thinks that the plaintiff will be suing a group of people who, among themselves, imposed a substantial share of the risk. And what precisely counts as a substantial share of the risk? By contrast, (a) lends itself easily to generalization: apportion damages for a harm in accordance with probability of having caused it. And in passing: under a generalization of (a), a victim of a harm has an incentive to join in his action as many of the possible causers of the harm as he can reach, which seems likely to be the more efficient deterrent to harm causing.

I asked earlier why the *Sindell* court did not hold that the defendants should be held jointly and severally liable. We might as well ask the analogous question about *Summers IV*. Thus suppose we think Summers should collect only .*m* of his costs, where .*m* = the probability that the harm-causer is among the shooters he sues. Why should he have to collect a part from each, rather than collecting all from any one he chooses—thus why prefer (a) to

> (c) Summers collects .*m* of his costs from any defendant he chooses, where .*m* = the probability that the harm-causer is among the defendants?

Collecting from a defendant may be hard, and Summers' burden of collecting damages is minimized under (c), maximized under (a); so on that ground we might think (c) the fairer choice—Summers after all is the innocent victim.[15]

Moreover, if the events take place in a state that allows suits for contribution, the defendant from whom Summers collects can sue the others.

There is a consideration that works in the opposite direction, however. In *Summers v. Tice*, there were only two defendants, and each was .5 probably the harm-causer. So whichever defendant Summers fastens onto for his costs, he anyway fastens onto a person who was .5 probably the harm-causer. In *Summers IV*, each shooter is only .1 probably the harm-causer. Is it fair that someone who only .1 probably caused the harm have the burden of collecting their shares of Summers' costs from the other shooters?

That consideration is still more serious if we imagine a final variant on *Summers*, namely, *Summers V*, in which (again) there are ten shooters, and one has quit the country, but the nine remaining shooters vary in the degree of probability that they caused the harm—though none is more than .5 probably the harm-causer. (Let it be that they

---

15. But remember Wigmore: "The real reason for the rule that each joint tortfeasor is responsible for the whole damage is the practical unfairness of denying the injured redress simply because he cannot prove how much damage each did, *when it is certain that between them they did all* . . ." (emphasis added). In *Summers IV* it is not certain that, among them, the defendants caused the harm.

shot different numbers of pellets in Summers' direction.) Under damage rule (c), Summers will surely collect from the shooter with the "deepest pockets"; but that shooter might have been the least probable of all to them to have caused the harm.

Compare *Sindell:* the largest drug company (which therefore has the deepest pockets) might have had the smallest share of the DES market at the time Sindell's mother took DES. Was that possibility among the reasons why the *Sindell* court preferred apportioning damages in accordance with market share to imposing joint and several liability? The Court unfortunately did not explain its preference.

For my own part, (a) does seem a fairer damage rule than (c), given a large number of defendants, each of whom is only in small degree probably the harm-causer. But that intuition is not a hard one. Summers, to repeat, is the innocent victim; and its seems to me that appeals to fairness do not really fix that (a) is preferable to (c).

We should notice, however, that in *Summers V*, there is a further possible damage rule. In that the shooters in *Summers V* vary in the degree of probability that they caused the harm,

(d) Summers collects $.m$ of his costs from that one of the defendants who is the most likely of the defendants to have caused the harm, where $.m$ = the probability that the harm-causer is among the defendants

suggests itself as a possibility. Or even more strongly, if one of the defendants is the most likely of all of the ten shooters to have caused the harm,

(e) Summers collects all of his costs from that one of the defendants who is the most likely to have caused the harm of all of the possible causers of the harm.

It has been argued in fact that it is the generalization of (e) which is the most efficient damage rule.[16]

Proposition (e) would impose liability for all of Summers' costs on someone the probability of whose having caused the harm might be small. We might well feel that to be objectionable.

Don't we feel it to be the more objectionable when we remember that the evidence against the defendants in *Summers V* is 'merely

16. See David Kaye, "The Limits of the Preponderance of the Evidence Standard: Justifiably Naked Statistical Evidence and Multiple Causation," *American Bar Foundation Research Journal* 2 (Spring 1982).

statistical'? (The first shooter shot so many pellets, the second shooter shot such many pellets, and so on.)

Indeed, the evidence against the defendants in all of the cases we have been attending to (other than *Summers II*) is 'merely statistical.' I suspect that that fact may have been responsible for a nagging suspicion that there is something wrong with imposing liability on anyone in *any* of those cases. We should take a closer look at it.

8. Consider the following hypothetical:

[T]here are two taxicab companies in town who have identical cabs except that one has red cabs and the other green cabs. [S]ixty percent of all cabs in town are red. Plaintiff has been knocked down on a deserted street by a cab. He is color blind and cannot distinguish red from green. Shortly after the accident a taxicab driver said over the air, "I just hit someone at (the accident location). I should have seen him, but I was drinking and going too fast." The static was such that no identification of the voice was possible, but the frequency is used only by cabs from that town. Neither company keeps dispatch records, so [neither knows] what drivers were in what parts of town. And to make things complete, the garage in which all the cabs of the two companies [were] housed was burned down the night of the accident.[17]

On the facts, Red Cab Company is .6 probably the harm-causer. The familiar "more probable than not" rule of tort law yields that Red Cab should be held liable for all of the plaintiff's costs. So also does the generalization of damage rule (e) of the preceding section—not surprisingly, since that generalization yields the "more probable than not" rule for the special class of cases in which a defendant is more than .5 probably the harm-causer.

Would it be fair for Red Cab to be held liable for all of the plaintiff's costs? I think we feel it would not.

It is possible that one source of this feeling lies in the fact that the rule which imposes liability of Red Cab alone, in light of its owning 60% of the cabs in town, will always impose liability on Red Cab alone, in all similar situations in future (so long as Red Cab continues to own more than half the cabs in town), which seems too harsh to Red Cab, too lenient to Green Cab.

17. Kaye, ibid., pp. 487–488. Compare *Smith v. Rapid Transit, Inc.*, 317 Mass. 469, 58 N.E.2d 754 (1945). For references to other cases, and a discussion of a wide range of questions that are raised by the use of statistical evidence in court, see Lawrence H. Tribe, "Trial by Mathematics," *Harvard Law Review* 84 (April 1971).

On the other hand, it is hardly to be expected that there will in future be many situations like this one in the relevant respects.

And there surely is in any case a deeper source of the feeling, lying in the nature of the evidence against Red Cab. But what exactly is wrong with it?

What we need is a general characterization of the difference between what I shall call "internal evidence" and what I shall call "external evidence." (I prefer "external evidence" to "merely statistical evidence," since it is certainly arguable that all evidence rests ultimately on mere statistics.) Consider the following hypothesis:

(H)   A red cab caused the accident.

The truth of

(E)   60% of the cars which might have caused the accident are red cabs

is what I shall be calling external evidence that (H) is true; if we were to find out that

(I)   A red cab went speeding away from the area moments after the accident

is true, we would have what I shall be calling internal evidence that (H) is true. We do feel there to be an important difference between the ways in which (E) and (I) support (H)—and that if our only evidence for (H) is (E), then there really is something wrong with our evidence for (H).

Indeed, the difference between the ways in which (E) and (I) support (H) is so dramatic that we may feel inclined to think that calling the truth of (E) external evidence for (H) is a misnomer. No doubt the truth of (E) is some reason to think (H) true; no doubt you would bet on (H) if told (E); no doubt (E) makes (H) probable. But is the truth of (E) *evidence* for (H)?[18] I think not. But it is not terminology

18. Compare the following, from *Sargent v. Massachusetts Accident Co.*, 307 Mass. 250, 29 N.E.2d 825 (1940): "It has been held not enough that mathematically the chances somewhat favor a proposition to be proved; for example, the fact that colored automobiles made in the current year outnumber black ones would not warrant a finding that an undescribed automobile of the current year is colored and not black, nor would the fact that only a minority of men die of cancer warrant a finding that a particular man did not die of cancer." The fact that only a minority of men die of cancer is some reason to think that Jones, who just died, did not die of cancer, and makes that probable; but could it at all plausibly be called *evidence* that Jones did not die of cancer?

that matters to us. What we need is an account of what is wrong with (E) which issues in this disinclination to call it evidence for (H).

What is wrong with (E) is that it stands in no explanatory relation with (H).

Let us begin with something simpler. Suppose "Alfred" is the name of a cabdriver and that the hypothesis under consideration is this:

(H_A) Alfred caused the accident.

The truth of

(I_A) Alfred went speeding away from the area moments after the accident

is internal evidence that (H_A) is true. I suggest that what is crucial is this: (I_A) stands in an explanatory relation with (H_A). Here the explanatory relation is simple: the truth of (H_A) would explain the truth of (I_A). How would it do this? Well, suppose we learn that (I_A) is true. *Why* was Alfred speeding away from the area moments after the accident? We have an explanation if we suppose that (H_A) is true: that is, we can explain Alfred's speeding away from the area if we suppose that he just caused the accident, and therefore wished to get away from the area as quickly as possible.

That is not of course the only possible explanation of (I_A): Alfred might have been speeding away, not because he caused the accident, but because he had just received an emergency call to bring a doctor to the hospital. But further inquiry might block alternative explanations, and bring out that Alfred's having caused the accident is the best explanation.

By contrast, (E) stands in no explanatory relation whatever to (H_A). Learning of the truth of one does not help us in any way to arrive at an understanding of why the other is true.

The relation between (H) and (I) is slightly more complicated. Suppose we learn that (I) is true. *Why* was a red cab speeding away from the area moments after the accident? We have an explanation if we suppose that it (that very red cab) had just caused the accident; but if it had just caused the accident, then a red cab caused the accident, and (H) is therefore true.

That supposition that that cab had just caused the accident is plainly not the only possible explanation of (I). But further inquiry might block alternative explanations.

By contrast, (E) stands in no explanatory relation whatever to (H)—not even this slightly more complicated explanatory relation.

Statement (I) reports on something that happened after the accident, and so we might call the truth of (I) "backward-looking internal evidence" for the truth of (H). But not all internal evidence is backward-looking. Consider

(I') A red cab went speeding into the area moments before the accident.

This reports on something that happened before the accident, and so we might call its truth "forward-looking internal evidence" for the truth of (H). The explanatory relation in which (I') stands to (H) is different from that in which (I) stands to (H). Let us again look at something simpler. It is plain enough that the truth of

(H$_B$) Bert caused the accident

would not explain the truth of

(I'$_B$) Bert went speeding into the area moments before the accident:

one could hardly hope to explain Bert's speeding into the area by appeal to his later having caused the accident. The explanatory relation goes in the opposite direction in the case of (I'$_B$) and (H$_B$): that is, Bert's speeding into the area would explain his having caused an accident in the area. Similarly, the truth of (I') would explain the truth of (H). If a red cab went speeding into the area moments before the accident, then that is why it, and therefore a red cab, caused the accident.

Internal evidence, then, stands, in an explanatory relation to the hypothesis for which it is evidence. External evidence does not. In the simple examples I gave, the bit of forward-looking internal evidence pointed to a (putative) cause of the event we were interested in, and the bit of backward-looking internal evidence pointed to a (putative) effect of the event we were interested in. But the explanatory relation might be more complex—for example, the evidence might point to a (putative) common cause of both it and the event we are interested in. In any case, internal evidence helps us to see the event we are interested in as causally embedded in a series of events, and thus as forming part of history.

It is very hard to see why the difference between internal and external evidence matters to us. It might be argued that internal evidence makes a hypothesis more probable than any external evidence alone could have done. But I doubt that such an argument could be made to work.[19] Consider the hypothesis that my ticket—let us suppose my ticket was ticket #3428—lost yesterday's lottery. That hypothesis is made probable by the fact that Jones says that ticket #6324 won the lottery. Jones' saying that #6324 won is backward-looking internal evidence that #6324 won, and therefore that my ticket lost, and it makes the hypothesis that my ticket lost the most probable, the less likely it is that Jones' saying that #6324 won can be explained in some other way than by appeal to the (putative) fact that ticket #6324 did win. But however probable that bit of evidence makes the hypothesis that my ticket lost, we can imagine a bit of external evidence such that, had we had only that external evidence, the hypothesis that my ticket lost would have been just as probable—we need merely imagine that there were appropriately many tickets sold.

Alternatively, it might be argued that the difference between internal and external evidence matters to the law because justice to a defendant requires not merely that it be made more probable than not (or, in a criminal case, beyond a reasonable doubt) that he caused the harm, but that this be made probable in a particular way—thus by a body of evidence that includes internal evidence. But actually producing such an argument would require explaining why this is a requirement of justice, and the explanation is by no means obvious.

Moreover, it is by no means obvious that the difference between internal and external evidence matters only to the law.

What calls for more attention than I can give it here is the fact (I think it a fact, indeed, an important fact) that we seem to be reluctant to conclude that a supposition is *true*, and then act on it, unless we have internal evidence for it, however probable the available external evidence makes it.[20] Sixty percent of the cabs in town are red? Ninety-nine percent of the cabs in town are red? That makes it highly probable that a red cab caused the accident. But it does not help us causally

19. Unless it appeals to a nonstandard concept "probability"—see L. Jonathan Cohen, *The Probable and the Provable* (Oxford: Clarendon Press, 1977).

20. A number of judicial opinions seem to me to show their authors to have this idea in mind. See again, for example, *Sargent v. Massachusetts Accident Co.*: "The weight or preponderance of evidence is its power to convince the tribunal which has the determination of the fact, of *the actual truth* of the proposition to be proved. After the evidence has been weighed, that proposition is proved by a preponderance of the evidence if it is made to appear more likely or probable in the sense that *actual belief in its truth*, derived from the evidence, exists in the mind or minds of the tribunal notwithstanding any doubts that may still linger there" (emphasis supplied).

connect any red cab with the accident, so although we would cheer-fully bet on its having been a red cab that caused the accident, we are not prepared to conclude, flatly, that a red cab did cause the accident, and impose liability on Red Cab Company.

Again, I tear up my ticket in yesterday's lottery when I hear a radio announcement that a different ticket won. I do not tear up my ticket in yesterday's lottery when I hear only that a million more tickets had been sold than I thought had been sold.

It was this idea which lay behind my dark saying (in section 4 above) that we think it not unfair to a defendant that he be out of pocket for the plaintiff's costs, where he is more probably than not the harm-causer, insofar as we think its being more probable than not that he is the harm-causer entitles us to conclude that he *did* cause the harm. Where there is internal evidence that the defendant is the harm-causer, internal evidence strong enough to make it more prob-able than not that he is the harm-causer, and thus where no back-ground information blocks the explanations which it points to, we do feel entitled to draw that conclusion. Not so where only external evidence is available, however probable it makes the hypothesis that the defendant caused the harm.

If this is right, then there is yet another way in which causation is important to us in imposing liability: not only do we (ideally) wish liability to be imposed only on those who actually caused the injury, we also are reluctant to attribute causality unless we can see the evidence for it as causally connected with the injury.

And its being right (if it is) would explain why we feel that where only external evidence is available, then if liability is to be imposed at all, it should be apportioned in accordance with probability of being the harm-causer. Sixty percent Red Cab, forty percent Green Cab. Fifty percent Tice, fifty percent Simonson. Ten percent each of the shooters in *Summers IV*. Market share in *Sindell*.[21]

If liability is to be imposed at all. There remains a sense of unfairness in imposing any of it on such evidence—even in face of the innocent victim.

9. *Sindell* forces us to confront a battery of questions about caus-ation and liability, but I have preferred to concentrate on variants on

21. John E. Coons recommends division of liability in a considerably broader range of cases than that in consideration here. See his "Approaches to Court Imposed Com-promise—the Uses of Doubt and Reason," *Northwestern University Law Review* 58 (1964), and "Compromise as Precise Justice," *California Law Review* 68 (March 1980).

Summers, since the variants on *Summers* raise those questions more cleanly and clearly. *Sindell* differs from *Summers V* in a number of ways. *Sindell* was a class action. A long time elapsed between the alleged negligent acts of the *Sindell* defendants and the harm allegedly caused by them. The defendants in *Sindell* are drug companies, not private persons, and therefore (as the Court said) better able to bear the costs of the harm than is any victim of the harm, and better placed to discover and guard against product defects. But those considerations have no bearing on the particular questions about causation and liability that I wished to attend to.

Moreover, those considerations do not seem to me to speak to the *fairness* of imposing liability on the defendants; indeed, they seem to me to be more properly addressed to the legislature in support of a request for a certain kind of statutory solution to problems like that presented in *Sindell*. The Dissent says "the problem invites a legislative rather than an attempted judicial solution," and on this point it seems to me to be right. But these comments must here remain mere bits of autobiography, since a study of the large question where decisions of this kind should be made is far beyond the scope of this essay.[22]

22. Many people made helpful comments on earlier drafts of this essay—too many to name, unfortunately. But I owe special thanks to J. Robert S. Prichard, who introduced me to *Sindell* in the first place.

13 · *Liability and Individualized Evidence*

1. Cases like *Smith v. Rapid Transit, Inc.*[1] present a problem to students of tort law. Here is a typical hypothetical case—I will call it *Smith v. Red Cab*—which presents the problem more cleanly than the actual case does. Mrs. Smith was driving home late one night. A taxi came towards her, weaving wildly from side to side across the road. She had to swerve to avoid it; her swerve took her into a parked car; in the crash, she suffered two broken legs. Mrs. Smith therefore sued Red Cab Company. Her evidence is as follows: She could see that it was a cab which caused her accident by weaving wildly across the road, and there are only two cab companies in town, Red Cab (all of whose cabs are red) and Green Cab (all of whose cabs are green), and of the cabs in town that night, six out of ten were operated by Red Cab. Why is that the only evidence she can produce against Red Cab? She says that although she could see that it was a cab which came at her, she could not see its color, and as it was late, there were no other witnesses to the accident—other than the driver himself, of course, but he has not come forward to confess.

If we believe Mrs. Smith's story, and are aware of no further facts that bear on the case, then we shall think it .6 probable that her accident was caused by a cab operated by Red Cab. I think it pays to spell this reasoning out; what follows is one way of doing so. If we believe Mrs. Smith's story, then we believe that a cab, indeed exactly one cab, caused the accident, so that there is such a thing as *the* cab

---

1. 317 Mass. 469, 58 N.E.2d 754 (1945). Mrs. Smith's evidence against the defendant bus company consisted in evidence that she was caused harm by a negligently driven bus on Main Street, and that the defendant bus company had the sole franchise for operating a bus line on Main Street.

which caused the accident; and we believe that it was a cab in town that night. Thus we believe:

(1)   The cab which caused the accident was a cab in town that night.

If we believe Mrs. Smith's story, we also believe:

(2)   6 out of 10 of the cabs in town that night were operated by Red Cab.

Relative to the facts reported by (1) and (2),

(3)   The probability that the cab which caused the accident was operated by Red Cab is .6

is true. But those are the only facts such that we are both aware of them and aware of their bearing on the question who operated the cab which caused the accident. (Perhaps we are aware that the accident took place on, as it might be, a Tuesday. Even so, we are not aware of any reason to think that fact bears on the question whose cab caused the accident.) Other facts whose relevance is clear might come out later: For example, a Green Cab driver might later confess. But as things stand, we have no more reason (indeed we have less reason) to think that any facts which later come out would support the hypothesis that the cab which caused the accident was operated by Green Cab than we have to think they would support the hypothesis that the cab which caused the accident was operated by Red Cab. We are therefore entitled to conclude that (3) is true—in fact, rationality requires us to conclude that (3) is true, for .6 is the degree of belief that, situated as we are, we ought to have in the hypothesis that the cab which caused the accident was operated by Red Cab.[2]

Is it right that Mrs. Smith win her suit against Red Cab? The standard of proof in a tort suit is "more probable than not," which is plausibly interpretable as requiring only that the plaintiff establish a

2. Some commentators on earlier versions of this essay have suggested that perhaps we ought not be entirely confident of the truth of (3), given only the truth of (1) and (2), on the ground that there just might have been more green cabs than red cabs in the part of town in which, and at the time at which, the accident took place. This suggestion seems to me to be a mistake—but one which it is not worth going into here. Anyone who is similarly moved may suppose we are provided, in addition to (1) and (2), with an admission by Red Cab that there is good reason to think (and no reason not to think) that cab-distribution at the time, in the part of town south of the tracks (where the accident took place), was the same as over-all cab-distribution in town that night.

greater than .5 probability that the defendant (wrongfully) caused the harm. But most people feel uncomfortable at the idea of imposing liability on Red Cab on such evidence as Mrs. Smith here presents. Why? That is the problem.

2. *People v. Collins*[3] and its typical descendant hypotheticals raise an analogous problem for the student of criminal law, but less cleanly, so let us set them aside for the time being. Consider, instead, a hypothetical case which I shall call *People v. Tice*.[4] Two people, Tice and Simonson, both hated Summers and wished him dead. Summers went hunting one day. Tice followed with a shotgun loaded with ninety-five pellets. Quite independently, Simonson also followed, but *he* had loaded his shotgun with only five pellets, that being all he had on hand. Both caught sight of Summers at the same time, and both shot all their pellets at him. Independently: I stress that there was no plot or plan. Only one pellet hit Summers, but that one was enough: It hit Summers in the head and caused his death. While it was possible to tell that the pellet which caused Summers's death came either from Tice's gun or from Simonson's gun, it was not possible to tell which. So what charges should be brought against Tice and Simonson? In the event, Simonson is charged with attempted murder, and in *People v. Tice*, Tice is charged with murder.

Well, why not? To win its case against Tice, the prosecution must show that it is beyond a reasonable doubt that the pellet which caused Summers's death was a pellet fired by Tice. But given the information in hand, that seems easy, for given the information in hand, we can say both:

(1′) The pellet which caused Summers's death was a pellet fired at Summers

and

(2′) Ninety-five out of the 100 pellets fired at Summers were fired by Tice.

3. 68 Cal. 2d 319, 438 P.2d 33, 66 Cal. Rptr. 497 (1968). Collins and his wife had been convicted of second degree robbery on evidence that the robbers, like the defendants, were an interracial couple, the man black, with mustache and beard, who drove a yellow car, the woman white, with blond hair in a ponytail—the prosecution alleged on statistical grounds that there was only one chance in twelve million that a couple would possess all these features.

4. With apologies to *Summers v. Tice*, 33 Cal. 2d 80, 199 P.2d 1 (1948).

The facts these report are the only facts such that we are both aware of them and aware of their bearing on the question whose pellet caused Summers's death. We therefore may, indeed should, conclude that

(3') The probability that the pellet which caused Summers's death was fired by Tice is .95

is also true. And isn't a proposition beyond a reasonable doubt if it is .95 probable?[5]

I hope you will feel at least as uncomfortable at the idea of convicting Tice of murder on such evidence as this that he caused the death as you feel at the idea of imposing liability on Red Cab in *Smith v. Red Cab*.

There are differences, of course. In *Smith v. Red Cab*, the information we have in hand gives no reason at all to think that both cab companies were at fault: It gives reason to think that one cab company was at fault, namely the one, whichever it was, that caused the accident. So if Mrs. Smith wins her suit, then Red Cab may be being held liable for her costs despite the fact that it not only did not cause her injury, but was entirely without fault.

By contrast, the information we have in hand in *People v. Tice* gives reason to think that both Tice and Simonson were at fault: It gives reason to think that both committed attempted murder. So if the people win their case against Tice, then while Tice may be being held liable for murder without having caused Summers's death, he was all the same gravely at fault, having at a minimum tried to bring that death about.

This difference brings in train yet another. If Tice did not cause Summers's death, then his failure to do so was—relative to the evidence we have in hand—just *luck*, good or bad luck according to the view you take of the matter. He did everything he could to cause the death, and if he did not cause it, well, that was certainly no credit to him. By contrast, if Red Cab did not cause Mrs. Smith's injury, that was a credit to Red Cab, for—relative to the evidence we have in hand—if Red Cab did not cause the accident, it was not at fault at all.

5. Rita James Simon invited a sample of judges to translate "beyond a reasonable doubt" into numerical probabilities. It is interesting to learn that almost a third of them translated it as a probability of 1. Over two thirds, however, translated it as a probability of .95 or less. See Simon, "Judges' Translations of Burdens of Proof into Statements of Probability," *Trial Lawyer's Guide* 13 (1969), 103.

We could have eliminated these differences by altering the details of *People v. Tice* so as to make the evidence suggest only that one of the actors (Tice or Simonson) was at fault, the evidence that it was Tice who was at fault issuing from nothing other than the evidence that it was a pellet from Tice's gun which caused the death—just as the evidence that it was Red Cab that was at fault issues from nothing other than the evidence that it was one of Red Cab's cabs which caused Mrs. Smith's accident. It is not easy to alter the details in that way without introducing a measure of weirdness. But I think we ought to feel that there is no need to do so; that is, I think we ought not be moved by the differences I pointed to between *Smith v. Red Cab* and *People v. Tice*.

No doubt it was just luck for Tice if he did not cause Summers's death. But that does not justify convicting him of murder. Anyone who attempts murder, and goes about things as carefully and well as he can, is just lucky (or unlucky) if he does not cause the death he wishes to cause, and that does not warrant holding him for murder. So also for Simonson, in fact. He too attempted murder, and it is also just luck for him if he did not cause Summers's death.

It is arguable that if a man attempts murder, and it is just luck for him that he does not cause the death he wishes to cause, then morally speaking he has acted as badly as he would have acted had he succeeded.[6] Many of those who take this view regard it as morally suspect that the penalty for murder should be heavier than the penalty for attempted murder. (Perhaps they view it as flatly unacceptable that there is such a difference in penalty. Perhaps they think the difference is just barely acceptable in light of the fact that imposing the same penalty might give unsuccessful attempters a motive to try again, or in light of some other, or additional, considerations.) At all events, the penalty for murder is everywhere heavier than the penalty for attempted murder. Or at least so I suppose; and we can anyway assume this true in the jurisdiction in which Tice is to be tried. So it is not enough to justify the charge of murder against Tice that it is just luck for him if he did not cause the death: To warrant imposition of the heavier penalty, the prosecution has positively to prove beyond a reasonable doubt *that* he caused it.

Well, isn't it beyond a reasonable doubt that Tice caused Summers's death? After all, it is .95 probable that he did.

6. Thomas Nagel denies this claim in his very interesting "Moral Luck," reprinted in his *Mortal Questions* (Cambridge: Cambridge University Press, 1979).

3. It is often said that the kind of evidence available in *Smith v. Red Cab* and *People v. Tice* merely tells us the "mathematical chances"[7] or the "quantitative probability"[8] of the defendant's guilt. And it would be said that what is missing in those cases, the lack of which makes conviction suspect, is "real"[9] or "individualized"[10] evidence against the defendant.

I strongly suspect that what people feel the lack of, and call individualized evidence, is evidence which is in an appropriate way causally connected with the (putative) fact that the defendant caused the harm.[11]

Consider the evidence that it was Red Cab which caused the accident in *Smith v. Red Cab:* It consists entirely of Mrs. Smith's testimony that a cab caused her accident, and that six out of ten of the cabs in town that night were operated by Red Cab. If we believe her, we believe there are such facts as that a cab caused her accident, and that six out of ten of the cabs in town that night were operated by Red Cab. But those facts lack an appropriate causal connection with the (putative) fact that Red Cab caused the accident.

What sort of causal connection would be appropriate? Well, if a witness came forward to say he saw the accident, and that the cab which caused the accident looked red to him, *then* we would have what would be called individualized evidence against Red Cab; and my suggestion is that that is because the accident-causing cab's actually being red (and therefore being Red Cab's) would causally explain its looking red to that witness. We might call this "backward-looking individualized evidence" of the defendant's guilt because the bit of evidence (the witness' believing the cab looked red to him) points back toward the (putative) fact that Red Cab caused the accident.

Or if it turned out that Red Cab had given a party for its drivers on the evening of the accident, a party which turned into a drunken brawl, then too we would have what would be called individualized evidence against Red Cab; and my suggestion is that that is because

7. From *Smith v. Rapid Transit, Inc.*

8. From *Day v. Boston & Me. R.R.*, 96 Me. 207, 217, 52 A. 771, 774 (1902).

9. From *Day v. Boston & Me. R.R.*

10. See (among many other examples) Laurence H. Tribe, "Trial by Mathematics: Precision and Ritual in the Legal Process," *Harvard Law Review* 84 (April 1971).

11. An earlier version of these ideas appears in section 8 of my "Remarks on Causation and Liability," essay 12. What I here call "individualized evidence," in light of this term's frequency in the literature, I there called "internal evidence." Neither term strikes me as a particularly happy choice.

the party would causally explain its having been a Red Cab which caused the accident. We might call this "forward-looking individualized evidence" of the defendant's guilt because the bit of evidence (the party) points forward towards the (putative) fact that Red Cab caused the accident.

Or more complicated (since it involves a common cause), if a red cab crashed into a parked car shortly after Mrs. Smith's accident, and four blocks past the place of it, the driver giving all signs of being drunk, then that too would be called individualized evidence against Red Cab; and my suggestion is that that is because that driver's having been drunk would causally explain *both* his crashing into the parked car *and* his (and therefore Red Cab's) having caused Mrs. Smith's accident.

In the actual *Smith v. Red Cab*, no such further evidence came out. The facts available to us provide no forward-looking individualized evidence that Red Cab caused the accident, for they neither supply nor suggest any causal explanation of its having been a red cab which caused the accident. Moreover, the facts available to us neither supply nor suggest anything which might have been a common cause *both* of those facts available to us *and* of the (putative) fact that Red Cab caused the accident.

What is of interest is that we do have in the actual *Smith v. Red Cab* a piece of backward-looking individualized evidence for *a* hypothesis. Mrs. Smith says she could see it was a cab which came towards her, and its actually being a cab which came towards her would causally explain her believing this; so her saying she could see it was a cab which came towards her is backward-looking individualized evidence that it was a cab which caused her accident.

No one, of course, supposes that individualized evidence is (deductively valid) proof. In particular, our having backward-looking individualized evidence that a cab caused Mrs. Smith's accident is logically compatible with its not having been a cab which caused the accident.

Moreover, different bits of individualized evidence may differ in strength. For example, it is possible for a private car or bus or truck, or for all I know a gorilla, to be disguised as a cab, and the more non-cabs there are on the roads that are disguised as cabs, the less weight we are entitled to place on the causal hypothesis that Mrs. Smith's believing it was a cab which caused her accident was caused by its being a cab which caused her accident, and thus the less weight her believing it was a cab which caused her accident lends to the causal hypothesis that it was a cab which caused her accident. Still, her believing it was a cab which caused her accident is backward-looking individualized evidence that it was a cab which caused her accident, for her having that belief would be causally explained by its having been a cab which caused her accident.

Mrs. Smith's believing it was a cab which caused her accident would also be causally explained by its having been a red cab which caused her accident. (Again, her believing it was a cab which caused her accident would also be causally explained by its having been a cab once ridden in by a Presbyterian minister which caused her accident.) That does not mean that her believing it was a cab which caused her accident is backward-looking individualized evidence for the hypothesis that it was a red cab which caused her accident (or for the hypothesis that it was a cab once ridden in by a Presbyterian minister which caused her accident.) For there is no reason to think that the redness of a cab (or its past ridership) is causally relevant to its looking to a person like a cab. Mrs. Smith of course might be unusual in this respect: It might be that her retinas are so structured as to record cabbiness only when caused to do so by red-cabbiness. If we were given reason to think that that is true of her, we would thereby have been given reason to think her believing it was a cab which caused her accident *was* backward-looking individualized evidence that it was a red cab which caused her accident. But in the absence of reason to think her odd in some such respect as that, what we have is backward-looking individualized evidence only for the hypothesis that it was a cab which caused her accident.

For Red Cab to be guilty, the cab that came at Mrs. Smith (supposing it was a cab that came at her, as we do suppose if we believe her story) has to have had the features which distinguish Red Cab's cabs from the other cabs in town that night. Redness is one such feature, and no doubt there are indefinitely many others. But we have in hand no facts about the accident in which the (putative) redness of the accident-causing cab, or its (putative) possession of some other feature which distinguishes Red Cab's cabs, can be assigned an appropriate causal role. The facts available to us, then, provide (backward-looking) individualized evidence that a cab caused Mrs. Smith's accident, but no individualized evidence that the cab that caused the accident was one of Red Cab's cabs.

The point, then, is not that the only evidence we actually have in hand in *Smith v. Red Cab* is numerical or statistical,[12] for we do have in that case a piece of individualized evidence for the hypothesis that it was a cab that caused the accident.

More important, numerical or statistical evidence too can be causally connected in an appropriate way with the (putative) fact it is presented to support. Suppose a plaintiff alleges that he was refused a job with a certain organization on grounds of race; in evidence, he presents statistics showing that the racial composition of the organization's workforce diverges widely from that of the local population. Those data suggest a causal hypothesis, namely that the organization intends to discriminate in its hiring practices, and the organization's intending to discriminate in its hiring practices would causally explain *both* the existing divergence in racial composition, *and* the (putative) fact that it refused to hire the plaintiff on grounds of race. So that evidence too is individualized, although it is numerical or statistical.

If we had individualized evidence (and thus, on my hypothesis, appropriately causally connected evidence) against Red Cab, in addition to the evidence we already have in hand, then we would feel considerably less reluctant to impose liability on Red Cab. Why is that? That seems to me to be a very hard question to answer.

It cannot plausibly be said that the addition of individualized evidence against Red Cab would make us feel less reluctant to impose liability on it because the addition of individualized evidence against Red Cab would raise the probability that Red Cab caused the accident. Even in the absence of individualized evidence, the probability that Red Cab caused the accident is already .6, which on a plausible interpretation of the requirements of tort law is higher than it need be.

Friends of the idea that individualized evidence is required for conviction have not really made it clear why this should be thought true. That has encouraged their enemies to suppose they have the idea because they think that individualized evidence is uniquely highly

12. It is of interest that although the court in *Smith v. Rapid Transit, Inc.* stated that "the most that can be said of the evidence in the instant case is that perhaps the mathematical chances somewhat favor the proposition that a bus of the defendant caused the accident," the evidence in that case was entirely nonstatistical. I suggest that what the court felt the lack of was, not nonstatistical evidence, but appropriately causally connected evidence.

probabilifying.[13] The enemies have then found it easy to make mincemeat of the friends. The enemies draw attention to the fact (and it is a fact) that eyewitness testimony, for example, which is paradigm individualized evidence, may be quite unreliable, that is, may probabilify to a lower degree than would some pieces of purely numerical or statistical evidence. And they draw attention to the mistakes about probability (and they are mistakes) which have been studied by Tversky and Kahneman, in particular, those which issue from ignoring base rates.[14]

But I think that is at best an ungenerous diagnosis of what is at work in the friends of individualized evidence. What is at work in them is not the thought that individualized evidence is uniquely highly probabilifying, but rather the feeling that it supplies something which nonindividualized evidence does not supply, which further something is not of value because it raises the probability of the hypothesis in question.

4. I think it is helpful at this point to look at an analogous problem faced by the student of the theory of knowledge. What is currently called the classical, or traditional, account of knowledge says that a person A knows that a proposition p is true if and only if three conditions are met. First, p actually is true. Second, A believes that

13. Some friends of individualized evidence do seem to think it uniquely highly probabilifying. Consider, for example, the court's comment in *Day v. Boston & Me. R.R.*:

> Quantitative probability, however, is only the greater chance. It is not proof, nor even probative evidence, of the proposition to be proved. That in one throw of dice there is a quantitative probability, or greater chance, that a less number of spots than sixes will fall uppermost is no evidence, whatever, that in a given throw such was the actual result. Without something more, the actual result of the throw would still be utterly unknown. The slightest real evidence that sixes did in fact fall uppermost would outweigh all the probability otherwise.

But the passage is obscure, and perhaps not to be understood in the way that at first suggests itself. In any case, I take it that friends of individualized evidence who would express their view in words such as these are in a very small minority.

14. See the very helpful survey (and further references) in Michael J. Saks and Robert F. Kidd, "Human Information Processing and Adjudication: Trial by Heuristics," *Law and Society Review* 15 (1980–81). Judging from that article, I think that Saks and Kidd would say, not only that the friends of individualized evidence are mistaken in thinking it of any special interest, but also that it is a mistake to suppose there is a problem to be solved here—thus that it is a mistake to think it would be worrisome for Mrs. Smith to win her case in *Smith v. Red Cab* or for the people to win its case in *People v. Tice*.

p is true. And third, A has a reason, and indeed, not just any old reason, but a good enough reason, for believing that p is true.[15] (Some people prefer to express this third condition in the words "A is justified in believing that p is true." Others express it in the words "A has adequate evidence for p.") Not surprisingly, it is this third condition which has generated the controversy. Nobody argues about the first or second conditions: It is plain enough that you know that the sun is shining only if it is shining and you believe it is. What is unclear is exactly what is required for A to have a reason which is good enough for it to be true that A satisfies the third condition.

But one thing is clear: If A's satisfaction of those three conditions is supposed to be sufficient for A's knowing that p is true, then A is not marked as satisfying the third condition by virtue of its being the case that in light of all of the facts available to A, he is entitled to conclude, indeed is rationally required to conclude, that p is highly probable. Suppose Alfred believes, truly, that Bert bought five tickets in a lottery, and that a hundred tickets were sold altogether. Suppose also that those are the only facts such that Alfred is both aware of them and aware of their bearing on the question whether Bert will win the lottery. (For example, Alfred is not aware of any reason to believe that the lottery is rigged, or, if he is aware of a reason to believe it rigged, there is no ticket such that he is aware of a reason to believe the lottery is rigged in favor of that ticket.) The following is therefore true:

(iii) In light of all of the facts available to Alfred, he is entitled to conclude, indeed is rationally required to conclude, that it is .95 probable that Bert will lose the lottery.

Alfred is aware that he is so situated, and for that reason concludes that Bert will lose the lottery, so that

(ii) Alfred believes that Bert will lose the lottery

is also true. Suppose, lastly, that Bert will actually lose the lottery (though of course Alfred does not, and we may suppose we ourselves do not, find this out until later). Then

(i) Bert will lose the lottery

15. It is arguable that we should add: "and it is because of having a good enough reason for believing that p is true that A does believe that p is true." (For it is arguable that a man might have a good enough reason for believing that p is true, and yet believe that p is true for no reason at all, or for a bad reason.)

is also true.[16] But

> Alfred knows that Bert will lose the lottery

is plainly *not* true.

It pays to stress: Not merely is it not true to say now that Alfred knows that Bert will lose the lottery, it will also not be true to say later, after Bert has already lost the lottery, that Alfred then knew (that is, in advance) that Bert would lose the lottery.

There is something missing in Alfred, something the lack of which makes it false to say he knows that Bert will lose. The point obviously is not that .95 is not a sufficiently high probability. Pick any probability you like, as high as you like, and we need only suppose that the appropriate number of tickets were sold to entitle Alfred to conclude it probable in that degree that Bert will lose the lottery. Still, even if in fact Bert will lose, Alfred does not know that he will.

Should we say that what is missing in Alfred is something which would make him satisfy a further, fourth, condition on knowledge? That is, it could be said that Alfred's reason for believing Bert will lose the lottery is good enough for him to satisfy the third condition, and that what the case shows is that knowledge requires something more than satisfaction of the three conditions laid out in the classical account. Or should we instead say that although Alfred has good reason for believing Bert will lose the lottery, what is missing is something which would make his reason be *good enough* for him to satisfy the third condition on knowledge? It makes no theoretical difference which choice we make, for the question what is missing in Alfred remains to be answered whichever choice is made. But I prefer the second, for the classical account of knowledge is so natural and intuitively plausible as to incline one to want to interpret it in such a way as to have it be immune to such cases as that of Alfred and Bert.

To get at exactly what is missing in Alfred, then, one would have (as I shall put it) to get at exactly what is required for A to have a

16. Some people think that sentences which are contingent and in the future tense have as yet no truth-value. If that were true, then it would be wrong to say we speak truly if we say "Bert will lose the lottery," even if Bert does later lose the lottery. I say "if that were true" because I think it false. No matter. Anyone who holds this view is invited to substitute for the lottery a game in which Bert just drew five cards at random from a Superdeck (which contains 100 successively numbered cards), and then replaced them without looking. Alfred believes none of Bert's cards said "73." Let us suppose that is true; and so on, and so on.

reason which is good enough for it to be true that A satisfies the third condition on knowledge. That, alas, is a hard problem.

But it is easy enough to say very roughly what is missing in Alfred: What he lacks is something which would make it not be just luck for him that Bert will lose the lottery.

This is a helpful way of expressing what Alfred lacks[17] because it points towards anyway one of the things which is required for A to have a reason that is good enough for it to be true that A satisfies the third condition on knowledge. What I have in mind is this: It seems very plausible to think that A's reason for believing that p is true must ensure, or *guarantee*, that p is true. Alfred's reason for believing that Bert will lose the lottery does not in any way guarantee that Bert will lose it. By contrast, consider Alice. Alice believes that Bertha bought one ticket in a certain lottery, and that unbeknownst to Bertha, the ticket seller tore up her ticket stub directly after selling it to her, and that the drawing will be made from among the stubs. Suppose that belief of Alice's is true. Then Alice has good reason for believing that Bertha will lose her lottery, namely the fact that Bertha bought one ticket, the ticket seller tore up her stub, and the drawing will be made from among the stubs. Suppose Alice does therefore believe that Bertha will lose the lottery. Suppose, lastly, that time passes, and that it has now turned out that Bertha did lose the lottery, and that her losing it *was caused by* the ticket seller's tearing up her stub. Then the fact which was Alice's reason for believing that Bertha would lose her lottery caused, and thereby guaranteed, that Bertha would lose it. This makes it seem much less implausible to think Alice knew that Bertha would lose her lottery than it did to think Alfred knew that Bert would lose his.

Again, consider Arthur. Arthur believes he is having, and is in fact having, a visual impression as of a chicken in front of him, and his having that visual impression is his reason for believing there is a chicken in front of him. If it later turns out that there was then a chicken in front of him, and that there being a chicken in front of him *was causally necessary for* his having that visual impression, then his having that visual impression guaranteed that there was a chicken in front of him. This makes it seem much less implausible to think

17. It was suggested by Thomas Nagel's remarks on epistemology in "Moral Luck," in his *Mortal Questions*.

Arthur knew that there was a chicken in front of him than it does to think Alfred knew that Bert would lose his lottery.

Similarly for more complicated cases, in which the guaranteeing proceeds via common causes.[18]

On most views about knowledge, even this is not enough. Suppose that A believes there is such a fact as q, and takes q to be reason for believing that p is true. On most views about knowledge, it is not enough to secure A's satisfying the third condition on knowledge that there actually is such a fact as q, and that q actually guarantees that p is true: In addition (on those views) A must have good reason for believing that there is such a fact as q, and A must believe, and have good reason for believing, that q does guarantee that p is true. Or perhaps, more strongly, that *these* good reasons must themselves contain guarantees. On some views about knowledge, if there is luck anywhere at all in A's route to his belief that p is true, then it is just luck for A if p is true, and A therefore does not know that p is true.

Those (most restrictive) views about knowledge had better be false, for down this road lies scepticism, that is, the thesis that nobody knows anything. (Only people who are excessively charmed by philosophy can regard it as a happy outcome that nobody so much as knows he has hands or feet.)

I think it helpful at this point to turn from knowledge itself to saying one has it. That in any case is what will matter for us.

If A says to B "I know that p is true," then A does something more than just assert something: He gives B his word that p is true, and in one of the strongest ways we have of doing this. Indeed, A positively invites B to take his word for the truth of p, and to rely on it. That being so, and because it is so, there are rather strong moral constraints governing the acceptability of saying "I know that p is true." Plainly A's saying this is not made acceptable by the mere fact that p turns out to be true. Suppose Boris will suffer a loss if he relies on the truth of p where p is not true. He trusts Andrew; he tells Andrew he will suffer a loss if he relies on the truth of p where p is not true, and asks Andrew if Andrew knows whether p is true. Andrew says "Yes, I know that p is true," but he says this in awareness that he has not the slightest idea whether p is true—he does so because he decided to flip a coin, heads I say it, tails I don't, and the

18. The guaranteeing required for knowledge need not proceed via causes at all. Compare mathematical knowledge: The truth of one statement may guarantee the truth of another via entailing it.

coin came up heads. Then Andrew has acted improperly in saying what he said, even if, as it turns out, p is true.

One way, the weaker way, of explaining the impropriety in Andrew is to point to the fact that he said "I know that p is true" without having any reason at all, and a fortiori without having good reason, to think p true. Boris had said he would suffer a loss if he relied on the truth of p where p is not true; lacking good reason to think p true, Andrew could not be sure that p was true, and thus could not be sure that Boris would not suffer that loss if he relied on the truth of p—yet he all the same, and therefore wrongly, invited Boris to rely on it.

But that *is* weak. Consider Alfred again. Alfred has good reason to think Bert will lose the lottery he entered, for Alfred is entitled to believe it .95 probable that Bert will lose the lottery. Suppose the lottery works like this, and that Alfred knows it does: The winner must prove he is the winner by producing his ticket, or he must wait six months for his prize, during which time the lottery organizers will assure themselves that he is who he says he is. Nevertheless Alfred says to Bert: "Look, it's silly of you to hang on to those five, by now grubby, lottery tickets. I *know* you are going to lose that lottery." Bert will suffer a loss (six months' interest on a large sum of money) if he accepts Alfred's invitation to rely on his losing the lottery, throwing out his tickets, and it then turns out that he wins the lottery; and Alfred knows this. The fact that Alfred is sure that Bert will lose the lottery, and thus that Bert will not suffer that loss, does not make it acceptable for Alfred to have said what he said.

Let us call the loss a person will suffer if he relies on the truth of p where it turns out that p is not true that person's "potential mistake-loss." Then we can say: the fact that Alfred is sure that Bert will lose the lottery, and thus that Bert will not suffer his potential mistake-loss, does not justify Alfred's saying to Bert "I know you will lose the lottery."

What Alfred implies by saying "I know you will lose" is not merely that he is sure that Bert will lose, and thus that Bert will not suffer his potential mistake-loss, but that Alfred has a certain kind of ground for being sure of this—"insider's information" (about rigging, perhaps) in the case of lotteries, stockmarkets, and other gambler's games. Alfred implies he has a guarantee of some kind that Bert will lose, so that not merely will Bert not suffer his potential mistake-loss if he relies on Alfred's word, but that Bert does not even risk suffering his potential mistake-loss if he relies on Alfred's word. (Think on Bert's reaction if he accepts Alfred's invitation to rely on his losing, and tears up his tickets, and then later learns that the ground on which Alfred issued his invitation was merely the large number of tickets sold, which made it highly probable that Bert would lose. Bert himself knew it was highly probable he would lose at the time of buying his tickets; and he will correctly view himself as having no less right to complain about Alfred's behavior if he loses the lottery than if he wins it.)

It is plausible to think, quite generally, then, that if A is aware that B will suffer a loss if he relies on the truth of p where p is not true, then A ought not say to B "I know that p is true" unless A is more or less sure that he has a guarantee that p is true[19]—so that B not only will not suffer, but does not even risk suffering, his potential mistake-loss. There are, after all, considerably weaker sentences than "I know that p is true" which the language makes available to A: He can say instead "I believe that p is true" or "It is highly probable that p is true" or "I believe that p is true because it is highly probable that p is true" and so on. To assert some such weaker sentence as this is not to do nothing: Assertions of them are governed by moral constraints too. But none of them is such that to assert it is to invite one's intended hearer to take one's word for the truth of p and rely on it. Doing *that* calls for being more or less sure that one has a guarantee of the truth of p—at any rate, where a potential mistake-loss is in the offing.

By way of making connection with what was said earlier, we could restate this point as follows: doing *that* calls for being more or less sure that it would not be just luck for one if p turns out to be true—at any rate, where a potential mistake-loss is in the offing.

This gives us a second, and stronger, way of explaining the impropriety in Andrew. He told Boris he knew that p was true because the coin he flipped came up heads. This was wrongful behavior on

19. Usage is slippery, and there are cases which suggest that this quite general claim may be over-broad. Suppose Alfred says to Bertha "I know that Bert will not pay you the money he owes you," and says this on the ground that Bert has no money other than that which he will get if he wins the lottery, and that a large number of tickets were sold; wouldn't *that* be all right? (I owe this example to David Gauthier.) I strongly suspect, however, that this seems to us acceptable (if it does) only because we are not imagining the further details which would be required to make plain what Bertha's potential mistake-loss is; and I predict that the supplying of such further details would make Alfred's behavior seem unacceptable.

his part because he invited reliance without being in the slightest degree sure of having a guarantee, despite his awareness of Boris's potential mistake-loss.

As I said, A need only be "more or less sure" that he has a guarantee, for circumstances differ. Suppose you ask me now, in the afternoon, if there's cold chicken in the ice-box. I say "Yes, I'm certain there is, in fact I know there is." Why do I say that? Because I believe I put some there this morning, and believe my putting some there this morning guarantees that there is some there now. In the normal course of events, my saying these words is acceptable, even if it turns out that there is no cold chicken in the ice-box now, for example, because some burglars broke in at noon and ate it while burgling. That is because in the normal course of events I know your potential mistake-loss is small—you will merely waste a bit of energy on a trip to the ice-box, and suffer a minor disappointment if it is chickenless. But we could imagine a series of cases in which your potential mistake-loss increases; that would be a series of cases in which the burden on me to make sure that I really do have a guarantee increases proportionately. Where I know your potential mistake-loss is truly terrible, then the burden on me is very heavy indeed. Did my putting cold chicken in the ice-box this morning really guarantee that there is some there now? Your potential mistake-loss being so great, I ought not ignore the possibility that it did not. (Burglars are only one of many more or less weird possibilities.) I had better not invite you to run the risk of suffering that truly terrible loss unless I make *very* sure I have a guarantee—as, for example, by getting up out of my chair and going to have a look, and perhaps also a sniff and taste.

In light of these considerations it might well be wondered why we ever say anything so strong as "I know that p is true." Well, we do not normally say this unless we believe our hearer will gain something if he acts on the supposition that p is true where it is true, or suffer a loss if he fails to act on the supposition that p is true where it is true. (In the normal course of events, a person who asks whether there is cold chicken in the ice-box wants to eat some, and thus has something to gain by acting on the supposition that there is some there if it turns out that there is.) A foregone gain is what is sometimes called an "opportunity cost," and thus itself a kind of loss, so it could have been said, instead, more briefly: We do not normally say "I know that p is true" unless we believe our hearer will suffer a loss (if only a loss which is an opportunity cost) if he fails to act on the supposition that p is true where it is true. What would be the point of inviting a hearer to rely on the truth of p if the hearer has nothing at all to lose by failing to rely on it even if p is true?

There might, then, be a case in which A believes both of the following about B. (i) B will suffer a loss if he acts on the supposition that p is true where it is not true; that is B's potential mistake-loss. (ii) B will suffer a loss if he fails to act on the supposition that p is true where it is true; I will call this B's "potential omission-loss." Here A has some more or less delicate balancing to do. But perhaps this much is clear enough: The greater the amount by which B's potential mistake-loss exceeds B's potential omission-loss, the more sure A must be that he has a guarantee that p is true before saying "I know that p is true."

It is not knowledge itself, but rather saying one has knowledge, that will matter for us. But I think it is worth indicating, just briefly, why (as I said) I think it helps a student of knowledge to attend to what is required for acceptably saying one has it. According to the classical account of knowledge, A knows that p is true if and only if p is true, A believes that p is true, and A has good enough reason for believing that p is true. What marks A as having good enough reason for believing that p is true? I suggest it is enough if A takes himself to have a guarantee that p is true, and if also what he takes to guarantee this does guarantee it. Thus, for example, suppose (again) that I believe there is cold chicken in the ice-box because I believe I put some there this morning, and believe my putting some there this morning guarantees that there is some there now. Suppose also that my believing I put some there this morning guarantees that I did put some there this morning, and that that guarantees that there is some there now. Then I do know that there is some there now. I could have been wrong: for example, my putting cold chicken in the ice-box this morning could have failed to guarantee that there is some there now. (Burglars, perhaps.) I suggest we should take that fact to have a bearing, not on whether I know, but only on what I may acceptably say.

5. I fancy it may already be clear from this long digression on knowledge what, on my view of them, is at work in the friends of individualized evidence.

The jurors do not say "We know that the defendant is guilty" at the close of the trial, they say only "The defendant is guilty"; but in saying that they do something of great significance. It is not strong enough to say they declare the defendant guilty. If you and I have been watching the trial, I may say to you as we leave the courtroom "The defendant is guilty"; I have declared the defendant guilty, but have not done, because I am not so situated as to be able to do, what the jurors do when they say these words at the close of the trial. The institution in which they are participating is so structured that their saying these words then is their imposing liability on the defendant—for if they say these words at that time, appropriate others will act on the supposition that he is guilty, which includes imposing the relevant penalty on him. So they do not merely invite reliance, they act in awareness that reliance will follow.

Under what conditions is it acceptable for the jurors to agree to say those words at the close of the trial? One thing which is perfectly plain is that their agreeing to say those words is not made acceptable by the mere fact that the defendant actually is guilty of what he is charged with. That what the jurors declare true turns out to have in fact been true does not by itself make it acceptable for them to have declared it true.

This point is obvious, but it pays to make its source explicit. Suppose that a jury is puzzled by the evidence which has been presented to it, and cannot arrive at a consensus as to its weight. "I know," says one juror, "let's decide by flipping a coin—heads we impose liability, tails we don't." They agree; they flip a coin, which comes up heads; so they return and say "The defendant is guilty." Their doing that is not made acceptable by the fact (supposing it a fact) that the defendant actually is guilty. If the defendant is guilty, then he deserves the penalty which this jury causes to be imposed on him; but that the defendant not suffer the relevant penalty unjustly is not all that matters to us. It matters to us, not just that a defendant not suffer a penalty unjustly, but also that the penalty not be imposed on him unjustly.

The defendant will suffer the penalty unjustly if he is not guilty, and so does not deserve the penalty; that means that it is unjust to impose liability on him, and thereby cause him to suffer the penalty, unless one believes one has good reason to believe that he is guilty, and therefore deserves the penalty. That being so, we can say, and we have an explanation of why we can say, that the jury I just described imposed liability unjustly: They imposed liability without believing they had good reason to believe that the defendant was guilty.

There is a second, and stronger, possible explanation of why we can say that that jury imposed liability unjustly: It was just luck for those jurors if what they declared true was true—just luck for them if it actually was the case that the defendant was guilty.

That *is* stronger. Consider the jury in the hypothetical case I called *People v. Tice* in section 3 above. Suppose it declares Tice guilty of murder, not on the ground that a coin was tossed and came up heads, but on the following two grounds. First, the evidence makes clear (perhaps Tice has even confessed) that he attempted to kill Summers. Second, Summers was killed by one of 100 pellets fired at him, and ninety-five of the pellets fired at him were fired by Tice. Then the jury imposes liability on Tice on the ground of what is on any view good reason to believe Tice guilty. (Its situation in respect of Tice's being guilty is exactly like Alfred's situation in respect of Bert's losing his lottery: In both cases, rationality requires believing the conclusion highly probable.) If it is required of a jury only that it not impose liability without good reason to believe the defendant guilty, then this jury does not impose liability unjustly. All the same, it is just luck for the jury if it actually was Tice who killed Summers, and thus if Tice committed murder. So if it is required of a jury that it not impose liability unless it has, not merely good reason, but reason of a kind which would make it not be just luck for the jury if its verdict is true, then this jury imposes liability unjustly.

On my view of them, what is at work in the friends of individualized evidence is precisely the feeling that just imposition of liability requires that this stronger requirement be met.[20] They believe, as they say, that "mathematical chances" or "quantitative probability" is not by itself enough; on my view of them, that is because they feel, rightly, that if a jury declares a defendant guilty on the ground of nonindividualized evidence alone, then it is just luck for the jury if what it declares true is true—and they feel, not without reason, that it is unjust to impose liability where that is the case. I say "not without reason" because I feel in considerable sympathy with them.

What would make it not be just luck for the jury if what it declares

20. To say this is to rest the importance of individualized evidence on what the jurors do, rather than on something external to the trial. Compare Laurence H. Tribe, who rests it on the symbolic or expressive function of trials; see his "Trial by Mathematics." Compare also Charles Nesson, who rests it on the messages communicated by trials; see his "The Evidence or the Event? On Judicial Proof and the Acceptability of Verdicts," *Harvard Law Review* 98 (May 1985).

true is true? A guarantee. I suggested that individualized evidence for a defendant's guilt is evidence which is in an appropriate way causally connected with the (putative) fact that the defendant is guilty, and hence (putatively) guarantees the defendant's guilt; so to require individualized evidence of guilt just is to be requiring a guarantee.

None of this is incompatible with the fact that there is a difference made in our law between the standard of proof required in criminal cases on the one hand, and cases in torts on the other hand. Our law requires the jury in a criminal case to be sure beyond a reasonable doubt that the defendant is guilty before imposing liability on him; the friend of individualized evidence may be taken to say that the jury must be sure beyond a reasonable doubt that the defendant is guilty *because of* being sure beyond a reasonable doubt that there are facts available to it which guarantee that the defendant is guilty. Our law requires the jury in a case in torts to believe no more than that it is more probable than not that the defendant is guilty; the friend of individualized evidence may be taken to say that the jury must believe it is more probable than not that the defendant is guilty *because of* believing it more probable than not that there are facts available to it which guarantee that the defendant is guilty.

We met an analogous difference in section 4 above, and the differences have analogous sources. Our society takes the view that, in a criminal case, the loss to society if the defendant suffers the penalty for a crime he did not commit is very much greater than the loss to society if the defendant does not suffer the penalty for a crime he did commit. (That is, in particular, we think it would be considerably worse that an innocent defendant be punished than that a guilty defendant go free.) This point might be reexpressed as follows: Our society takes the view that in a criminal case, the society's potential mistake-loss is very much greater than the society's potential omission-loss. It would be no wonder, then, if our law imposed a heavy standard of proof on the jury in a criminal case; and according to the friend of individualized evidence, that means the jury must be very sure of having a guarantee before imposing liability for a crime. The fact that the standard of proof in a case in torts is more relaxed by itself suggests that our society takes the view that, in a case in torts, the society's potential mistake-loss is not much greater than the society's potential omission-loss. (Thus that, in particular, we think it would be worse that an innocent defendant be forced to pay a plaintiff who either was not really harmed at all, or who anyway was not harmed by the defendant, than that a guilty defendant go free and the plaintiff he injured go uncompensated—but not by much.)

6. The typical hypothetical cases which descend from *People v. Collins* raise the problem we are dealing with less clearly than *People v. Tice,* and that in two ways.

Here is an example. Mrs. Smith testifies that she saw a man, indeed exactly one man, kill Bloggs, and that she could see he was one-legged, left-handed, entirely bald, and extremely tall. Mrs. Jones is a biologist-statistician, and she testifies that men with all four of those features are very rare: Only one man in 10 million has all four of them. There is the defendant Mullins, and we can see that *he* has all four of them. So we may be inclined to think we may conclude, on the basis of that evidence alone, and without hearing or seeing anything more, that it is highly probable that Mullins killed Bloggs.

As the commentators on this kind of case enjoy pointing out, however, this would be a mistake on our part. After all, there are a lot more than 10 million men in the world. How many are there? Let us suppose there are a billion men in the world, thus 1,000 million. If, as Mrs. Jones's data suggest, one in 10 million men have all four features, then 100 in 1,000 million have all four features; so we are entitled to conclude only that the probability that Mullins killed Bloggs is 1 in 100, thus .01—not at all a high probability.

I think it helps to see this point if we lay our information out in the way in which I laid our information out in *People v. Tice* and *Smith v. Red Cab.* Thus we believe, on the basis of what we can see on looking at the defendant Mullins:

(1″) Mullins is a man who is one-legged, left-handed, entirely bald, and extremely tall.

If we believe Mrs. Smith's story, we believe that exactly one man killed Bloggs, and that the man is one-legged, left-handed, completely bald, and extremely tall. If we also believe Mrs. Jones's story, we believe that one in 10 million men have those four features. If we believe there are 1,000 million men, we are committed to believing that 100 men all told have those four features. So we are committed to believing:

(2″) 1 of the 100 men who are one-legged, left-handed, entirely bald, and extremely tall killed Bloggs.

The conclusion we are entitled to draw is only:

(3″) The probability that Mullins killed Bloggs is .01.

Our problem was this: What should we think of the idea of convicting a defendant on the basis of evidence which makes it highly probable he is guilty, but which is nonindividualized evidence against him? So the first way in which the typical hypothetical descendant of *People v. Collins* is less clean than *People v. Tice* is this: In that kind of case, the available data do not even entitle us to conclude that it is highly probable that the defendant is guilty.

This may seem to be a relatively trivial difficulty, for there are a number of different ways in which the case against Mullins could be revised so as to raise the probability of his guilt, despite its anyway seeming to remain a case in which no individualized evidence is produced against him. We might suppose, for example, that Mrs. Smith testifies that the man she saw kill Bloggs had, not merely the four features I have mentioned, but in addition, only one eye—not one good eye and one bad eye, but exactly one eye, right in the middle of his forehead. Mullins, as we can see in the revised case, has not merely the four features, but exactly one eye, right in the middle of his forehead. Our biologist-statistician, Mrs. Jones, assures us that she would have said this was impossible if she had not seen Mullins: It is due to a freak genetic mutation which may be expected to occur no more often than once in 100 billion men. There being in existence only 1 billion men, it is highly probable that Mullins is the only existing man with all five features, and thus (if we believe Mrs. Smith's story) it is highly probable that Mullins did kill Bloggs.

This kind of move has to be watched, however, for once the probability is made high in this way, our problem does not come out more cleanly, it instead disappears. What I have in mind is this. In the original case against Mullins, Mrs. Smith believes she saw a one-legged, left-handed, entirely bald, and extremely tall man kill Bloggs. That is individualized evidence that a man with those four features killed Bloggs, for the (putative) fact that a man with those four features killed Bloggs would causally explain Mrs. Smith's believing she saw a man with those four features kill Bloggs. (Compare the fact that in *Smith v. Red Cab*, Mrs. Smith's believing she saw a cab come towards her was individualized evidence that it was a cab that came towards her.) Our further evidence also suggests there are other men than Mullins, ninety-nine other men in fact, who have all four features, so getting individualized evidence against Mullins requires getting some fact in respect of which an appropriate causal role is played by a feature which distinguishes Mullins from the others. (Compare the need of a fact in respect of which an appropriate causal role is played by a feature which distinguishes Red Cab's cabs from the other cabs we believe were in town on the night of the accident in *Smith v. Red Cab*.)

In the revised version of the case, Mrs. Smith believes she saw a one-legged, left-handed, entirely bald, extremely tall, *and* one-eyed man kill Bloggs. That is individualized evidence that a man with those five features killed Bloggs, for the (putative) fact that a man with those five features killed Bloggs would causally explain Mrs. Smith's believing that she saw a man with those five features kill Bloggs. But *here* our further evidence suggests that only Mullins has all five features, and therefore that there is no such thing as a feature which distinguishes him from the other men who have all five features, and therefore that there is no possible fact in respect of which such a distinguishing feature so much as could play an appropriate causal role. To the extent to which we believe that further evidence, then, we shall take ourselves to have individualized evidence, not merely that a man with those five features killed Bloggs, but that Mullins did—he being the only available candidate with the five features.

There is more to be said here, but I bypass it, because whatever revisions might be made in the case against Mullins, there remains the second way in which the typical hypothetical descendant of *People v. Collins* raises our problem less cleanly than *People v. Tice*: In that kind of case, the sources of the statistical information are typically softer than the source of the piece of statistical information in *People v. Tice*. For example, that exactly one man in 10 million has all four of the features which interested us in the original case against Mullins may be true; but we may well be pardoned if we do not feel much confidence in those figures. By contrast, I was inviting you to suppose that the evidence presented in court entitles us to feel entirely confident that exactly 100 pellets were fired at Summers, and that exactly ninety-five of them were fired at him by Tice. (And compare *Smith v. Red Cab*. Perhaps we do not feel *entirely* confident that six out of ten of the cabs in town that night were operated by Red Cab, since we are so familiar with gypsy cabs. But we may have good reason to believe in the figures Mrs. Smith gives us, and no positive reason to disbelieve in them, perhaps in that Red Cab itself gives us no reason to think them wrong.)

On the other hand, I am not arguing that no hypothetical descendant of *People v. Collins* raises our problem cleanly. Quite to the contrary: *People v. Tice* itself descends from it.

7. Commentators of this kind of case very commonly say that all evidence is "ultimately" statistical or probabilistic,[21] and that this itself means there is muddle in the friends of individualized evidence. Such comments are decidedly not transparent, and they can be interpreted in a number of different ways. The interpretation which makes them most plausible, however, seems to me to be one under which they do not really constitute a difficulty for the friends of individualized evidence.

Under that interpretation, "All evidence is ultimately statistical" says about causal hypotheses in particular that such evidence as we have for them is itself statistical (or anyway, is ultimately itself statistical), so that we can have no more confidence in the truth of a causal hypothesis than we have in the statistical data which (ultimately) supports it. This does not strike me as obvious, but perhaps it is true. Perhaps it is true that I am entitled to place no more confidence in the hypothesis that my pressing the button marked "T" just now caused a "t" to appear on the page than I have in some set of statistical data—alas, I do not know what exactly the members are, but perhaps one member of the set is, not quite that every time I press the button marked "T" a "t" appears on the page, for sometimes I have previously pressed the button marked "shift," so that a "T" appeared on the page instead, and sometimes the machine had not been turned on, so that nothing appeared on the page, and so on, but something *like* this.

Now why might it be thought that this should trouble the friend of individualized evidence? He is familiar with the idea that a causal hypothesis may be supported by statistical data. Compare, for example, the kind of race discrimination case mentioned in section 3 above, in which statistical data about the divergence between the racial composition of an organization's workforce and that of the local population suggests the causal hypothesis that the divergence was caused by an intention to discriminate in hiring.

Moreover, he is familiar with the fact that being presented with

21. Tribe himself says "I am, of course, aware that *all* factual evidence is ultimately 'statistical,' and all legal proof ultimately 'probabilistic' " *op. cit.*, p. 1330, fn 2. And compare Saks and Kidd, "Human Information Processing": "Invariably, all information is really probability information," p. 153.

statistical data may entitle us to feel more or less confidence in the truth of a causal hypothesis. As I said in connection with *Smith v. Red Cab*, the more non-cabs there are on the roads that are disguised as cabs, the less confidence we are entitled to place in the hypothesis that its being a cab that came towards Mrs. Smith does causally explain her believing she saw a cab come towards her. Similarly for a surprise witness, who comes forward to say he saw the accident, and that the accident-causing cab looked red to him: The more often non-red things look red to that witness when he is placed in similar circumstances, the less confidence we are entitled to place in the hypothesis that the cab's being red does causally explain his believing that it looked red to him.

One can, after all, be more or less sure of having the kind of guarantee that, as I said, is what the friends of individualized evidence thinks some degree of assurance of is necessary for just imposition of liability. That our assurance of having a guarantee of the appropriate kind rests (ultimately) on statistical data seems to me to be something he can in consistency agree to.

And it need not trouble the friend of individualized evidence that the particular causal hypothesis that this or that bit of individualized evidence points to may not be well supported by the available statistical data, and hence that the bit of individualized evidence may not lend much weight to the hypothesis that the defendant is guilty. As I said, it is an ungenerous diagnosis of what is at work in the friends of individualized evidence to take them to think it of value because of thinking it uniquely highly probabilifying. What interests them is something else—a something else that I have been trying to bring out, and to invite others to take an interest in.[22]

22. A great many people made helpful criticisms of earlier drafts of this essay; I am particularly indebted to Jonathan Bennett, David Gauthier, Gilbert Harman, Paul Horwich, Mary C. Potter, and the participants at the Conference on Responsibility (Duke University, April 1985) at which parts of the essay were first presented.

Afterword

I am grateful to William Parent for thinking that it would be useful to collect these essays, and for doing the work required to see them through to publication. I would not have done this myself. While it still seems to me that the central ideas at work in the essays are correct, many of them contain mistakes, and I cannot reread any of them except the most recent without wanting to rewrite them. I think that attitude toward earlier work is fairly common among practicing philosophers. Even when one still agrees with ideas one had in the past, one's sense of how they should be presented and argued for changes, in some cases radically, as the years pass. On the other hand, to rewrite an old essay is to write a new one; and perhaps Professor Parent is right in thinking that the old ones themselves continue to be of interest, if only because what they say they say with enthusiasm and a sense of discovery (these are rarely found in rewritings of old essays), and because people interested in the problems they raise and discuss continue to find it a good question what exactly their mistakes are.

It might pay, however, to mention three things which strike me on looking back over these essays now.

1. Although most of the essays are centrally concerned with the concept "has a right to," they say precious little about what rights we have. The reason is that that seems to me to be a question which moral theorists are not yet in a position to begin to answer. We cannot produce a reasoned account of what rights we have until we are clearer than we currently are just what it is to have a right. What have you *got* when you've got a right?

It was William James, I think, who recommended that when confronted with a puzzling concept, one should ask for its cash value. What is the cash value of having a right? Suppose that Alfred (as it might be) has a right to life or liberty or property, or less grandly, suppose that Alfred has a right that Bertha not drive her car through his greenhouse. So what? The answer, very roughly, is this: Alfred having the right, there are ways in which others may, and more importantly, may not treat him. For example, Alfred having a right that Bertha not drive her car through his greenhouse, Bertha must not do this.

But that *is* very rough. One difficulty comes out as follows. Suppose Bertha discovers to her horror that she will die unless she drives her car through Alfred's greenhouse. (How on earth could that be? Let us imagine that an avalanche is headed towards her, and that her only available escape route passes through Alfred's greenhouse.) Then what? Most people would be prepared to say that Bertha may proceed: surely one may wreck a greenhouse if doing so is necessary to save one's life! Should we conclude that Alfred never had a right that Bertha not drive her car through his greenhouse? Or that although he once had this right, he ceased to have it when it became true that Bertha needed to do this if she was to save her life? Or that although Alfred once did, and still has, this right, it is in some circumstances (as when life is at stake) permissible to proceed despite the fact that to do so is to infringe the right?

What does it matter which of these conclusions we draw?—so long as we are agreed that it is morally permissible for Bertha to drive her car through Alfred's greenhouse, given she needs to do this to save her life. Well, if all we want to know is whether it is morally permissible for Bertha to drive her car through Alfred's greenhouse in those circumstances, then there is no need for us to decide which of those conclusions to draw. But if what we want to know is the cash value of having a right, then we need to know how others may or may not act, given a person has this or that right, and that means we need to know whether it is ever morally permissible to infringe a right—so, in particular, whether Bertha would be infringing a right of Alfred's in driving her car through his greenhouse.

And we need to know also in the name of what it is permissible (if it ever is permissible) to infringe a right. Bertha may surely drive her car through Alfred's greenhouse to save her life; she equally surely may not do this just for the pure pleasure of it.

Indeed, we need to know these things if we want to know what having a right *is*. For my own part, it seems to me that to have a right just *is* its being the case that people may and may not treat you in these and those ways. (Rights are in this respect unlike tables and chairs, which are not identical with their cash value.) This means, then, that figuring out what it is for Alfred to have a right that Bertha not drive her car through his greenhouse requires figuring out what it is that Bertha (and others) may or may not do to him, in these or those possible circumstances.

So also for the grander rights of political theory. To have rights to life, liberty, and property, just is to have clusters or bundles of simpler rights; and each of the simpler rights in a cluster just is a moral status, which would be exhaustively characterized if it were exhaustively characterized what we may or may not do to a person who has it.

But these questions have not yet been answered to the satisfaction of all who have been concerned with them. Several of the essays in this collection argue that it is sometimes permissible to infringe *some* rights. For example, it seems to me that Alfred does not cease to have a right that Bertha not drive her car through his greenhouse in consequence of its coming to be the case that Bertha needs to do this to save her life; thus it seems to me that Bertha does infringe a right of Alfred's in driving her car through his greenhouse, despite its being permissible for her to do so. The argument for this claim issues from the fact that certain acts leave "moral traces," as it were, and that to understand why they do, we must suppose that the acts are infringements of rights. What I have in mind is this. Suppose Bertha proceeds: she drives her car through Alfred's greenhouse to save her life. She cannot now simply wash her hands of the matter: she *owes* Alfred something—she must at a minimum contribute to repairing the damage she did. If things had been different, if Bertha had been under no risk, if Alfred had simply invited her to drive her car through his greenhouse (perhaps for the fun of watching her do it), then Bertha would owe him nothing. So far as I can see, the only adequate explanation of this difference is that if Bertha drives her car through the greenhouse at Alfred's invitation, then he has waived his right that she not do this, and she therefore infringes no right of his in doing so; by contrast, if she drives her car through the greenhouse not at his invitation, but instead to save her life, then he has not waived any right, and she *has* infringed a right of his.

Arguments to the effect that such and such is the only adequate explanation of a phenomenon are very hard to make convincing. (Have *all* the other possible explanations been ruled out?) And since there are, as it seems to me, two good reasons for preferring that we be able to say it is never permissible to infringe a right, it is no surprise that many people have not been convinced by this argument. In the first place, assertions of rights have a kind of moral force that no other moral assertions do. As Ronald Dworkin expressed the point, in a metaphor from bridge: rights are trumps.[1] Do we think it would be better on balance if we curtailed certain liberties?—for example, refused to permit certain kinds of political speech, or preventively detained people who have as yet committed no crime, but who meet conditions which we have found in the past to be highly correlated with criminality? It might well be that the consequences of doing so would be on balance beneficial, but that does not justify doing so: those who would be affected have the right that we not treat them in these ways, and their right trumps the benefits to be got, and thus morally blocks our so treating them.

On some views, human self-respect itself rests on the belief that one possesses such trumps, which make it impermissible for one to be used as a means for the securing of benefits for others.

The second reason why we might well prefer to be able to say it is never permissible to infringe a right is theoretical: it is because a moral theory which takes rights to be absolute is simpler than one which does not. A right it is permissible to infringe seems to be an excrescence on a moral theory—like a Ptolemaic epicycle it should be the aim of a theorist to eliminate.

But though I think these are good reasons, I do not think them good enough. The right to speak one's mind on matters political, the right to not be imprisoned without guilt, these are fundamental rights, and it is hard to imagine a benefit to be got by infringing them which would justify infringing them—that is precisely what marks them as fundamental rights. But on the one hand, we do also have other rights, rights which are not in the same way fundamental. You have a right that I not here and now kick you in the shin, Alfred has a right that Bertha not drive her car through his greenhouse, these are not fundamental rights, but for all that, they are not nothing either; and we misconstrue what a right is if we ignore them. And on the

1. Ronald Dworkin, *Taking Rights Seriously* (Cambridge, Mass.: Harvard University Press, 1977).

other hand, while it is hard to imagine circumstances which would justify infringing a man's right to speak his mind on matters political, it is not impossible to imagine them. (I leave it to the reader to invent some sufficiently desperate and dangerous circumstances.) For my own part, it seems to me that very very few of the rights a human being can plausibly be thought to have are truly absolute. So self-respect had better not turn only on the belief that one possesses absolute rights.

The good moral theorist, like the theorist in any other branch of study, loves simplicity and hates an epicycle. It is right to say (I here emend Occam's Razor) that complexity ought not be introduced beyond necessity. All the same, however, complexity ought not be avoided where it is necessary, that is, where it can only be avoided at the cost of diminished explanatory power. *Can* a moral theory which does not allow for rights it is permissible to infringe explain the moral phenomena which need explaining as well as one which does? The argument from "moral traces" which I pointed to earlier is intended to lend weight to the idea that the answer to that question is No.

2. This brings me to the second of the three things which (as I said) strike me on looking back over these essays: One of their central messages, as I can now see, is precisely that a moral theory adequate to its explanatory job is going to have to be a more complex affair than we might have expected it to be. An interesting question lurks here. Nobody expects chemistry or physics to be simple; why do so many people expect moral theory to be simple? (My students seem to think that if you have a moral theory, you ought to be able to say what it is without having to draw a second breath.) Consider, for example, the greatest of all the classical moral theories: Hedonistic Act Utilitarianism. It is among the simplest of all moral theories. It says that if you want to find out what you ought to do in a given set of circumstances, all you need do is find out which of the acts open to you at the time would cause the greatest happiness, on balance, and in the long run, for everybody affected—what you ought to do is to choose that act. No doubt it is not always, or perhaps even very often, easy to find out which of the acts open to you at a given time would cause the greatest happiness; but the difficulty of finding this out is a difficulty of fact, not of value—according to this theory, when once the facts are clear, the moral question is easy. Most moral theorists nowadays think that Hedonistic Act Utilitarianism is false; but

they continue to feel a need to rebut it, and no one feels free just to ignore it. One (though only one) source of its continuing life is the very fact that it is so attractively simple.

I hazard a guess that there are two reasons why we expect a moral theory to be simple. In the first place, there is nothing recondite about the data which the theory must explain. What the moral theorist attends to is human action, and what wants explaining is what makes those acts right which are right, and what makes those acts wrong which are wrong; and we need no microscope, no telescope, no Geiger counter to observe a human act and detect the rightness or wrongness in it. Second, we have very powerfully the inclination to think that it is within everyone's capacity to act well, and not just within the capacity of specialists and experts; and how could that be if it were not within everyone's capacity to reason out what ought and ought not be done?

But the fact is that there is no end to the range of possible situations in which human beings may find themselves, or to the range of beliefs, intentions, and motives they may act on in those situations. If we need no special equipment to observe the data, we do all the same need to remind ourselves from time to time of the wide variety of possible human action, and of the fact that a wide array of considerations bear on all but the simplest of moral problems.

This comes home to us particularly vividly when we turn to the literature of law. Case books are like anthologies of short stories, each of which ends in a moral problem. Defendant Smith was driving his car down Main Street when a child ran out from between two parked cars, and to avoid him, Smith swerved. Unfortunately, Smith had not been watching quite as carefully as he should have been, so he swerved to the right instead of to the left—and drove smack into Plaintiff Jones. Should Defendant Smith be placed under the duty of paying Plaintiff Jones' medical bills? If so, why? If not, why not? The judge's answer is constrained in ways in which the moral theorist's is not; but the moral theorist can learn, not merely from the story itself, that is, not merely from the possibilities of human action which the story reminds us of, but from the judge's decision and his or her argument for it.

Many moral theorists came to the literature of law by way of what still seems to me the most interesting work ever written on its topic, namely *Causation in the Law*, by H. L. A. Hart and A. M. Honore.[2]

2. H. L. A. Hart and A. M. Honore, *Causation in the Law* (Oxford: Oxford University Press, 1959).

No moral theorist, however ingenious, could have invented the stories which Hart and Honore told us about what actual people actually did to each other. Contact with law has been immensely enriching to moral theory in recent years.

3. The reader of these essays will see that I regard examples, stories, cases—whether actual or invented—as of central importance to moral theory; that is the third of the three things which seemed to me worth mentioning. There are two reasons for thinking them of central importance. In the first place, we do not even know what accepting this or that candidate moral principle would commit us to until we see what it tells us about what people ought or ought not do in this or that (so far as possible) concretely described set of circumstances.

Second, and more interesting, it is precisely our moral views about examples, stories, and cases which constitute the data for moral theorizing. I said earlier that there is nothing recondite about the data which a moral theory must explain. What the moral theorist attends to is human action, and what wants explaining is what makes those acts right which are right, and what makes those acts wrong which are wrong. But which acts *are* the right ones? Which acts *are* the wrong ones? Well, among the right ones are the ones which strike us as clearly, plainly, on any plausible moral view, right; and so also for the wrong ones.

Here is an example. (It is discussed at greater length in essays 6 and 7 in this collection.) A surgeon has five patients who will die unless they are provided with certain essential bodily parts. A young man has just come in for his yearly check-up, and his parts will do: the surgeon can cut him up and transplant his parts among the five who need them. The surgeon asks the young man if he is willing to volunteer his parts, and thus his life; the young man says "Sorry, I deeply sympathize with your five patients, but no." Would it be morally permissible for the surgeon to proceed anyway? Hardly! That it would be wrong for the surgeon to proceed seems to me to be as certain as anything in life, and thus as among the data which a moral theory should explain.

What is to be done with a person who asks "But how do you *know* that it would be wrong for the surgeon to proceed?" That is a good question, but what it asks for is not moral theory. Compare the chemist. He put a bit of paper in a certain liquid, and it turned pink. That it did is something he takes as a datum; and what he wants is a theory which will explain that datum. It is of course open to us to ask "How do you *know* that the bit of paper turned pink?" But what we are asking for if we do say this is not chemistry, it is, rather, what has traditionally been called Epistemology, or Theory of Knowledge. Moral knowledge may well be special in this or that way, and the moral theorist can learn from the epistemologist in ways in which the chemist is not likely to be able to; all the same, chemistry can proceed in advance of the solution of the central problems of epistemology, and so also can moral theory. I shall come back to this point again shortly.

The person who asks "But how do you *know* that it would be wrong for the surgeon to proceed?" is very different from the person who says "I disagree: I believe it would be quite all right for the surgeon to proceed." Is there such a person? Does anybody really have this belief? (Students often pretend they have it, to see how the teacher will react.) I have yet to meet anyone so peculiar as really to have it. No matter: it seems to be possible that someone might, and what if someone did? If we had an account of moral knowledge under which it was possible to demonstrate that we know it would be wrong for the surgeon to proceed, then we would a fortiori be in a position to demonstrate that it would be wrong for the surgeon to proceed—and thus in a position to demonstrate to the peculiar person that anyway this one of his moral beliefs is mistaken. Unfortunately, we have no such account of moral knowledge: the central problems of epistemology have not been solved. The reply we have to make to the peculiar person, then, is this. "The rest of us are agreed that it would be wrong for the surgeon to proceed, and we agree also on a good many other instances of actual and possible human action, and what we are in search of is *our* moral theory: that body of principles which will explain what *we* take to be the moral facts. (That does not mean we're going to ignore you. It's not every day in the week one meets a person with truly odd moral ideas, and we fully expect to find it a fascinating question what *your* moral theory is—that is, what body of principles explain what *you* take to be the moral facts.)" That is how moral theory can proceed in advance of the solution of the central problem of epistemology: it can simply bypass them.

The first requirement on a moral theory is that it explain the data it sets itself to explain. The second is that it correctly predict further data, and explain them too. So far, the requirements on a moral theory are the same as the requirements on a theory in any area of study.

However there is a third requirement on a moral theory which has no *exact* analogue elsewhere. Consider Hedonistic Act Utilitarianism again. What does it predict in the case of the surgeon? If the surgeon proceeds, he saves five lives at a cost of one, and thus produces a net saving of four lives; this makes it seem likely that Hedonistic Act Utilitarianism would predict that the surgeon not only may proceed, but ought to. But it would be wrong for the surgeon to proceed. So if Hedonistic Act Utilitarianism does predict that the surgeon ought to proceed, one of its predictions is incorrect, and the theory therefore fails to meet the second of the requirements I mentioned.

But a friend of Hedonistic Act Utilitarianism could deny that it predicts the surgeon ought to proceed. He might say: "Look, if the surgeon proceeds, others will hear about it—you can't keep such enterprises a secret. And if others hear about it, they will come to mistrust their doctors. And they will therefore avoid their doctors. Much unhappiness would therefore be caused by the surgeon's proceeding, more unhappiness than would be caused by the loss of those four lives. So on balance, and in the long run, more happiness would be produced by the surgeon's *not* proceeding. So it really would be wrong for the surgeon to proceed."

And what if the surgeon could carry out the plan for saving his five patients in secret? Then what would Hedonistic Act Utilitarianism predict about his doing so? For my part, I think we believe it would be wrong for the surgeon to proceed, whether or not he could do so in secret.

But let us set this aside, because what I want to get to is the third requirement on a moral theory, which (as I think) Hedonistic Act Utilitarianism fails to meet even if the surgeon could not carry out his plan in secret, and thus even if the theory does make the right prediction in his case. What I have in mind is that even if the theory predicts that the surgeon ought not proceed, the theory's explanation of that prediction is, morally speaking, unsatisfactory.

The surgeon must not operate on the young man, and give his parts to the five who need them. Why not? Well, that is what a theory should tell us: It should explain why the surgeon must not proceed. But consider what Hedonistic Act Utilitarianism offers as the explanation why the surgeon may not proceed: the fact that doing so would cause much unhappiness to others. That locates the moral source of the prohibition on proceeding in the wrong place. Surely the reason why the surgeon must not proceed has to lie, not in what proceeding would cause other people, but in what proceeding involves doing to the young man. The unhappiness which would be caused others by the surgeon's proceeding seems to be utterly insignificant by comparison with, and thus not adequately explanatory of, the enormity of the wrong which the surgeon would be doing to the young man himself.

It is not easy to say what it is about the young man himself which is the source of the prohibition on the surgeon's proceeding. One feels intuitively that the surgeon would be violating a right of the young man's, a fundamental right, in fact, and that that is why the surgeon must not proceed. I am sure that something like this must be correct. But it brings us full circle: for as I indicated earlier, we do not yet fully understand how the concept "has a right to" itself works.

What is clear, at all events, is that a moral theory ought not merely explain the data it sets itself to explain, it ought not merely make correct predictions and explain them, it also ought to give morally satisfying explanations of what it explains—its explanations ought to be morally adequate to what it explains. Hedonistic Act Utilitarianism fails to meet this third requirement.

It is arguable that the third requirement collapses into the first two, that is, that the moral inadequacy of a theory's explanations must show itself somewhere in incorrect predictions. Indeed, I suspect that this is true.

But what matters for present purposes is only that, whether or not it is true, the moral theorist must attend to his or her own moral beliefs about examples, stories, and cases, actual or invented, looking to see how those beliefs do (or do not) change as the details of the stories are altered. For it is precisely those beliefs which supply the data for moral theorizing, and which go a long way—if not all the way—to setting the constraints on what constitutes an acceptable moral principle, and thus on what constitutes an acceptable way of understanding what we ourselves take morality to require of us.

Sources
Index

Sources

The following is a list of the original places and dates of appearance of the essays in this collection; they are listed in order of the book's sequence and are reprinted by permission of the publishers.

"A Defense of Abortion," *Philosophy and Public Affairs*, 1 (Fall 1971). Copyright © 1971 by Princeton University Press.

"Rights and Deaths," *Philosophy and Public Affairs*, 2 (Winter 1973). Copyright © 1973 by Princeton University Press.

"Self-Defense and Rights" was presented as the 1976 Lindley Lecture at the University of Kansas.

"Some Ruminations on Rights," *The University of Arizona Law Review*, 19 (1977). Copyright © 1977 by the Arizona Board of Regents.

"Rights and Compensation," *Nous*, 14 (1980). Copyright © 1980 by Indiana University.

"Killing, Letting Die, and the Trolley Problem," *The Monist* (1976).

"The Trolley Problem," *The Yale Law Journal*, 94 (1985).

"The Right to Privacy," *Philosophy and Public Affairs*, 4 (1975). Copyright © 1975 by Princeton University Press.

"Preferential Hiring," *Philosophy and Public Affairs*, 2 (1973). Copyright © 1973 by Princeton University Press.

"Some Questions about Government Regulation of Behavior," in *Rights and Regulation: Ethical, Political, and Economic Issues*, ed. Tibor R. Machan and M. Bruce Johnson (Cambridge, Mass., Ballinger, 1983). Copyright © 1983 by the Pacific Institute for Public Policy Research.

"Imposing Risks," in *To Breathe Freely*, ed. Mary Gibson (Totowa, N.J., Rowman and Allanheld, 1983).

"Remarks on Causation and Liability," *Philosophy and Public Affairs*, 13 (1984). Copyright © 1984 by Princeton University Press.

"Liability and Individualized Evidence " will also appear in a forthcoming volume of *Law and Contemporary Problems*.

Index